FINANCIAL ACCOUNTING:

GET IT STRAIGHT

The Why's and How's of Financial Accounting

Errol Deacon

Deacon Media Company
Internet: deaconmedia.com

This book isn't intended to provide personalized, legal, accounting, financial or investment advice. Readers are encouraged to seek the counsel of competent professionals with regard to such matters as interpretation of the law, financial planning and investment strategies.

The Author and Publisher specifically disclaim any liability, loss or risk, which is incurred as a consequence, directly or indirectly, of the use and application of any of the contents of this book

Rights to this manual will be enforced worldwide. No part may be reproduced or utilized in any form, media, or technology, now known or later developed.

Published By: Deacon Media Company

ISBN 0-9770173-0-3

CONTENTS

WHO AM I
WHY I WROTE THIS BOOK,
WHY THIS BOOK IS DEFFERENT,
WHO NEEDS IT,
WHO DOESN'T NEED IT AND WHY
THEY SHOULD READ IT ANYWAY.

In addition to my academic training, my practical accounting career began over thirty years ago, at the first step of the ladder as accounting clerk climbing every step up that ladder through the ranks to corporate accountant. This didn't take the most direct route, acquiring practical experience in credit and collections, purchasing and cost controls before stepping off at the top. In the mid eighties, I founded and operated an accounting practice, targeting the small to medium size businesses, before returning to the corporate workplace.

A few years ago, I attended a presentation that aimed to explain the fundamentals of accounting specifically to the non-accountants. It was the first time the promoters even attempted this type of event, so it was a make, break or die for the speaker! They had over two hundred enthusiastic attendees. There are a lot of hungry non-accountants out there that needs this information urgently.

It didn't take long for me to evaluate speaker. He was exceptionally knowledgeable. Unfortunately, during break, attendees walked around with blank looks on their faces, and dare I say, most of them looked more confused than they were when the presentation began. An attendee interrupted during one of the segments, complaining, that all she was getting out of this was a rehash of a textbook that she couldn't understand to begin with. The only visual aid was a blackboard.

Criticizing the speaker is easy. The doors opened at 6:30pm and the room had to be completely vacated by 9:30 pm sharp. The sponsor's preprinted literature stated that, during the break attendees could purchase a handbook based on the subject matter covered during the event.

They replaced the speaker the following month, but this time they attracted about ten attendees. The speaker was extremely articulate, but didn't cover the subject matter. Instead of covering the subject matter, most of the time she promoted her practice, and how the day-to-day duties of the accountant have changed with modern software!

In the mid-eighties, accounting software began revolutionizing Financial Statement preparation. Thanks to inputting data, a few clicks later, the Balance Sheet, Income Statement and Statement of Cash Flows would came off the printer, that would have taken more than a week to prepare by hand and a typewriter.

The clear line between bookkeeper and accountant became blurred. Clicking the mouse didn't require accounting qualifications and experience, so bookkeepers, with a click entered new territory. Accounting isn't just input, and few bookkeepers were anywhere near qualified for the role of accountant.

Small business, in particular, were tempted to replace accountants with, what I called "Input Bookkeepers" What did I get out of that seminar? "The more things change, the more things stay the same"

In my experience, the dislike and the problems in understanding accounting, begin at the first baby steps. So we start at the very beginning. We must get those that hate this subject so engrossed and interested, that they let go of the beliefs that held them back without them having to do anything.

The quantity of material in this book compares favorably to Accounting 101. This is the absolute minimum level of accounting knowledge needed get by in the world of business today, as well as getting a glimpse in understanding the Financial Statements prepared by the listed companies. The

Questions and Answer format helps control the reader's focus. Some questions recap, some move us along, and some challenge.

This isn't a traditional textbook or a "How To" book. It couldn't have been written without substantial practical experience in the field.

The accountant is only as good as his or her client! The entities and individuals, that defer critical decision making to their accountants without their input, may initially not agree. This goal of this book isn't to make you a professional accountant, but the goal is that you learn and master the accountant's language, and challenge them intelligently, but don't be surprised if you become an accountant after this, or you enroll in college accounting or related courses. Most professional accountants will love the challenge, as long as you are knowledgeable and make sense. Witness your return on professional fees skyrocket

This book is ideal for Accountants and managers in training their staff, and passing it on to their clients. Accountants are only as good as their clients! I urge accountants out there, to purchase this book for your clients, or sell it to them. It will provide them with practical hands on knowledge, scrutinize their accounting operations, and with that knowledge, enhance the relationship with their advisors and their employees.

Even the non-accountant, that understands accounting procedures, but hasn't been exposed to the How's and Why's of Accounting have been cheated out of truly understanding this "Language of Business" then this book is also for you!

The Deacon 3Q's™ The quality of the financial reports depends on the quality of the input and the quality of the management of that input. I attended a meeting on whether or not to replace an existing computerized system or upgrade it. There was widespread dissatisfaction with the current programs and despite years of spending money on upgrades the product didn't deliver. They asked my opinion: It went this way:

"You can't fix what is clearly junk. There is only one place for junk and that is the trash. You can be no worse off going back in time twenty years doing the job manually than holding on to what you have, not alone an upgrade"

Are you guilty of upgrading your accounting system when you should be doing a complete overhaul? If you aren't proficient in the baby steps of accounting, how can you make the decision to upgrade or install a new system not alone stay in business?

Chapter 1

A Short History of Accounting

What is Accounting?

 So accounting can be presented in a casual story-book fashion?

 Students of accounting usually have rigid preconceived ideas that were acquired long before the first session. An alternative approach, to get past this powerful, almost always negative programming is vital.

A student has an examination in Geography or History, and preparation has been non-existent. A couple of nights before the examination, the student crams ten chapters, takes the examination and passes, perhaps with an A+. Within days, whatever was crammed is forgotten. For accounting, if the student understands the rules and procedures, they might live to take the examination and achieve a passing grade. Unlike most other subjects they will retain what they understood. This subject cannot effectively be mastered by rote. Understanding it is vital.

 The column accountants pad is almost replaced by computerized spreadsheets and accounting software. Does this book go through one of these programs in detail?

 No. Data entry is mechanical. Reading and understanding Financial Statements is one thing. The master uses them as a critical tool for making decisions, but sees through, and deals with those producing them, if they are no more then smoke and mirrors.

 "The Sound of Music" when Julie Andrews played the bedroom scene with the children, she sang: "Let's start at the very beginning. A very good place to start" Where is the beginning?

 For example, take the project of developing a New York City skyscraper, it isn't going anywhere without solid foundations. Is that the beginning?

For the physical construction part, it is. Is the beginning the purchase of the land? I can't pinpoint the exact starting point of the project as it could have taken months of dreaming and talk. Purchasing the land is useless if it can't handle the skyscraper building, not to mention zoning, permits, financing etc. Accounting functions took place long before the foundations are laid.

 Your accounting career began before computers became part of every day life. Does your generation understand accounting better than the generation graduating today? Accounting is as old as civilization. Can accounting be modernized?

 Many graduated high school and college in the mid sixties have issues with accounting to this day, so don't blame computers and technology. Accounting is as old as civilization. Terminology won't change that fact.

This book begins at the individual level, but before we go there it's essential to get a grip on what accounting can, and cannot do.

We can't demand more from accounting than it can deliver, but the majority of those having their own businesses should demand more from their Financial Statements than they are likely receiving. Computers don't replace the need to UNDERSTAND accounting principles and procedures, as the computer is nothing more than a high-speed idiot. Despite that, most of us wouldn't exchange it for a manual system.

The Deacon 3 Q's™ is more than a passing statement and will be referred to throughout this book. The quality of the financial reporting depends on the quality of the input and the quality of the management of that input. Quality input is vital. No matter whether the system is fully automated, semi automated or manual.

How in studying accounting history, will bring light to its limitations and strengths? Is accounting a follower or a leader?

 Accounting is a follower not a leader. Accounting certainly played a role even in 8000BC but evidence SUGGESTS double entry bookkeeping systems were developed in the Genoa-Venice Florence area in the 1200 to 1250 period. Each account had a separate debit and credit with the equivalent of journals and ledgers.

It took a mass produced volume to have impact. Apparently, generally accepted the first accounting textbook printed and distributed throughout Europe by Gutenberg's Printing Press going back to Luca Pacioli (1447-1517). A Franciscan monk and mathematician Published "Suma de Arithmetica, Geometrica, Proportioni et Proportionalite" in 1494 summarizing all mathematical knowledge at the time, including a section on double entry bookkeeping applicable to the Venice area.

 What is it about the period of the mid 1600s? Is it an important step in the growth of "Accounting"?

 The first textbook owed its success to the fact that the printing press was established. As accounting doesn't anticipate, events must have occurred before accounting reacts.

Accounting responds to needs, and it took off after the birth of the Industrial Revolution in England, which created for the first time the business cycle, depressions and bankruptcy.

In the UK, 1834 legislation required all public companies to be audited. In the United States, US Steel became in 1902 the worlds first Billion Dollar Corporation!

The earliest of the big accounting practices, William Deloitte opened in London 1845. Samuel Price and Edwin

Waterhouse Cooper began in 1854, their brothers joining in 1861. William Peat began in 1867. Often overlooked, British and American Cost Accountants and Engineers developed calculations and reporting techniques making control of huge empires possible.

Frank Broaker located in Manhattan in New York is the first Certified Public Accountant in the United States. Price Waterhouse and Haskins and Sells had branch offices. A booming stock market, with mergers, acquisitions, initial public offerings almost daily, accountants worked almost round the clock. US Steel hired Price Waterhouse to prepare and post the first audited financial statements in 1903.

 Had the accounting profession been regulated, could the aftermath of the 1929 Wall Street crash been avoided? What about uniform audit standards?

 In the late 1880's Royal Charter in the UK allowed the public to acquire stock in public companies irrespective of their financial knowledge. This market crash in the UK gave birth to the British Companies Act.

 You didn't answer my question. The 1929 Wall Street crash had an enormous ripple affect throughout the world. If the United States had acted as the British had, could this crash been avoided?

Again, accounting doesn't anticipate. Regulators sincerely believe additional regulations in themselves will solve problems.

In the early 19th Century Railroads crisscross the United States. Tracks are expensive and had a life of many years. For the first time the question came up. How long do they last? Answers depended on who asked the question, and to whom the question was addressed. These events gave birth to the concept of depreciation. After years of talk and no action, Congress enacted the Interstate Commerce Commission Act of 1887.

 How did we get from almost zero accounting standards and procedures in a space of a little over one hundred years?

 It's much less than one hundred years. The aftermath of the 1929 crash changed accounting forever. The Roosevelt Administration enacted The Securities Exchange Commission, the Payroll Tax, among others.

The Securities Act of 1933 was modeled on state regulations, British Companies Acts and earlier congressional regulation.

The Act of 1934 Securities and Exchange Commission created the SEC, which made accountants liable to the public as well as the companies they audited. The McKesson and Robbins scandal demonstrated major flaws in auditing practices. Out of this scandal standardized accounting and General Accepted Accounting Principles. (GAAP) is born. The pronouncements, SEC Accounting series releases, accounting research bulletins of the committee of accounting procedures, the accounting standards board opinions and Financial Accounting Standards Board Statements which continue and grow to this day

The SEC by legislation has the power to regulate accounting. They elected to hand this jointly to the private sector and the successor to the AIA – The American Society of American Certified Public Accountants. The Financial Accounting Standards Board established in 1973, an independent body. In 1984 Emerging Issues Task Force provides advice to the FASB on new areas and technical issues.

 Is this legislation a failure?

I think we are building a paper castles, but that's a subject for another time. The SEC has failed miserably is some areas, but they have contributed as well. The ruling, accountants are responsible to the entities they audit, as well as the investing public cannot be argued against.

Early in 2001 the world - wide stock market bubble burst. The bursting of this bubble didn't discriminate between the professional traders, or those that had absolutely zero knowledge of the market or accounting. I thought the legislation enacted in the UK in the late 1880's and the host of legislation over the past fifty years was supposed to take care of this. It may take twenty years or longer, but there will be more Enron's, and WorldCom's

To be fair, the SEC requires an additional reporting that if the investors read those reports, they might not have invested, but these reports are almost without exception not user friendly. When stocks are rapidly appreciating regulations in themselves don't control a market bubble.

 Hasn't accounting failed miserably as the "language of business?"

 Knowing precisely what and when accounting delivers, and the opposite, knowing precisely what it cannot deliver, takes understanding and knowledge. If those in charge of input, or managing that input integrity sucks, then they might be guilt of the following: I am not the author of: "Figures never lie, sometimes liars figure"

Accounting did communicate as the language of business during the mania and the dot com fiasco. Accounting DID communicate no earnings, no cash, outrageous rent and other overhead expenses. A figure is accepted regardless of the intent for foul play, a genuine error, or the best determination of facts available. Figures don't lie and they don't discriminate either. It's the interpretation of those figures that make, break or even kill.

How does accounting <u>officially</u> define itself?

 Accounting communicates primarily through <u>three main Financial Statements.</u>

Accounting reports history! These are: The Balance Sheet, Income Statement (additionally known as the Profit and Loss, or P&L for short) giving birth to the accounting terms, Historical and Periodic Accounting.

 If accounting communicates primarily through three main financial statements, there wouldn't be a big deal complying with the SEC reporting requirements.

 These three Financial Statements are the least they have to file. If it were all they had to file, more companies would go to big boards. The 10K, and 10Q's compared to the Financial Statements, make them a light night novel by comparison.

Where is the auditors' opinion located? What does it include? Does the opinion transfer blame or responsibility to the management?

It's usually a standardized statement. Typically the first paragraph covers the scope of the opinion that responsibility rests with management. The second paragraph confirms the auditor applied a standard, including references the auditor relied on audited statements from other subsidiaries or data from other periods. The third paragraph is the key. It's qualified or unqualified. The majority of them are <u>unqualified.</u> The auditor describes no exceptions.

 Business days consume time for meetings, sales calls, taking orders, employee matters, purchasing, contract negotiations etc, What does accounting ignore and which ones are taken seriously?

Accounting can only translate events into currency, that's dollars, pound sterling, yen, etc.

If your daughter hounds you for permission to go on a school outing that includes a week at Disneyland, accounting is interested when and if a check or credit card charge is processed

 How are changes handled?

 Accounting takes into account the number of units, and the changes in those units. Accounting for <u>changes</u> is as vital as paying for the air and accommodation expenses for your daughters outing to Disneyland.

If a car dealership receives into Inventory fifteen automobiles commanding an AVERAGE retail price of $50,000, this inventory has projected revenue of $750,000 for those cars.

A client presents a check for $96,000 for some automobiles. Out of 15 automobiles, excluding inventory on hand before the delivery, how many automobiles does the customer receive for $96,000? Accounting records, and monitors the changes in inventory. You will be hearing a lot more: The Deacon slogan: Timing Timing Timing Timing™. These rules are very specific and accounting places great emphasis on the Timing rules.

My sister provided the entire financial backing for a start up restaurant. The Accountants commented on the financial results "It isn't a pretty picture" Explain.

 Financial Statements are mere SNAPSHOTS of the financial position at a definite period in time on a certain date. Failure to understand this reality can create unnecessary pain on the one hand, and uncalled pleasure on the other.

A photographer takes a picture of you engrossed in a conversation. A minute later the word "Smile" is uttered and another photograph is taken. There are two SNAPSHOTS of you taken a within minutes of each other. One photograph may be loved, the other despised.

 If the Financial Statements are pictures, take them to another professional. They may be viewed more favorably?

 Financial Statements are scrutinized for acceptable debt levels, trade payables outstanding etc. The statements may now get a clean bill of health, but it might go the other way.

The Deacon 3Q's™: The quality of the financial reports depends on the quality of the input and the quality of the management of that input. The Accountant is only as good as his or her client. The decision to replace an accountant must never be taken lightly, but no matter the qualifications and experience of the professional, rapport between the professional and the client are essential.

 Great. Just as technology can edit regular pictures, the then the pictures of the Financial Statements can be edited as well?

 Year-end tax reporting can be a blessing. If it weren't for this deadline many entities wouldn't ever get their books straight.

Great pictures assume to mean a healthy net profit, healthy cash flow and the lenders falling in love with all the respective ratios. Poor pictures represent the exact opposite. There is editing and there is editing.

If after editing, the transactions are booked properly and there's a loss, that's what the picture should report!

 Out of six months data, half reflect reality. Does she start again?

She is the sole provider of capital. She has a choice. She can let things go as they are, or she can take control and demand up to date accurate reporting.

That's all well and good, but reality is, accounting can only report events denominated in currency such as dollars and that have already occurred. The reports are SNAPSHOTS at a given period in time.

This explains the SNAPSHOT factor, and clears up the fool-hardiness of concentrating on financial statements that aren't sufficiently updated. Investors in public companies don't get reports that are close to real time, but that doesn't prevent investors providing all or most of the capital in privately held entities demanding up to date, and almost real time information.

A restaurant secures business for $50,000.00 for a catered event. The agreement requires payment of $10,000.00 at the time of signing the contract. The balance is due fourteen days prior to the event. Of course the deadline passes and the day before the event, and after the banks have closed for the weekend, the clients increase the number of attendees and request additional services.

They pointed out the check will come from the identical account that paid the original down payment.

Monday morning the check was deposited. A SNAPSHOT of the financial health for that day reports financial health. On Friday the check was returned. "Account Closed" What went from joy now turns to tears? Did accounting communicate as the "language of business?" Yes! It communicated the status of the business, at the moment in time a report is requested. A SNAPSHOT was taken of the financial condition.

That's the reason you don't get too excited, or you don't get too upset over past results if you have only the basic information.

Chapter 2

The Brown Family

T-Account Concept

Debits and Credits

Capitalization

The best place to start is at the beginning. The family isn't getting financial planning advice from you, so why begin at this level?

 Is there a better way to conquer people's fear of accounting than beginning at the level they are comfortable and secure, using that as a base and move up aggressively from there?

The Brown family has two children attending private school. The pretax combined income is $1 million a year. Fig 2:1: The left side lists the family's Investments, Assets and Debts at the end of February 2003. The right side lists all the monthly outflows for the following month, March 2003 per the checking account.

 Is the after tax monthly income of $56,518.75 their take home pay? Does the negative variance means more cash went out than came in?

 Yes. The Balance Sheet it the most <u>critical</u> of all the Financial Statements. The Income Statement came along later, and theoretically it's for convenience only. Income Statements can only report one result. Net Income or Net Loss.

Now move on to Fig 2:2. On the left hand side, do you see the items, Checking Account, Money Market Account and Brokerage Account? Do you notice the arrows grouping them together? Follow the arrows, and that's the exact location where those items located on the Balance Sheet. (Never mind the categories for now)

Moving on down, the 401k has its own position. If the Brown Family had an IRA, or Keogh Plans, then those would be included. The three automobiles are listed under Other Assets. Investment in Time Share, Principal residence and the Condominium in Florida are long-term and they get grouped together.

Brown Family
Investments Assets and Debts
February-03

Checking Account	5,500.00
Money Market Account	23,000.00
Brokerage Account	118,076.00
Company 401(k)	213,000.00
Personal Affects	73,902.00
Automobile 1-Honda	20,000.00
Automobile 2-BMW	37,000.00
Automobile 3 Mercedes Benz	63,250.00
Investment in Time Share	12,400.00
Principal Residence FMV	3,100,000.00
Condominium Florida	630,000.00
Owed Banks - Line of Credit	876,091.00
Mortgage Fixed Principal Residence	2,000,000.00
Mortgage Due 5 Years Baloon	521,000.00
Credit Card Balances	73,000.00
Automobile Loan Honda	10,000.00
Automobile Loan BMW	30,000.00
Automobile Loan Mercedes Benz	61,100.00

Monthly Cash Outflows for March 03

Mortgage, Taxes Utilities &Repairs	17,100.00
Term Life Insurance	800.00
School Tuition (Private School)	5,100.00
Food	3,200.00
Clothing	1,760.00
Transportation	860.00
Combined Automobile Payments	3,300.00
Credit Cards	8,000.00
Florida Condo	5,300.00
Entertainment	1,876.00
Line of Credit - Monthly Payments	3,000.00
Monthly - Brokerage Account	4,000.00
Vacations	4,000.00
Outflows	58,296.00
After Tax Monthly Income	56,518.75
Cash Shortfall	1,777.25

Fig 2:1

14

Brown Family
Investments Assets and Debts

Balance Sheet for the Brown Family as February 2003

	February-03
Checking Account	5,500.00
Money Market Account	23,000.00
Brokerage Account	118,076.00
Company 401(k)	213,000.00
Personal Affects	73,902.00
Automobile 1-Honda	20,000.00
Automobile 2-BMW	37,000.00
Automobile 3 Mercedes Benz	63,250.00
Investment in Time Share	12,400.00
Principal Residence FMV	3,100,000.00
Condominium Florida	630,000.00
Owed Banks - Line of Credit	876,091.00
Mortgage Fixed Principal Residence	2,000,000.00
Mortgage Due 5 Years Baloon	521,000.00
Credit Card Balances	73,000.00
Automobile Loan Honda	10,000.00
Automobile Loan BMW	30,000.00
Automobile Loan Mercedes Benz	61,100.00

ASSETS

Current Assets		
Checking Account	5,500.00	
Money Market Account	23,000.00	
Brokerage Account	118,076.00	146,576.00
Non Current Assets		
401k	213,000.00	213,000.00
Other Assets		
Personal Effects	73,902.00	
Automobile 1 Honda	20,000.00	
Automobile 2 BMW	37,000.00	
Automobile 3 Mercedes Benz	63,250.00	194,152.00
Long Term Assets		
Investment in Time Share	12,400.00	
Principal Residence	3,100,000.00	
Condominium Miami Florida	630,000.00	3,742,400.00
Total Assets		4,296,128.00

LIABILITIES

Current Liabilities		
Credit Card Debts		73,000.00
Other Liabilities		
Automobile Honda	10,000.00	
Automobile BMW	30,000.00	
Automobile Mercedes Benz	61,100.00	101,100.00
Long Term Liabilities		
Line of Credit	876,091.00	
Mortgage Miami	630,000.00	
Mortgage Residence	2,000,000.00	3,506,091.00
Total Liabilities		3,680,191.00
Net Worth		615,937.00
Total Assets & Liabilities		4,296,128.00

Fig 2:2

It might be fun listing the Assets, but no Balance Sheet would be complete without listing the Liabilities. (For the Brown Family those Liabilities are Debts!) All the items from the Line of Credit, to the Automobile Loan- Mercedes Benz are located to the right of the Assets under Liabilities. The difference between the two is the Net Worth or Net Loss.

Go to Fig 2:3 Here we jump right into the river with the Income Statement, or Profit and Loss Account (P&L for short) The left hand side lists the cash outflows per the checking account. The cash outflows exceed the cash inflows for the month.

Those items, Term Life Insurance, School Tuition, Food Clothing, Transportation, Entertainment and Vacation are moved over dollar for dollar. What about the others?

Go to right hand side under the Income Statement and you will find, Interest on Mortgage Obligations for $14,140.00 Ah! Out of $16,000.00 to be allocated, we have located $14,140.00 but that still leaves $1,860.00! OK, that goes against the Mortgage Outstanding on the Balance Sheet.

Exactly the same system applies to the Combined Car Payments, Credit Card Payments and the Miami Condominium. A portion of the cash outlays comprise of interest and reduction of the total amount of the loans outstanding. You will find the interest portion directly under Interest on Mortgage on the Income Statement side of Fig 2:3

The last of the monthly Brown Family Monthly Cash Disbursements is the "Monthly standing commitment to the Brokerage Account". Recall that the Brokerage Account is listed under the Asset Side of the Balance Sheet? The $4,000.00 is building up the Asset and this cannot be classified as an expense.

I told you the amounts that reduce the principal balances outstanding for mortgages, loans and credit card payments are Balance Sheet items.

Monthly Cash Disbursements for the Brown family March 2003

Mortgage Taxes, Utilities and Repais	17,100.00
Term Life Insurance	800.00
School Tuition	5,100.00
Food	3,200.00
Clothing	1,760.00
Transportation	860.00
Combined Car Payments	3,300.00
Credit Cards	8,000.00
Miami Condo	5,300.00
Entertainment	1,876.00
Line of Credit Monthly Payments	3,000.00
Monthly Standing Commitment Brokerage	4,000.00
Vacation	4,000.00
Outflows	58,296.00
After Tax Monthly Income	56,518.75
Variance	(1,777.25)

Income Statement for The Brown Family as of March 2003

After Tax Income All Sources	
Untilites and Repairs	1,100.00
Term Life Insurance	800.00
School Tuition	5,100.00
Food	3,200.00
Clothing	1,760.00
Transportation	860.00
Entertainment	1,876.00
Vacation	4,000.00
Interest on Mortgage Obligations	14,140.00
Interest on Automobile loans	505.00
Credit Card Interest	909.00
Total	34,250.00
Net Gain or Loss	

Fig 2:3

Balance Sheet for the Brown Family as February 2003 | Balance Sheet for the Brown Family as March 2003

February 2003			March 2003		
ASSETS			**ASSETS**		
Current Assets			Current Assets		
Checking Account	5,500.00		Checking Account	3,722.75	
Money Market Account	23,000.00		Money Market Account	23,000.00	
Brokeage Account	118,076.00	146,576.00	Brokeage Account	122,076.00	148,798.75
Non Current Assets			Non Current Assets		
401k	213,000.00	213,000.00	401k	213,000.00	213,000.00
Other Assets			Other Assets		
Personal Effects	73,902.00		Personal Effects	73,902.00	
Automobile 1 Honda	20,000.00		Automobile 1 Honda	20,000.00	
Automobile 2 BMW	37,000.00		Automobile 2 BMW	37,000.00	
Automobile 3 Mercedes Benz	63,250.00	194,152.00	Automobile 3 Mercedes Benz	63,250.00	194,152.00
Long Term Assets			Long Term Assets		
Investment in Time Share	12,400.00		Investment in Time Share	12,400.00	
Principal Residence	3,100,000.00		Principal Residence	3,100,000.00	
Condominium Florida	630,000.00	3,742,400.00	Condominium Florida	630,000.00	3,742,400.00
Total Assets		4,296,128.00	Total Assets		4,298,350.75
LIABILITIES			**LIABILITIES**		
Current Liabilities			Current Liabilities		
Credit Card Debts		73,000.00	Credit Card Debts		65,909.00
Other Liabilities			Other Liabilities		
Automobile Honda	10,000.00		Automobile Honda	9,496.90	
Automobile BMW	30,000.00		Automobile BMW	29,161.50	
Automobile Mercedes Benz	61,100.00	101,100.00	Automobile Mercedes Benz	59,646.60	98,305.00
Long Term Liabilities			Long Term Liabilities		
Line of Credit	876,091.00		Line of Credit	874,591.00	
Mortgage Miami Condominium	521,000.00		Mortgage Miami Condominium	517,790.00	
Mortgage Principal Residence	2,000,000.00	3,397,091.00	Mortgage Principal Residence	1,994,550.00	3,386,931.00
Total Liabilities		3,571,191.00	Total Liabilities		3,551,145.00
Net Worth		724,937.00	Net Worth February	724,937.00	
			Current Earnings (March)	22,268.75	747,205.75
Total Assets & Liabilties		4,296,128.00	Total Liabilities & Net Worth		4,298,350.75

Fig 2:4

Fig 2:4 compares the Balance Sheets for two months, showing with the use of the arrows the affects of those transactions.

The left side is the Brown Family Balance Sheet at the end of February 2003. The right side is the Brown Family Balance Sheet at the end of March 2003.

The checking account at the end of February is $5,500.00. Add monthly "After Tax Monthly Income" of $56,518.75 less monthly outflows (For Reference See Fig 2:1) $58,296.00 is $3,722.75. The outstanding Credit Card Balances and the Mortgage both decreased. The amounts you can see for yourself.

The checking account reports a net outflow of $3,722.75. Had the checking not funded the Brokerage Account for $4,000.00 the shortage would have turned into a surplus for the Checking Account, but if you take the three items Checking Account, Money Market Account and Brokerage Account from the end of February to the end of March this category increases by $2,222.75. Now that you have a grasp on the affects on cash flows, take a look at the increase in net worth for the Brown Family for the month of March alone. The net worth for this family increased $22,268.75!

This is an excellent example illustrating an Asset rich, Cash poor. This is as common in business, from the home operation to the worldwide multi national operation.
Another valuable lesson: Governments' levy taxes on Net Income, not Net Cash Inflows.

<u>INCREASES IN NET WORTH DON'T AUTOMATICALLY TRANSLATE INTO INCREASES IN CASH.</u>

<u>INCREASES IN CASH DON'T AUTOMATICALLY RESULT IN DECREASES IN NET WORTH.</u>

 Both sides of the Balance Sheet have the same Dollar amounts. Did you do this to make it easier to comprehend as a teaching tool?

 The reason it's called the Balance Sheet. It MUST balance. Assets = Liabilities + Shareholders Equity. This is a legitimate equation. It's equally valid as Liabilities = Assets − Owners Equity, and so forth.

The definition proves the double entry system at work.

There is no legitimate plug account, and it requires ZERO knowledge of Mathematics to master and understand accounting.

Take the balance sheet for the Brown Family as of March 2003.

Assets = $4,298,350.75   Liabilities &
Liabilities = $3,551,145.00   ⟶   Owners Equity
Owners Equity = $747,205.75   Equals Total Assets

 The Balance Sheet for the Brown Family has sub categories within the Assets and Liabilities. This has no effect on the equation, why are they categorized?

 The accounting cycle is typically the period making up twelve consecutive months. All Current Assets, with the exception of Cash should complete the cycle within the accounting period returning to the Cash position from where it started. Current Liabilities are obligations falling due and paid within the accounting period of twelve months from the transaction dates.

For those that want the technical definitions, here they are: They will be clearer later:

Assets are economic resources having the ability or the potential to provide economic benefits now as well as for the future.

Liabilities: These are claims creditors have on all the assets, unless otherwise specified in the case of a mortgage secured to specific property. Even employees have claims on the asset in the form of labor supplied.

Retained Earnings: The net effect of the operating results on an ongoing basis after dividends paid.

<u>Shareholders Equity:</u> The owners have a claim on the assets after all claims have been met. (Capital for a sole proprietorship, Net worth for the Brown Family)

 Assets = Liabilities + Shareholders Equity is an equation proving Total Debits must equal Total Credits. There isn't one negative on the Brown Family Balance Sheet. Which items are negatives?

 They are NOT negatives. They are credit balances! Overall debits MUST equal overall credits. In practice the term negative in accounting is used very loosely. Negatives MUST be replaced by credits, at least in the learning stage.

The word Account stands out. Anything that gets a transaction in accounting is called an Account.

 Can the accounts with debit balances be segregated from those having credit balances?

 All Accounts are held in the GENERAL LEDGER. Sales, Purchases and Cash Receipts are JOURNALS and they FEED into the GENERAL LEDGER.

Total Liabilities represent the debts or the total amount owed to others. There can be no Liabilities without having Assets. Liabilities must have credit balances in the GENERAL LEDGER. If the house mortgage outstanding for the Brown Family becomes a debit balance, in absence of an accounting error, they are paying the mortgage long after it is paid off!

Assets must have debit balances in the GENERAL LEDGER. In the absence of an accounting error, if the Cash Operating becomes a credit balance, then that account is overdrawn in the books. All accounts get both debits and credits.

 Textbooks seldom advise on how to memorize the mechanics of debit and credit leaving it to the instructors. As this isn't a traditional textbook, how about coming up with something?

A friend shared a technique she acquired in college. Debits are good. Credits are bad.

Accounting is yin yang. Interfering with "what is" by demanding an answer to the question of whether it is good or bad is a recipe for failure. Why is accounting "what is?' "Figures never lie, sometimes liars figure" but let's play with it: "Figures never lie, but they don't tell the truth either"

With the exception of Contributed Capital all accounts have both debits and credits posted to that account.

Cash and Accounts Receivable are both asset accounts. Accounts Receivable is the total outstanding amount the entity has extended credit to their clients. If a client pays the bill for $1 million, the Cash account is debited and Accounts Receivable is credited. They are both asset accounts. I thought credits are supposed to be bad! How can it be bad news receiving cash from a customer, particularly if the entity is carrying the paper? This one is used throughout the book and as repeated as repetition is the mother of learning.

THE ACCOUNT RECEIVING THE BENEFIT IS ALLOCATED THE DEBIT

THE ACCOUNT PROVIDING THE BENEFIT IS ALLOCATED THE CREDIT.

An advantage of manual systems is as it takes so much time booking entries there's ample time to think it through.

Out of the debit or the credit, one will always jump out in front. This is particularly so after asking the right questions. The opening Balance Sheet amounts are: For the Checking Accounts the opening balance is $3,722.75.

The Money Market Account is $23,000.00

The technical definitions for those that want them: Debits increase Asset Accounts. Credits decrease Asset Accounts. The opposite applies: Debits decrease Liability Accounts, Credits increase Liability Accounts.

It takes a transaction to change an account. The transactions are $3,000.00 for the Mortgage. Mercedes Benz $1000.00

THE ACCOUNT RECEIVING THE BENEFIT IS ALLOCATED THE DEBIT

THE ACCOUNT PROVIDING THE BENEFIT IS ALLOCATED THE CREDIT.

For simplicity, $4000 is moved from the Money Market to checking.
Which one receives and which one gives?
One of them always pops up real fast.
The receiver is the checking account
The receiver is ALWAYS the DEBIT.
Which account is allotted the credit?
The giver or provider is ALWAYS the CREDIT
This case the Money Market

The T- Accounts would look like this

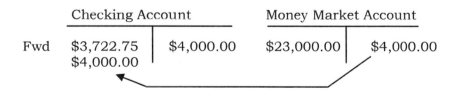

	Checking Account		Money Market Account	
Fwd	$3,722.75	$4,000.00	$23,000.00	$4,000.00
	$4,000.00			

I sympathize with those having spent the entire time studying Accounting 101 through Accounting 1001 expending valuable energy in excessive analysis and still coming up with nothing.

The checking account RECEIVED the $4,000 and the

$4,000 is placed on the DEBIT SIDE. The Money Market Account provided, therefore it got the CREDIT entry. The same rule applies for the Liability Accounts. Now apply the monthly payments.

Which account is providing the funds?
They are funded from the checking account.
It would have been the money market account had a transfer from the money market account to the checking account not been done earlier.

The checking account PROVIDES, so that must be CREDITED. If the checking account is the yin, what is the yang? If the checking account is the yang, what is the other side?

What is the $1000.00 check for? The invoice is a reminder that it's the Mercedes Benz monthly installment.

The RECEIVER of the installment payment is the Automobile Mercedes Benz outstanding installment note. The installment payment includes interest and principal payment. Interest expense is an Income Statement issue, but for now, the Assets side reports a Mercedes Benz, and there is an outstanding obligation against the automobile. For our purposes here, the outstanding dollar amount of the liability is the amount outstanding to Mercedes Benz.

Here's the flow:

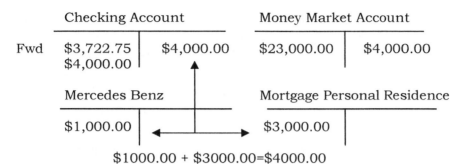

Checking Account		Money Market Account	
Fwd $3,722.75	$4,000.00	$23,000.00	$4,000.00
$4,000.00			

Mercedes Benz		Mortgage Personal Residence	
$1,000.00		$3,000.00	

$1000.00 + $3000.00=$4000.00

 Had the Brown Family acquired the residence and automobiles for cash, would the formula and procedures still apply?

 Had the Brown Family acquired the residence and automobiles for cash, there would be no corresponding liabilities. Liabilities on the Balance Sheet are reduced at the rate the debts are paid down.

If the house is acquired for cash, then the Asset account holding the house is debited immediately on acquisition, the Cash account is simultaneously credited. Every Liability recorded on the Balance Sheet, takes the resources of an Asset to clear, or pay down those Liabilities.

 "Every liability recorded on the Balance Sheet, takes the resources of an Asset to clear or pay down those Liabilities" Can you defend that definition in today's world for both business and individuals?

 That definition is true today as never before. The Brown family breadwinners loose their income due to a layoff from work, and as they don't have layoff insurance they turn to credit cards for cash advances for the mortgage payment.

Liabilities can be reduced without significant reduction in Assets as long as another Liability is created or increased!

Is it fact, the larger or more complex the organizational structure the more complex the accounting system? You began at the wage earner level. How much of this is transferable?

 The difference between the home based operation and a conglomerate, as GE, is that GE has more account categories more zeros when at the end

Tax accounting takes Financial Accounting net profit as the base then makes adjustments according to the applicable tax legislation. This book focuses on Financial Accounting, with the only noticeable differences between a sole proprietorship and the corporate form, is the Owners' Equity, or Shareholder Equity sections of the Balance Sheet. (Partnerships have Partnership Accounts with net profit or loss allocated to the Partners in accordance with the agreement)

 Established business change hands every day in this country. Financial institutions at times prefer extending debt financing if the funds are used to acquire an established business rather than a start up. Are all the assets <u>revalued</u> to market value?

 It's a definite no if the business assets are held in a corporation, and the <u>stock</u> is sold thereby leaving the Assets and Liabilities intact. If the actual <u>assets</u> are sold to another entity, then they are revalued to fair market value.

The excess of the amount paid and the fair market value of the assets is Goodwill. If Goodwill is $1 million, and the amortization of Goodwill is ten years, then Goodwill on the Balance Sheet is reduced $100,000 each year or sooner if the entity fails, or if Goodwill is no longer a measure of operating results.

In evaluating an existing business, there's no changing the fact fixed assets are lumped together on the Balance Sheet

That's no excuse for the buyer's failure to demand detailed analysis of these assets and failing to determine proper valuations of these assets in both current dollars and their condition and usefulness.

"Figures never lie, or tell the truth" Accounting transactions are history. This "language of business" can be very narrow minded in communicating and assisting in making quality decisions. Accounting requires physical counts of fixed assets and inventory, especially in take over situations. The figures on the financial statements must be taken very cautiously and without emotion attached, no matter the health of the economy. This isn't going to change and there is huge price to pay for ignoring this fact.

 Allocating assets if they are discarded, or if a building is gutted, isn't the headache compared to acquiring an existing business. Are assets grouped together? If a five family unit is acquired for $5 million, does this all get allocated to land and buildings?

 The market value for these assets may be significantly below book value, or they may be significantly higher. Sometimes new owners get garbage in relation to what they paid, which in most cases would have been avoided if they are not too proud to have the inventory verified and valued.

Don't spend hours of billable hours arguing over nonsense items, if they aren't major then ignore the boilers, the electrical system or even the condition of the building that might bc on its last legs.

Don't wait till after escrow to find out that the hallways had been painted to look good, but they hadn't bothered to remove the grease before lying on the first layer of fresh paint.

A family unit, acquired for $5 million allocates part of the purchase price to Land, and part to the building and its components.

Among other items escalators, elevators have lives of their own. When replaced, they are accounted for as separate items in accordance with the rules of the particular asset or asset categories.

 Aren't you making it too much of a big deal? It's a learning process acquiring a business, and getting legitimate valuations. Usually buyers are at the mercy of their advisors and appraisers.

 Due to the volume of material that must be covered I chose a hotel for this book, as the hotel has all the asset classes and categories that are more than sufficient to grasp the foundations of accounting.

 The hotel might not be such a good choice. What about the business functions that doesn't apply to hotels? Are we shortchanged?

 No. In instances where other industries need clarification, deviations will be made. In my opinion the hotel business is years behind, both in technology and management sophistication. As this goes to print, hotels are only now installing automatic check in and out.

The banks introduced ATM's more than twenty years ago, but it doesn't preclude it being an excellent product to teach accounting principles.

Hotels are real estate, including service and manufacturing aspects. This hotel has one thousand rooms with Restaurants, Functions and Meeting Space, Garage, Spa and leased facilities involving third parties sharing revenue. Food preparation has all the elements of basic manufacturing. Vital accounting functions for Inventories, Payroll, Depreciation and Accruals are covered. There is a chapter on Accounts Receivable, Accounts Payable, Petty Cash, Employee' Reimbursements.

How does accounting record the Capitalization of the hotel or any other entity?

 Assets contributed, including Labor and services in exchange for stock get the fair market value of those assets, or services rendered at the time. Textbooks state typically state stock is exchanged for cash. As this is mechanical I'm adopting the textbook version.

This is the pre-opening year-end Balance Sheet as of December 31st, 2003. Capitalizing a business is standard. For convenience of instruction the only items (assets) that have still to arrive and be accounted for are the Furniture Fittings and Equipment.

Excluding the Bank Operating Account balance of $100,000, Land and Buildings on the Balance Sheet is close to $960 million dollars. Textbooks tell you to debit the Land and Buildings accounts and credit Cash or Accounts Payable for the items that were acquired on credit.

Organization and Pre Opening Expenses for almost $619 million are valid expenses that would have been recognized if the property were open for business. Organization and Pre Opening expenses can't be written off in one shot either, they can only be written off over a period not less than five years.

After reviewing the Balance Sheet, take a look at the last page of this chapter and observe the multitude of Asset categories and by no means will this list include all items for a project as large as this. It will alert that allocating these Assets is more than debiting an Asset account and crediting another Asset or Liability account.

The items that don't have a dollar figure next to them are Inventory items or Furniture Fittings and Equipment. The Balance Sheet hasn't reported any of those items, as it's assumed they hadn't arrived

Balance Sheet For Deacon Properties
As of December 31st, 2002

ASSETS		LIABILITIES AND CAPITAL	
Current Assets		**Current Liabilities**	
		Accounts Payable Trade	
Cash - Operating Account	100,000.00	Deposits and Security Deposits	
Total Current Assets	100,000.00	Total Current Liabilities	
Furniture Fittings & Equipment		**Long-Term Liabilities**	
TL Furniture Fittings & Equipment		Construction Loan	600,000,000.00
		Total Long-Term Liabilities	600,000,000.00
Land and Buildings	959,952,120.00		
Total Land and Buildings	959,952,120.00	Total Liabilities	600,000,000.00
Other Assets		**Shareholders Equity (Capital)**	
Org Costs/Pre opening Exp.	618,954.00	Common Stock $1 Par Value	50,000.00
Total Other Assets	618,954.00	Common Stock Paid In Capital	360,621,074.00
		Total Capital	360,671,074.00
Total Assets	960,671,074.00	Total Liabilities & Capital	960,671,074.00

Fig 2:5

The Financial Statements is a picture of the financial affairs of the organization at a given moment in time. That picture may be loved or despised

Deacon Hotels

Acquisition Cost Land+A47	223,888,996.14	**FURNITURE FITTINGS EQUIPMENT.**
Building Frame, Windows, Glass, Flag Poles etc	385,330,627.86	Rooms - Drapes
Structure Essentials	208,541,887.00	Rooms - Bed Heads
Structure Essentials and Enhancements	30,650,609.00	Rooms - Bed Frames
Actual Facilities Construction	111,540,000.00	Rooms - Rollaway Beds
Furniture Fittings and Equipment		Rooms - Bedside Lamps
Non Depreciable Operating Inventory		Rooms - Bedside Lamp Shades
Inventory Cost of Doing Business		Rooms - Inside Carpeting
Inventory Cost of Sales		Rooms - Television
Organizational cost and Pre Opening Promotional	618,954.00	Rooms - Safe for Valuables
Total Through December 31st, 2002	**960,571,074.00**	Rooms - High Speed and Wireless Connections
		Rooms - Telephones Main Suite
STRUCTURE		Rooms - Telephones Bathrooms
Building Frame, Windows, Glass, Flag Poles etc	385,330,627.86	Rooms - Refrigerators
STRUCTUAL ESSENTIALS		Rooms - Coffee Makers
Boilers	49,870,000.00	Coffee Shop - Tables and Chairs
Main Electrical Plant	31,987,000.00	Fine Dining - Tables and Chairs
Back Up Generators	3,543,900.00	Steak House - Tables and Chairs
Air Conditioning Plant	11,000,000.00	Roof Top Rest & Lounge Tables and Chairs
Fire Sprinkler System	3,500,000.00	Functions and Catering - Tables and Chairs
Fire Hose and Fire Alarm System	1,760,000.00	Functions and Catering - Teleconferencing
Refrigeration - Main	12,000,000.00	Show Lounge - Tables and Chairs
Refrigeration - Seven Smaller Units	7,000,000.00	Show Lounge - Performing Stage
Elevators - Public Fifteen	38,000,000.00	Buffet Stands
Elevators - Private - Five	10,350,000.00	Pianos
Elevators - Freight - Six	19,490,000.00	Dance Floors
Elevators - Garage - Auto's and Mini Vans	6,400,000.00	Bar Stands and Bar Chairs
Escalators - Lobby and Conference Halls Four	8,400,000.00	Lobby Furniture
Escalators - Private Four	2,100,000.00	Lobby - Baggage Carts
Bathroom- Tubs	2,790,000.00	Closed Circuit Security Television Systems
Bathroom - Showers	350,987.00	General safe Deposit Boxes
Total Through December 31st, 2002	**208,541,887.00**	
STUCTURE ESSENITAL & ENHANCEMENTS		Telephone - Excluding Rooms
Kitchen – Main	2,860,113.00	Telephone - Main Communications Center
Kitchen – Fine Dining	261,873.00	Internal Security Systems including Cameras
Kitchen - Steak House	254,900.00	Showcases
Kitchen - Conference and Meeting Halls	543,123.00	Garage - Automatic Entry / Departure
Kitchen – Roof Top Restaurant and Lounge	321,000.00	Satellite and Communications Tower.
Kitchenette - Lobby Bar	133,600.00	Main Safe
Kitchenette - Room Service	211,000.00	Office Furniture
Indoor Swimming Pool	175,000.00	Printers
Indoor Squash Courts	250,000.00	Computer Hardware
Marble Flooring - Lobby	8,000,000.00	Scanners
Marble Flooring - Bathrooms	10,000,000.00	In House Teleconferencing Equipment
Bathroom - Shower Rods	300,000.00	Copier Machines
Bathroom - Towel Rods	430,000.00	**NON DEPRECIABLE OPERATING INVENTORY**
Spa - Swimming Pool	250,000.00	Kitchen Utensils
Spa – Pools	160,000.00	Room Towels
Chandeliers	1,500,000.00	Room Linen
Carpeting	5,000,000.00	Rooms - Door Stoppers
Total Through December 31st, 2002	**30,650,609.00**	
ACTUAL FACILITIES - CONSTRUCTION		Linen Tablecloths and Napkins
Coffee Shop	5,000,000.00	Bathroom - Bath Mats
Steak House	8,000,000.00	Cutlery and Crockery
Fine Dining	11,000,000.00	**INVENTORY - COST OF DOING BUSINESS**
Show Lounge	30,000,000.00	Regular Room Supplies
Roof Top Restaurant and Lounge	21,000,000.00	Cleaning Supplies
Meeting and Function Space	13,000,000.00	Spec Amenities, Stationery & Office
200,000 Sq ft Spa and Fitness Center	7,000,000.00	Engineering Supplies
Business Center	1,500,000.00	**INVENTORY- COST OF SALES**
Lobby Shop	540,000.00	Canned items, Peanuts
Garage	12,000,000.00	Liquor
Storage Areas	500,000.00	Non Alcoholic Beverages
Executive, Sales and Accounting Offices	2,000,000.00	Meat, Fish Frozen Foods
Total Through December 31st, 2002	**111,540,000.00**	

31

Chapter 3

The Balance Sheet - Introduction

Rules and Procedures

Introduction to Cost of Sales

Introduction to Inventory Flows

The Trial Balance

For independent business owners' can the Financial Statements provide too much detail?

 Fig 3:1 That's what I call the short Balance Sheet. Take a look at it. Although the format resembles textbook accounting it nevertheless provides the basic information.

 What other alternatives are available?

 The short Balance Sheet (Fig 3:1) won't work for teaching accounting theory and practice. <u>Even publicly held companies produce statements in the short format.</u> Fig 3:2 This is what I call the detailed Balance Sheet.

 What about Prepayments? Why are there so many of them?

 All entities have prepaid expenses such as Insurance before the doors open. The opposite applies. They had opportunities to collect Security Deposits from their commercial tenants.

Sometimes state and local legislation require deposits to be placed in trust. In that case they aren't included in the Financial Statements, as they don't have control of the funds

The mechanics for <u>initially</u> booking the <u>Prepayment</u> is mechanical. Prepayment accounts are debited (as that benefits) Cash Operating Account or Accounts Payable Trade (if purchased on credit) is credited. Booking the indoor swimming pool for $175,000 gets permanent residence in an Asset account for a long time.

Entries booked to Inventory, Prepaid Expenses, Accounts Payable, Accrued Payroll, Interest Payable among others have temporary resident status, and leave according to the accounting rules and procedures for each category.

Deacon Hotel Management Corporation
As at Januaary 31st. 2003

ASSETS

Current Assets			
Cash and Cash Equivalents			
Cash Equivalents		36,771,620.39	
Accounts Receivable	4,668,330.50		
Reserve for Bad Debts	(63,306.00)	4,605,024.50	
Other Assets		3,351,549.33	
Inventory		1,584,890.39	
Total Current Assets		46,313,084.61	
Property and Equipment			
Furniture Fittings/Equipment	10,614,884.00		
Accumulated Depreciation		10,614,884.00	
Other Assets			
Org Costs & Pre Opening	11,487,738.57		
Land and Buildings	959,952,120.00		
Total Other Assets	971,439,858.57	971,439,858.57	
Accumulated Depreciation			
Total Other Assets		982,054,742.57	
Total Assets		1,028,367,827.18	

LIABILITIES AND CAPITAL

Current Liabilities		
Accounts Payable Trade	6,458,610.55	
Payables Affiliates	800,710.61	
Taxes & Accrued Expenses	2,562,904.44	
Payroll Liabilities	1,162,618.64	
Trade & Security Deposits	2,689,082.50	
Total Current Liabilities		13,673,926.74
Long Term Liabilities		
Mortgage Payable	653,250,000.00	
Construction Loan		
Bond Issue 7% Coupon		
Total Long Term Liabilities		653,250,000.00
Total Liabilities		666,923,926.74
Capital		
Preferred Stock 7%		
Preferred Stock 5%		
Preferred Stock 9%		
Common Stock $1 Par	50,000.00	
Additional Paid in Capital	360,621,074.00	
Retained Earnings		
Treasury Stock		
Dividends Paid		
Net Income	772,826.44	
Total Capital		361,443,900.44
Total Liabilities and Capital		1,028,367,827.18

Fig 3:1

Fig 3:2

Deacon Hotel Management Corporation
As at January 31st, 2003

ASSETS

Current Assets			
Cash and Cash Equivalents			
Cash on Hand	40,000.00		
Cash Operating Account	16,731,620.39		
Cash Payroll Account			
Cash Certificate of Deposit	20,000,000.00	36,771,620.39	
Accounts Receivable	4,668,330.50		
Reserve for Bad Debts	(63,306.00)	4,605,024.50	
Prepayments			
Sales & Promotion Materials	40,000.00		
Insurance Fire	400,000.00		
Insurance General	40,000.00		
Insurance Other	7,999.33		
Insurance Terror	103,000.00		
Software Licenses	5,300.00		
Maintenance Contracts	4,800.00		
Postage Machine Rental	450.00		
Contract Cleaners	10,000.00		
Security Deposits			
Sales Tax	2,300,000.00		
Water and Power	133,000.00		
Telephone	57,000.00		
Food & Liquor Vendors	250,000.00	3,351,549.33	
Inventory			
Cleaning Supplies	4,787.40		
Regular Room Supp	16,544.80		
Other Room Supplies	55,692.75		
Food Inventory	148,184.27		
Liquor and Soft Drinks	68,021.33		
Stationery Office and Other	2,659.83		
Inventory - Other	1,289,000.00	1,584,890.39	
Total Current Assets		45,313,084.61	
Property and Equipment			
Furniture Fittings & Equipment	10,614,884.00		
Less Accumulated Depreciation	-	10,614,884.00	
Other Assets			
Org. Cost and Pre Opening Eq	11,487,738.57		
Land and Buildings	959,952,120.00		
Total Other Assets	971,439,858.57		
Less Accumulated Depreciation	971,439,858.57		
Total Assets		1,028,367,827.18	

LIABILITIES AND CAPITAL

Current Liabilities		
Trade and Affiliates		
Accounts Payable Trade	6,458,610.55	
Payables Affiliates	800,710.61	7,259,321.16
Other		
Taxes Payable Sales & Use	760,214.59	
Taxes - Income	-	
Interest Payable	1,153,225.81	
Commissions Payable	34,059.40	
Accrued Expense Payable	615,404.64	2,562,904.44
Spa Memberships	908,005.50	
Prepaid Customer Rooms	-	
Prepaid Customer Other	945,477.00	1,853,482.50
Payroll Liabilities		
Payroll Signed Gratuities	249,285.43	
Medical Insurance Payable	77,077.00	
Life and Disability Insurance	6,050.00	
401k Contributions Payable	40,794.43	
Payroll Taxes State	89,130.70	
Payroll Taxes Federal	268,547.37	
Payroll Net Payroll Payable	370,027.84	
Accrued Vacation/Sick	61,705.87	1,162,618.64
Tennant Security Deposits		
Show Case	90,060.00	
Lobby Shop	13,880.00	
Starbucks	16,800.00	
American Express Office	15,000.00	
Garage	700,060.00	835,600.00
Total Current Liabilities		13,673,926.74
Long Term Liabilities		
Mortgage Payable		
Construction Loan	653,250,000.00	
Bond Issue 30 year Coupon 7%		
Total Long Term Liabilities		653,250,000.00
Total Liabilities		666,923,926.74
Capital		
Preferred Stock 7% Interest		
Preferred Stock 5% Interest		
Preferred Stock 9% Interest		
Common Stock $1.00 Par Value	50,000.00	
Additional Paid in Capital	360,621,074.00	
Retained Earnings		
Treasury Stock		
Dividends Paid		
Net Income	772,825.44	
Total Capital		361,443,900.44
Total Liabilities and Capital		1,028,367,827.18

The official opening should be a time for celebration. Do accounting functions change on opening date?

 Opening date gives birth, <u>no matter the nature of the business</u> to the Income Statement. This milestone ends Organizational Costs and Pre Opening expenses. The Balance Sheet reports this at $11,487,738.57

Remember we are talking about expenses, not inventory or asset purchases. For example, after opening the hotel, inspections reveal a hole that should be the swimming pool. Even if the pool is purchased after opening, it's still a Capital Asset. Salaries paid to the management and staff prior to opening date, must be part of the Organizational Costs and Pre opening Expenses. After opening date those salaries become immediate expenses.

 The Balance Sheet reports total Assets of $1,028,368, which includes Land and Buildings, Prepayments, Inventories, etc. Assets don't just get there. What conditions have to be met to qualify as an Asset?

 Both of the following must be present: The rights to use the asset as a result of a transaction typically, a lease, purchase, or assignment. Future benefits must be able to be quantified with reasonable accuracy

<u>All assets generate future benefits, not all future benefits are assets.</u> Merchandise sold on credit creates a Note Receivable, or an entry to Accounts Receivable Trade. Actual delivery triggers the legal obligations to pay. <u>Title isn't required for booking an asset</u>. Copy machines purchased on installments might provide that title may be transferred at the end of the payment contract.

 How are Intangibles, such as excellent relations with employees and customers' booked?

Accounting ignores these matters due to the difficulty in valuing and quantifying them, both now and anytime in the future. Why? They are mutually unexecuted contracts.

The rights to acquire a property for $1 Billion Dollars for a definite period of time and in absence of a legal contract, no transactions are recorded in the books of either party. One requirement for a legal contract is "consideration" In legal lingo that's something of value, typically currency.

Before accounting can legitimately book Assets on the Balance Sheet, all valuation questions must be fully answered. Primarily, its Acquisition Cost otherwise usually the "Lower of Cost or Market" rules apply.

Current replacement cost is so infrequent it might as well not even be mentioned. That happens when market value is almost impossible to come by. The Internal Revenue Service, in most cases, requires Acquisition Costs.

 What are the rules of valuing not substantially declined Monetary Assets and Non-monetary Assets?

 GAAP (Generally Accepted Accounting Principles) require two valuation systems. Cash and Accounts Receivable are both recorded at their present value. Non-monetary assets are written down to the Lower of Cost or Market

Monetary assets are physical Cash on hand, Bank Operating Accounts, Payroll Accounts, Accounts Receivables and Marketable Securities. Accounts receivable is normally collected within one to three months, so for convenience, it's recorded at the amount the customer is billed. Marketable Securities, if they haven't declined substantially in value are recorded at their present value.

If Marketable Securities have declined, they must be written down to the current market value, complying with the "Lower of Cost or Market" rule. Appreciated assets are NOT revalued. If securities cost $50 per share and market price declines to $35, as the market price is below cost, the securities must be marked down.

Non-monetary assets are Merchandise Inventory, Land and Buildings, Furniture Fittings and Equipment. They are all valued at Acquisition cost, less Depreciation taken to date.

 Back to the real world, business assets are traded or exchanged at the blink of an eyelid. Do buyers' book the asset at exactly the same value the seller reported them on their Financial Statements at the time of transfer?

 GAAP (Generally Accepted Accounting Principles) require through trade in, exchange for stock, or other merchandise the acquisition cost, is the market value of the asset received. Accounting assumes the entity is a going concern. Acquisition costs provide objectivity over all other valuation methods.

Acquisition Costs seldom stir opposition, but for some other valuations there can be widespread differences of opinion. Acquisition Costs satisfy the Objectivity requirement and complying with the accounting concept of Conservatism.

 What conditions must be present before accounting recognizes a liability? The Balance Sheet (Fig 3:2) total for this category is almost $667 Million!

 Nearly all liabilities are obligations, but not all obligations are liabilities Assets require delivery, with an obligation to pay on delivery, or sometime in the future.

F ASB rules: Accounting generally recognizes a liability, when one or all of the following are present. In the future, an asset is sacrificed, which is usually cash. If cash isn't the asset that's sacrificed, the cash equivalent must be determined. There must be no option available to back out of the contract and the time of talk and making promises is over.

Accounts Payable is the total amount the entity owes all the vendors that have extended credit to them. If a custom designed automobile is ordered in December for delivery in March, with partial payment required in January the deposit is a Liability on the Balance Sheet.

 In our lawsuit crazy world, what are the rules for dealing with lawsuits?

 Lawsuits in themselves don't <u>automatically</u> trigger accounting entries. GAAP require entries when payment is probable and that's a judgment call. In practice, if probability of payment reaches 80-85% it's booked as a Liability.

 What is the Accounting Period and what is a Fiscal Year?

 Regardless of the accounting method, the accounting period is typically twelve months or one year. The natural year closes December 31st A year-end closing other than December 31st is called a fiscal year.

 Why are there "Current Assets" and "Current Liabilities?" What qualifies them to be "Current?"

Current Assets and Current liabilities are due within one year. They are booked for what the entity should pay or for what they should receive.

Liabilities exceeding one year (Long-term Bonds) are booked at the present value of future cash flows. Current Assets should return to the Cash position within one year from the transaction date.

Typical examples of Current Liabilities are: Accounts Payable, Employee Notes, Bonds Payable and Customer's

Customer Deposits.

Long-term liabilities most likely match long-term assets.

Shareholder's Equity isn't a Liability. <u>Common Stock</u> is recorded at Par value, or No Par value. Par or No Par is designed to meet the State's incorporation laws, and rarely equals the initial share price, and has no economic significance.

Typical examples of Current Assets are: Cash on Hand, Bank Operating Accounts, Payroll Accounts, Certificate of Deposits, Inventory and Prepaid Expenses.

 Why is there such intense focus on the Current Assets and the Current Liabilities?

 Don't concentrate these and ignore the rest. The Quick or the Acid Test Ratio tests the liquidity of the entity. For now, divide Current Assets by Current Liabilities.

Given my skepticism of financial reporting, (Figures never lie, but sometimes liars figure) I don't hold these ratios to the high standard many professionals do, despite lenders being very big on this one. Some of the rank and file, and even executives might be suspicious of this ratio, but they to have to live with it as corporate standards often dictates certain minimum ratios before funds can be expedited.

 Liquidity? Is this an indication how the Current Assets performed in relation to the Current Liabilities?

 Yes. If the beneficiary of a trust fund receives $20,000 a month for life and monthly expenses never exceed $5000 a month, then liquidity isn't rocket science.

Prior to the birth of credit, business start-ups required cash in order to acquire the furniture fittings and equipment, other assets and finally operating inventory purchases. This begins the accounting flow. This will be revisited.

 There is the Furniture Fittings and Equipment and a few Inventory segments. (See Fig 3:2) Is this standard procedure? If not, should it be adopted?

 Typically Balance Sheets do NOT list all the Inventory Account categories, From my experience, by default, the majority of the low end accounting software programs list all the inventory accounts on the Balance Sheet, they permit the data to be exported to other programs and modified. Fixed Assets require reconciled schedules and back up reports. Why? They are depreciated from a few years to many years.

 Furniture Fittings and Equipment are depreciable assets and can be compared to the landlord replacing the cooker. Why did you break up inventory?

 Linen, towels, tablecloths, bathmats, cutlery and crockery for the <u>hotel</u> is inventory. They wear out, or acquire legs and walk, and must be written off and replaced. Cleaning and regular room supplies are consumed as needed, and are regular expenses.

Look at the Industry! Budget hotels might provide only soap and towels. Middle of the road to luxury, they have items from soap, shampoo, chocolate, all the way to bathrobes. Some items will be consumed others will be left there for the next occupant.

 The cost of the towels and linen is booked when they are torn or acquire legs. Room supplies and cleaning materials become costs <u>immediately</u> when supplies are requested out of inventory? Are those items included in the Cost of Sales calculations?

Cost of Sales is a widely used term, and no industry or entity has a monopoly on it. You have two bottles of whiskey, and if the law permits: Option 1: One bottle is sold at the liquor store. Option 2: The second bottle is sold at a bar or hotel lounge.

Revenues from the bar or hotel lounge, compared to the liquor store, will be far greater. The bar has other costs to cover and that is another matter.

If whiskey and water sells for $5.00 per glass, and each bottle holds twenty measures, each bottle of whiskey <u>should</u> generate $100.00. In practice it's too easy.

Cocktails are a dash of this and a dash of that. Then there's wastage. The cost price of the whiskey is standard but what price customers will pay, will vary even within the same establishment. The whiskey served at the Roof Top Lounge will likely generate a higher price compared with the Lobby Bar location due to the exotic views! How is cost of beverage calculated?

This is covered in the chapter dedicated to Inventory, and it's an Income Statement issue too. As this is an extremely important area, I am introducing it here.

At the beginning of the month, the physical count of the inventory is valued at $100,000. During the month, requisitions are $50,000 making the total amount available for sale during the month of $150,000.00. The physical inventory count at the end of the month values it at $90,000.

To calculate the COST OF SALES, deduct the total available from the closing inventory valuation and that's $60,000 for the month.

That's comparable to Macy's buying $60,000 for shoes for sale at mark up. If the Bar generates Beverage revenue of $240,000 for the month, then the Gross Margin is $240,000 less $60,000 leaving $180,000.

Food is no different. The establishment buys 50 lbs of potatoes, and 500 lbs of beef. The potatoes and beef are used to satisfy patrons. That comparable to General Motors purchasing 500 engines and other components and producing completed vehicles.

 Cash and Inventory are Current Assets. For the hotel, bath towels and tablecloths are classified as Inventory?

 Inventory by default is a Current Asset. Before blindly accepting any ratios at face value, or any Balance Sheet valuations, ask what the Inventory will realize at a forced liquidation sale.

What would the linen generate with the Deacon Hotels name on them?

For example, the entity has no credit but has sufficient cash to purchase six shirts. In this case, the shirts were in inventory for six months until one customer purchased all six of them in on shot. The cycle is complete when the transaction completes the cycle back to the cash position.

 Now that the entity has acquired Inventory for resale or Inventory for use in serving breakfast, nothing changes without a buyer?

 Absolutely. That's the reason inventory purchases are NOT expenses. This is an excellent time to go through the steps. Inventory is an Asset and remains on the Balance Sheet, until all or part of those items are sold.

We move on to inventory flows. Fig 3:3: Reports the book value of Cash and Cash Equivalents and Other Assets before acquiring Inventory. (Inventory is zero)

Fig 3:4: Reports the movement of $3,000,000 of Inventory paid in Cash. Initial Inventory on hand is valued at

Current Assets		Current Liabilities
Cash and Cash Equivalents		
Cash Equivalents	10,000,000.00	Accounts Payable Trade
Accounts Receivable		Payables Affiliates
Reserve for Bad Debts		Taxes & Accrued Expenses
Other Assets	3,351,549.33	Payroll Liabilities
Inventory		Trade & Security Deposits
Total Current Assets	13,351,549.33	Total Current Liabilities

Fig 3:3

ASSETS		Tranactions		LIABILITIES
		Effect		
Current Assets			Current Liabilities	
Cash Equivalents	10,000,000.00	7,000,000.00	Accounts Payable Trade
Accounts Receivable			Payables - Affiliates
Reserve for Bad Debts			Taxes & Accrued Exp
Other Assets	3,351,549.33	3,351,549.33	Payroll Liabilities
Inventory		3,000,000.00	Deposits
Total Current Assets	13,351,549.33	13,351,549.33	Total Current Liabilities

Fig 3:4

Fig 3:5: Reports the movement of $3,000.000 of inventory acquired on Credit

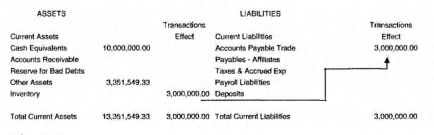

Fig 3:5

$3,000,000. In this case (Fig 3:6) $2,500,000 of inventory at cost is later sold for $4,200,000 (See Accounts Receivable) to one client on credit. At the time of sale, $500,000 of the original inventory remains. They place an additional order for $3,000.000 worth of inventory. The cash account is now $4,000,000 and Accounts Receivable at $4,200,000. Inventory is $3,500,000.

ASSETS			LIABILITIES
		Transactions	
Current Assets		Affected	Current Liabilities
Cash Equivalents	7,000,000.00	4,000,000.00	Accounts Payable Trade
Accounts Receivable		4,200,000.00	Payables - Affiliates
Reserve for Bad Debts			Taxes & Accrued Exp
Other Assets	3,351,549.33	3,351,549.33	Payroll Liabilities
Inventory	3,000,000.00	3,500,000.00	Deposits
Total Current Assets	13,351,549.33	15,051,549.33	Total Current Liabilities

Fig 3:6

Assets can only be classified within the Current Assets section if they are expected to return to the cash position within the accounting <u>period of one year.</u>

This time the original inventory is purchased on credit. (Accounts Payable shows $3,000.000; the Bank is $7,000,000 the original consignment was paid in cash) This time the entire inventory is sold to one client on credit for $3,700,000. See fig 3:7.

ASSETS			LIABILITIES	
		Transactions		Transactions
Current Assets		Affected	Current Liabilities	Affected
Cash Equivalents	10,000,000.00	7,000,000.00	Accounts Payable Trade	3,000,000.00
Accounts Receivable		3,700,000.00	Payables - Affiliates	
Reserve for Bad Debts			Taxes & Accrued Exp	
Other Assets	3,351,549.33	3,351,549.33	Payroll Liabilities	
Inventory	3,000,000.00	3,000,000.00	Deposits	
Total Current Assets	16,351,549.33	17,051,549.33	Total Current Liabilities	3,000,000.00

Fig: 3.7

Why are the Prepayments Current Assets? Why are Trade and Security Deposits Liabilities?

Security deposits for the apartment or membership dues are paid in advance sometimes over a year or more, and sometime over a few weeks.

What about selling or pledging Accounts Receivable?

Selling and pledging Accounts Receivable is big business, usually at very unfavorable interest rates for the borrower. If the Accounts Receivables are sold, they can't be part of the Balance Sheet. If they are given as security, they are shown on the Balance Sheet, but this reality must be disclosed in the notes to the Financial Statements

 How often is the Trial Balance prepared and what is the purpose of it?

 Due to the volume of work in manual systems, Trial Balances are prepared at the end of the month. From the Trial Balance the Financial Statements are generated.

There's an Unadjusted Trial Balance and an Adjusted Trial Balance. Unadjusted Trial Balances tells you adjustments are required. Today computers produce Trial Balances on demand. Fig 3:8 attempts to give you an idea of what a Trial Balance is, and what it does. A complete Trial Balance lists all the Revenue and Expense accounts. This one, for illustration, lists only the Balance Sheet items.

The Trial Balance (Fig 3:8) lists the Accounts Categories. The columns to the right list the outstanding balances, one column for Debit Balances, the other for Credit Balances. They must both add up to the same figure with no plug. The arrows show the exact position where those accounts are located on the Balance Sheet. If this Trial Balance included the Revenue and Expense Accounts, those would be located on the Income Statement.

 Some entities don't have Inventory for sale as their core product, some have little or no Fixed Assets, but every entity has purchases. We will find the answer when we get to the Income Statement, but for now, Inventory Purchases are not expenses. Are Purchases unique in having their own Journal?

Standard Balance Sheets lists totals for the accounts. Details are located elsewhere! Accounting terminology doesn't resemble Twenty First century

Manual Accounting systems have JOURNALS listing the amounts paid for items purchased, including other details. Computerized accounting still calls them journals such as the PURCASES JOURNAL. At the end of the period, the total is POSTED to the GENERAL LEDGER accounts.

"Have the results been posted to the General Ledger?" is still common throughout the world no matter the level of accounting technology

The Purchases Journal lists all the PURCHAES for the period. The Sales journal lists all the SALES for the month. The GENERAL LEDGER lists and holds all the accounts and transactions that make up the FINANCIAL STATEMENTS. These journals are NOT part of the GENERAL LEDGER. Totals are TRANSFERED to the general ledger.

 Is the Accounts Receivable the opposite of Accounts Payable Trade?

 For now, yes. A chapter is dedicated to both Accounts Receivable and Accounts Payable.

Account	Account Description	Debit Amt	Credit Amt	Balance Sheet for Deacon Hotel Properties as at December 31st, 2002	
				Current Assets	
10101	Cash Operating Account		1,337,169.00	Cash Operating Account	<1,337,169.00>
10302	Prepay-Sales & Promotion Mat	50,000.00		Prepay-Sales & Promotion Mat	50,000.00
10303	Prepay-Insurance Fire	500,000.00		Prepay-Insurance Fire	500,000.00
10304	Prepay-Insurance General	83,333.00		Prepay-Insurance General	83,333.00
10305	Prepay-Insurance Other	16,666.00		Prepay-Insurance Other	16,666.00
10306	Prepay-Insurance Terror	226,000.00		Prepay-Insurance Terror	226,000.00
10307	Prepay-Software Licenses	6,500.00		Prepay-Software Licenses	6,500.00
10308	Prepay-Server Maint Contracts	6,000.00		Prepay-Server Maint Contracts	6,000.00
10309	Prepay-Postage Machine Rental	900.00		Prepay-Postage Machine Rental	900.00
10310	Prepay-Contract Cleaners	20,000.00		Prepay-Contract Cleaners	20,000.00
10311	Security Dep Sales Tax	2,300,000.00		Security Dep Sales Tax	2,300,000.00
10312	Security Dep - Water and Power	133,000.00		Security Dep - Water and Power	133,000.00
10313	Security Dep - Telephone	57,000.00		Security Dep - Telephone	57,000.00
10314	Security Dep - Food Liquor Ven	250,000.00		Security Dep - Food Liquor Ven	250,000.00
10401	Furniture Fittings & Equipment	10,614,884.00		Cleaning Supplies	5,000.00
10500	Org Cost & Pre Opening Exp	1,200,000.00		Regular Room Supp	28,600.00
10501	Land and Buildings	959,952,120.00		Other Room Supplies	65,770.00
10602	Cleaning Supplies	5,000.00		Food Inventory	75,360.00
10603	Regular Room Supp	28,600.00		Liquor and Soft Drinks	196,984.00
10604	Other Room Supplies	65,770.00		Stationery Office and Other	2,700.00
10605	Food Inventory	75,360.00		Inventory - Other	1,289,000.00
10606	Liquor and Soft Drinks	196,984.00		Total Current Assets	3,975,644.00
10607	Stationery Office and Other			Property and Equipment	
10608	Inventory - Other	1,289,000.00		Furniture Fittings & Equipment	10,614,884.00
15100	Accounts Payable Trade		13,187,697.00	Total Property and Equipment	10,614,884.00
15109	Deposits - Customers Other		1,048,277.00	Other Assets	
15111	Security Deposits-Lobby Shop		13,800.00	Org Cost & Pre Opening Exp	1,200,000.00
15112	Security Deposits-Starbucks		16,800.00	Land and Buildings	959,952,120.00
15113	Security Deposits-Amex Office		15,000.00	Total Other Assets	961,152,120.00
26102	Construction Loan		600,000,000.00	Total Assets	975,742,648.00
26502	Common Stock $1.00 Par Value		50,000.00		
26503	Additional Paid in Capital		360,621,074.00	LIABILITIES AND CAPITAL	
		977,079,817.00	977,079,817.00	Current Liabilities	
				Accounts Payable Trade	13,187,697.00
				Deposits - Customers Other	1,048,277.00
				Security Deposits-Show Case	90,000.00
				Security Deposits-Lobby Shop	13,800.00
				Security Deposits-Starbucks	16,800.00
				Security Deposits-Amex Office	15,000.00
				Security Deposits-Garage	700,000.00
				Total Current Liabilities	15,071,574.00
				Long-Term Liabilities	
				Construction Loan	600,000,000.00
				Total Long-Term Liabilities	600,000,000.00
				Total Liabilities	615,071,574.00
				Capital	
				Common Stock $1.00 Par Value	50,000.00
				Additional Paid in Capital	360,621,074.00
				Net Income	0.00
				Total Capital	360,671,074.00
				Total Liabilities & Capital	975,742,648.00

Fig 3:8

Chapter 4

You told us the Income Statement (Profit and Loss) initially was for convenience only. Where is it in the hierarchy of reports?

 For example: The other side of the Current liabilities on the Balance Sheet is found on in the Income Statement. If the Income Statement (Profit or Loss) were declared illegal, those entries have no place to go accept to the Retained Earnings. The Income Statement is the number two in the hierarchy after the Balance Sheet, and before the Statement of Cash Flows.

 Income Statements prepared under the Accrual method report different results compared to the Cash method or the Hybrid methods. What are the differences between the various methods?

 Investors and lenders frequently demand the Financial Statements to be prepared under the accrual method. This applies to un-audited Financial Statements as well.

Financial Statements prepared under the Accrual method convert easily to the Cash method of accounting, but that can't be said for statements prepared under the Cash Method. Depreciation doesn't discriminate between the cash and accrual methods.

The Internal Revenue Service care less if taxes are filed under the Cash method and the Accrual method is used for financial reporting as <u>long as the conversion is proper and accurate</u>. It requires IRS approval to change from one method to another. Approval isn't automatic.

Outside (External) Auditors can't audit Financial Reports prepared under the Cash method, if one method doesn't qualify to perform an audit, there are some serious differences. For example, you are the seller and have shipped merchandise to a client that has an open account with you.

Under Accrual, you MUST book the shipment of that merchandise as Income. Shipping and insuring this merchandise costs $3,000.00. Under Accrual Accounting you MUST book the expense too.

 You tell me, the merchandise that's sold on credit, and the client will pay much later, and as you haven't paid the shipping, there shouldn't be any entries recorded? That's the Cash method.

 Accrual books the income the moment there is a contractual liability, and shipping the merchandise and granting credit triggered that contractual legal obligation. As the Accrual method requires booking income the moment there is a contractual obligation, the same procedure applies to expenses.

Shipping the merchandise created an obligation for you the seller, so you must book the freight as well.

Under Cash Accounting, when you pay the freight, you will book the expense. When and if your customers pay, then you will book the Income.

Only Accrual complies with the Matching Principle. Income for the period is matched with expenses for the period. As this is vital to understand, I am using a few long examples:

If the landlord allows the tenant to pay rent six months in arrears, (I wish!) under Accrual, the rental income is booked effective the first day of each month if, that's the contractual due date.

Service industries typically, law and accounting firms are almost all on the Cash method. The end result doesn't make much difference as payment for the services rendered comes in shortly after the services are rendered, satisfying the Matching concept. Retainers are spread over the length of the contract, follows the Accrual method, as the Cash method doesn't provide for it.

A catering outfit hosts a wedding reception for $200,000.00. Management dropped the ball by not collecting the cash up front or obtaining a hold on their credit card. By the time the organizers received the bill for this unsecured debt, they have zero incentive to pay. To the extreme, $200,000.00 is collected two years later, under the Cash method, only then will it be taken into income. If entities could delay the cost of their payroll for this function for two years, then the Cash method would satisfy the Matching Principle.

Cash accounting recognizes expenses when they are paid, and income when received. In the case of the catering outfit there would be a two-year gap for this event! Imagine General Electric deferring income based on the Cash method for $1 Billion for a couple of years! "Oh by the way, we recently collected on some significantly past due bills"

 How does the Cash method deal with Bad Debts? "Figures never lie, sometimes liars figure" Do liars figure easier under the Cash Method as they might have better opportunities to cover their tracks?

 The Cash method on the books, don't have ANY Bad Debts. Cash Accounting takes into Income WHEN and IF the customer pays.

Entities must keep track of Receivables as they would under the Accrual Method, but from the Financial Statements, you would never know the entity experienced any losses from extending in-house credit.

Those committed to graduating top of their class to become masters of "Figures never lie, sometimes liars figure" have many more opportunities under the cash method, but accrual accounting is far from perfect, and coming up with a plan and some creativity can achieve remarkable results.

The hybrid method handles Inventory on the accrual method with expenses under the cash method. So the hybrid method is the best of both worlds?

 No! Cash and accrual accounting aren't interchangeable. Recall, if the entity requires audited Financial Statements, the hybrid method isn't fitting the bill either.

The only way the statements will get a clear bill of health from the outside auditors, is that they must be prepared under the accrual method

 Accounting has definite rules before assets can be recorded. How is Income measured? How are the expenses measured?

 For income it's selling price. For expenses it's the amount paid or the invoice price, whichever is lower.

 Explain the terms, Posting and Journalizing?

 The General Journals, Purchases Journal, Sales Journal etc accumulate transactions. The totals from these Journals are transferred to the General Ledger. This specific process is called "Journalizing"

 Could we have a look how one of these Journals actually looks like? Is the layout the same for the Purchases Journal and the Sales Journal?

 The Purchases Journal (Fig. 4:1) is a partial list. You don't need to see pages and pages of data. This is sufficient to understand what these Journals contain, and yes, the Sales Journal will have a similar layout.

Date	A/C ID	Account Description	Invoice/CM #	Line Description	Debit Amount	Credit Amount
1/1/03	10309	Prepay-Postage Machine Rental	Post Machine	Postage Machine Contracts	900.00	
1/1/03	15100	Accounts Payable Trade	Post Machine	POSTAGE MACHINE CONTRACT		900.00
1/1/03	10306	Prepay-Insurance Terror	Insurterr1	Insurance - Terror Related	226,000.00	
1/1/03	15100	Accounts Payable Trade	Insurterr1	INSURANCE TERROR		226,000.00
1/2/03	10401	Furniture Fittings & Equipment	Hotbed001	Bed Boards	550,000.00	
1/2/03	10401	Furniture Fittings & Equipment	Hotbed001	Bed Frames	300,000.00	
1/2/03	10401	Furniture Fittings & Equipment	Hotbed001	Rollaway Beds	12,000.00	
1/2/03	10401	Furniture Fittings & Equipment	Hotbed001	Drapes for the Rooms	300,000.00	
1/2/03	15100	Accounts Payable Trade	Hotbed001	HOTEL BEDDING SUPPLIES		1,162,000.00

Transaction Date
General Ledger Account Number
Supplier Reference Number
Description of Services
Debit Allocation   Credit Allocation

Fig 4:1

The Bookkeeper can't present pages upon pages of T-Accounts for processing, but surely, computerized accounting has replaced doing Journal entries?

The high-speed idiot (the computer) hasn't eliminated the Purchases, Sales and Payroll Journals. As the Journals haven't been eliminated, Journal Entries can't be eliminated, because the totals from these Journals must be transferred to the General Ledger, which holds the Financial Statements. It just isn't as obvious!

We used the T-Account extensively in the previous chapters. The left side houses the debit entries, the right side the credit entries. Repetition is the mother of learning, so back to the Brown Family transactions. We'll bring back the T-Accounts then journalize them!

For simplicity, $4000 is moved from the Money Market to Checking.
Which one receives and which one gives?
The receiver is the checking account
The receiver is ALWAYS the DEBIT.
Which account is allotted the credit?
This case the Money Market Account

The T- Accounts would look like this

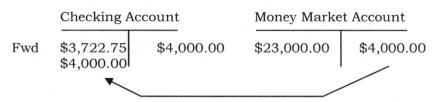

Checking Account		Money Market Account	
Fwd $3,722.75 $4,000.00	$4,000.00	$23,000.00	$4,000.00

The Journal Entry in recording the transfer of $4,000 from the Money Market Account to the Checking Account:

Jan 15th Checking Account $4000.00
        Money Market Account $4000.00
        Monthly bill payment Money Market to Checking

Now apply the monthly payments. What account provides funding? Here is the flow

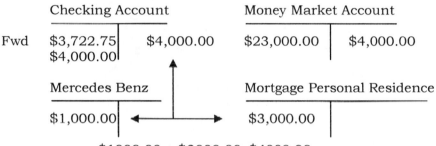

Checking Account		Money Market Account	
Fwd $3,722.75 $4,000.00	$4,000.00	$23,000.00	$4,000.00

Mercedes Benz		Mortgage Personal Residence	
$1,000.00		$3,000.00	

$1000.00 + $3000.00=$4000.00

Jan 15th. Mortgage Personal Residence $3000.00
        Automobile Mercedes Benz $1,000.00
        Checking Account $4000.00
        Monthly bill payment Automobiles January 2002

 Explain the accounting term "Closing the Revenue and Expense accounts"?

 This is the common terminology calling for the transfer of the net result produced by the Income Statement to the Retained Earnings account on the Balance Sheet.

The procedure: Closing the Revenue and Expense accounts moves those amounts to the Retained Earnings.

Treasury Stock is part of the Shareholders' Equity section of the Balance Sheet. Treasury stock is NOT United States Government Securities, rather it's the corporations' own stock that's been acquired for cash on the open market and the shares are not being cancelled.

Corporations often buy their stock on the open market, hold them for a while, and then sell them. If the shares are cancelled, the number of shares outstanding is reduced. If the corporation buys 10,000 shares of it's own stock at $50.00 per share for $500,000. The shares are later sold for $55.00 per share realizing a gain of $50,000.00. Gains and losses from the sale of treasury stock aren't recognized for tax purposes. The rationale is the corporation is trading its own equity. The gains and losses remain in the shareholders' equity section and do NOT affect the income statement.

The Retained Earnings contains the total gains and losses minus dividends and other distributions from the beginning of time. All Income statement accounts begin their balances at the year with zero and accumulate to the end of the year. Balance Sheet accounts have running balances and never close.

 Explain the accounting term "The Closing Process" Is it interchangeable with "Closing the Revenue and Expense Accounts"

 Technically, this process closes the EXPENSE accounts to the new period (the following month)

There are two separate procedures. The <u>Closing Process</u> closes or completes the month. For example, the books for February aren't yet closed and the water bill for the month is $10,000.00. The accumulated expense for water at the end of January is $8,000.00. The Closing Process at the end of February takes the $8,000.00 plus the current $10,000.00 reporting a total water expense of $18,000.00.

There are two separate procedures. The <u>Closing Process</u>

closes or completes the month. For example, the books for February aren't yet closed and the water bill for the month is $10,000.00. The accumulated expense for water at the end of January is $8,000.00. The Closing Process at the end of February takes the $8,000.00 plus the current $10,000.00 reporting a total water expense of $18,000.00.

Manual systems require each account to be closed, the amounts brought forward, and properly balanced. Accounting software handles this process.

 This might be too early in the game but large entities might not qualify to utilize Departmental Income Statements but the smaller entity might qualify. Would you post the different formats Income Statements can take, even though we haven't even scraped the surface with this Financial Statement? Although it might be bind boggling at first, we will have a reference to an actual Income Statement as you go through the concepts and the workings?

 Entities elect to file taxes under the Cash or the Accrual method and changes must have the IRS stamp of approval. With Departmentalized Income Statements net income is identical. Producing Income Statements in this format is an internal matter, and can be changed at will.

Macy's Sacks Fifth Avenue, Bloomingdale's etc sells, cosmetics, formal clothing, casual clothing, linens, jewelry, watches, etc. These are departments, and income and expenses can be clearly defined and allocated. As long as the revenue and expenses for these departments can be contained within each category, then each of those departments produce an operating profit or loss just as if they are a stand-alone operation.

A 150-room hotel can elect Departmentalized Income Statements so long as the revenue for Rooms, Coffee Shop, Business Center and the Meeting Space are segregated and the expenses matched. If they can't allocate the cost of labor, and other expenses to the respective departments, Departmentalized Income Statements are out of the door!

Subsidiaries are separate legal entities apart from the parent company. Legally they must produce their own Financial Results. Fig 4.2 reports Food and Beverage revenue of $6,576,973.35. Total Food and Beverage Expenses are $3,196,596.84. The difference between the two amounts produces a net Food and Beverage Departmental gain of $4,380,0376.92. This format provides a quick overview of all the other major operating departments as well.

Fig 4:3: This is a Deacon Hotel Coffee Shop and Room Service Department. Look at the bottom line of both these departments.

Now place yourself in the position of the management. How valuable, is having this information in making quality decisions? Now place yourself in the position of being the sole owner. Would management provide this kind of information, if you didn't demand it? Accounting is more than the limited Financial Statements the public corporations issue For owners of, or investors in small to medium size business, would management produce the very minimum, or would they volunteer to produce the kind of Financial reporting your really need?

 Do all departments get the same treatment? The Room Service has a loss to date of $635,391.68, which isn't obvious in the overall Food and Beverage performance.

 All departments are identical as long as they produce revenue. Non-revenue departments as Human Resources, Sales, Repairs and Maintenance, General and Administration are essential to the overall operation. They can't be allocated to any specific department.

The Financial Statements are found at the end of the last

Income Statement for Deacon Management Corporation
For the Month Ending May 31st, 2003

Revenues	Current Month	Percent	Year to Date	Percent
Room Revenue	9,611,778.18	56.04%	44,115,728.58	55.88%
Revenue Spa and Fitness	223,368.30	1.30%	1,436,311.32	1.82%
Revenue Rooms Generated Phone	187,937.76	1.10%	821,606.54	1.04%
Revenue Business Center	11,843.83	0.07%	121,129.76	0.15%
Revenue Other	56,139.95	0.33%	324,421.71	0.41%
Space Rental and Garage	483,203.82	2.82%	1,895,294.77	2.40%
Revenue Food and Beverage	6,576,973.35	38.35%	30,235,967.86	38.30%
Total Revenue	17,151,245.19	100.00%	78,950,460.54	100.00%
Rooms Department Expense	970,456.93	5.66%	4,400,755.30	5.57%
Food and Beverage	3,196,596.84	18.64%	14,029,248.77	
Spa and Fitness	93,624.12	0.55%	402,488.82	0.51%
Telephone Department	81,242.22	0.47%	500,227.19	0.63%
Business Center	58,202.95	0.34%	257,641.07	0.33%
Front of the House	124,871.05	0.73%	507,601.11	0.64%
Doormen and Other	70,054.40	0.41%	314,793.60	0.40%
Repairs and Maintenance	225,947.58	1.32%	1,376,578.47	1.74%
Security	72,516.82	0.42%	320,951.10	0.41%
Human Resources	98,643.08	0.58%	268,781.55	0.34%
Sales and Marketing	213,055.34	1.24%	1,264,354.07	1.60%
General and Administrative	728,213.88	4.25%	3,295,180.92	4.17%
Executive Offices	167,232.26	0.98%	794,345.17	1.01%
Total Non Food & Bev Operating Expenses	6,100,657.47	35.57%	27,732,947.14	35.13%
Net Operating Income or Loss	11,050,587.72	64.43%	51,217,513.40	64.87%
Non Operating Expenses				
Insurance	363,000.00	2.12%	1,494,999.00	1.89%
Management and Trademark Fees	2,099,349.62	12.24%	9,662,649.41	12.24%
Interest Expense	3,232,100.87	18.84%	16,263,065.29	20.60%
Property Taxes	474,308.20	2.77%	1,917,308.20	2.43%
Depreciation and Amortization	3,662,065.30	21.35%	14,744,796.82	18.68%
Excise and Other Taxes		0.00%		0.00%
Gain or Loss on Disposition of Assets		0.00%		0.00%
Gain or Loss Other		0.00%		0.00%
Total Non Operating Expenses	9,830,823.99	57.32%	44,082,818.72	55.84%
Profit or Loss before Income Taxes	1,219,763.73	7.11%	7,134,694.68	9.04%
Income Taxes Federal and State	417,864.69	2.44%	2,683,702.67	3.40%
Net Profit or Loss	801,899.04	4.68%	4,450,992.01	5.64%

Fig 4:2

Income Statement for Deacon Management Corporation
For the Month Ending May 31st, 2003

Revenues	Current Month	Percent	Year to Date	Percent
Revenue Coffee Shop Food	545,409.92	96.59%	2,620,007.02	97.18%
Revenue Coffee Shop Liquor	19,250.42	3.41%	76,050.96	2.82%
Total Revenue	564,660.34	100.00%	2,696,057.98	100.00%
Cost of Sales:				
Coffee Shop Cost of Food	236,162.50	43.30%	969,065.58	36.99%
Coffee Shop Cost of Liquor	6,006.13	31.20%	21,417.91	28.16%
Total Cost of Sales	242,168.63	42.69%	990,483.49	
Gross Profit Margin	322,491.71	57.11%	1,705,574.49	63.26%
Operating Expenses				
Coffee Shop Gross Payroll	146,544.00	25.95%	624,090.00	23.15%
Employer Payroll Taxes	13,227.43	2.34%	63,458.10	2.35%
Coffee Shop Vacation and Sick	11,317.86	2.00%	54,297.00	2.01%
Coffee Shop Employer Medical	4,200.00	0.74%	20,400.00	0.76%
Employer Life and Disability	384.00	0.07%	1,836.00	0.07%
Coffee Shop Employer 401k	2,640.83	0.47%	12,177.27	0.45%
Employee Benefits Other	0.00	0.00%	0.00	0.00%
Coffee Stationery and Office	255.17	0.05%	1,523.97	0.06%
Coffee Shop Copy Paper	0.00	0.00%	4,965.28	0.18%
Coffee Shop Managers Meals	116.46	0.02%	677.86	0.03%
Coffee Non Inventory Supplies	657.67	0.12%	1,018.65	0.04%
Coffee Shop Travel	244.87	0.04%	719.52	0.03%
Coffee Shop Uniforms	0.00	0.00%	5,239.49	0.19%
Coffee Shop Miscellaneous	0.00	0.00%	704.52	0.03%
Printing and Design	5,511.82	0.98%	19,793.92	0.73%
Coffee Shop Signage	0.00	0.00%	1,787.73	0.07%
Decorating Expenses	0.00	0.00%	1,723.93	0.06%
Coffee Shop Laundry	4,004.04	0.71%	24,117.52	0.89%
Coffee Shop Dry cleaning	312.22	0.06%	1,880.67	0.07%
Coffee Shop Postage	0.00	0.00%	0.00	0.00%
Total Non Cost of Sales Expenses	189,416.37	33.55%	840,411.43	31.17%
Coffee Shop Profit or Loss	133,075.34	23.57%	865,163.06	32.09%
Revenue Room Service Food	28,860.37	82.47%	131,058.96	81.98%
Revenue Room Service Liquor	2,317.92	6.62%	11,486.55	7.18%
Total Room Service Food & Bev	31,178.29		142,545.51	
Room Service Delivery Charge	3,815.51	10.90%	17,327.65	10.84%
Total Room Service Revenue	34,993.80	100.00%	159,873.16	100.00%
Room Service Cost of Food	12,207.94	42.30%	51,340.17	39.17%
Room Service Cost of Beverage	846.04	2.93%	3,952.66	3.02%
Total Cost of Sales	13,053.98	37.30%	55,292.83	
Gross Profit Margin	21,939.82	62.70%	104,580.33	65.41%
Operating Expenses				
Room Service Gross Payroll	130,032.00	371.59%	553,770.00	346.38%
Employer Payroll Taxes	15,864.21	45.33%	60,435.10	37.80%
Vacation and Sick	13,573.98	38.79%	51,710.40	32.34%
Employer Medical	2,800.00	8.00%	13,600.00	8.51%
Employer Life and Disability	256.00	0.73%	1,224.00	0.77%
Room Service Employer 401k	3,167.27	9.05%	12,065.77	7.55%
Employee Benefits Other	0.00	0.00%	0.00	0.00%
Stationery and Office	267.93	0.77%	1,180.17	0.74%
Room Service Copy Paper	1,500.40	4.29%	6,608.95	4.13%
Room Service Managers Meals	93.17	0.27%	542.29	0.34%
Non Inventory Supplies	644.87	1.84%	1,070.15	0.67%
Room Service Travel	244.52	0.70%	458.11	0.29%
Room Service Uniforms	0.00	0.00%	7,279.79	4.55%
Room Service Miscellaneous	0.00	0.00%	308.65	0.19%
Room ServicPrinting and Design	2,834.65	8.10%	10,179.73	6.37%
Room Service Signage	0.00	0.00%	3,828.13	2.39%
Room ServiceDecorating Expense	0.00	0.00%	2,398.29	1.50%
Room Service Laundry	2,002.02	5.72%	12,058.77	7.54%
Room Service Dry cleaning	206.14	0.59%	1,253.71	0.78%
Total Non Cost of Sales Expenses	173,489.16	495.77%	739,972.01	462.85%
Room Service Profit or Loss	(151,549.34)	-3971.93%	(635,391.68)	-3666.92%

Fig 4:3

60

chapter of this book. There are arguments for and against Departmentalized Income Statements. Know the difference and understand them

 Don't all Expenses offset Income under the Accrual method? What about Total Receipts and Total Income? Are they used interchangeably?

 There's a constant flow between the Balance Sheet and the Income Statement. Understanding and mastering this flow is vital. This will be revisited before the close of this chapter.

Fig 4:4 takes the Rooms Department. The left side lists Total Receipts. To the right are the required Journal Entries. Total Receipts include Sales Taxes. For the Rooms Department, Gross Income is Total Receipts less Total Sales Taxes. The amounts that don't qualify as Income are located on the Liability Side of the Balance Sheet

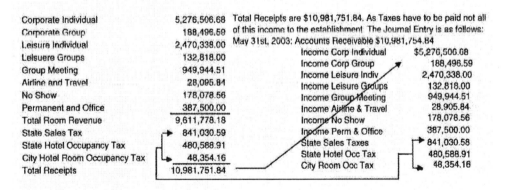

Corporate Individual	5,276,506.68	Total Receipts are $10,981,751.84. As Taxes have to be paid not all
Corporate Group	188,496.59	of this income to the establishment. The Journal Entry is as follows:
Leisure Individual	2,470,338.00	May 31st, 2003: Accounts Receivable $10,981,754.84
Leisuere Groups	132,818.00	Income Corp Individual $5,276,506.68
Group Meeting	949,944.51	Income Corp Group 188,496.59
Airline and Travel	28,095.84	Income Leisure Indiv 2,470,338.00
No Show	178,078.56	Income Leisure Groups 132,818.00
Permanent and Office	387,500.00	Income Group Meeting 949,944.51
Total Room Revenue	9,611,778.18	Income Airline & Travel 28,905.84
State Sales Tax	841,030.59	Income No Show 178,078.56
State Hotel Occupancy Tax	480,588.91	Income Perm & Office 387,500.00
City Hotel Room Occupancy Tax	48,354.16	State Sales Taxes 841,030.58
Total Receipts	10,981,751.84	State Hotel Occ Tax 480,588.91
		City Room Occ Tax 48,354.16

Fig 4:4

Move on to Fig 4:5. The current months Total Income is $17,151,245.19 (not Total Receipts) Income accounts are credited. The debit is either Cash or Accounts Receivable Accounts. That's the portion that's sold on credit.

Whenever gratuities are added for the restaurant server, the taxi driver, the hairdresser, etc to the bill that's paid by credit card, Signed Gratuities Payable, or some other

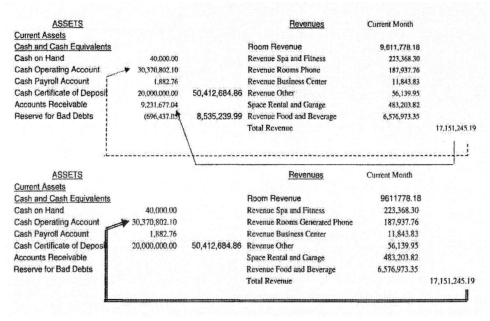

Fig 4:5

account having the same purpose is affected. Total Receipts now has Food and Beverage Sales, Sales Taxes plus Signed Gratuities.

Entities that don't fall into the trap and pay the recipients in cash at the end of the day or week, instead paying them through payroll, insures compliance with the tax code that all income is taxed, and helps avoid penalties for the employer.

 What are the standard procedures for Sales Discounts and Allowances?

 So long customers have rights to return merchandise, GAAP permits Revenue recognition only when the returns can be reasonably estimated, and the use of an Allowance account is mandatory.

 Where are the Sales Returns and Discounts located? How are they recorded?

The Income Statements reports the net effect of Sales less Sales Returns. In practice, Income Statements segregate Sales Returns. The Journal Entries report Gross Merchandise sales of $1 million. Sales Returns: $250,000

Journal Entries booking the Initial Sales:

May 31st   Accounts Receivable $1,000,000
               Merchandise Income $1,000,000
             Record Gross Sales for the Month May

The Sales Returns are:

May 31stMerchandise Income $250,000
              Allowances Merchandise Returns $250,000
              Merchandise Returns for the Month of May

Accounting calls this a Contra Entry, debiting Merchandise Income for $25,000.00 instead of the Allowance account. One benefit of utilizing Allowances accounts is that it leaves a permanent record providing an audit trail. The Income Statement could be presented in this format:

Merchandise Income $1,000,.000.00
Less Allow/Returns $ 250,000.00 $750,000.00

Adjusting entries utilize Journal Entries. The word adjust means fine tune or change. What do they accomplish in accounting? If they are ignored, is this a big deal?

Adjusting entries are used for reallocation purposes. Typically they're found among Prepayments, Accrued Expenses, Depreciation and the correction of errors.

Adjusting entries typically affect at least one Income, Expense, Asset or Liability account. As adjusting entries correct or fine-tune, their scope is unlimited. Ignoring or forgetting to do adjusting entries can trigger disastrous consequences.

The Trial Balance is an excellent tool that can be used to confirm the required entries have been done as well as being a check on pending items.

 Prepayments are Current Assets. Customers' Advance Deposits are Current Liabilities

 Complying with the Matching principle, expenses are booked at the time the legal obligation is triggered.

Take the payment for the Fire Insurance premiums for $24,000 that was sent in December, covering the period January through December of the following year. The payment is booked in December to the Prepayment account. That is a Balance Sheet item.

Dec 15th 20 Prepayment Fire Insurance $24,000.00
            Cash or Accounts Payable $24,000.00
      Prepayment January December 2003 Fire Insurance

Book the Adjusting Entry each month from January through December 2003.

Jan 1st 2004 Fire Insurance $2,000.00
            Prepayments Fire Insurance $2,000.00
      Allocation of Fire Insurance Expense January 2004

 Prepaying Fire Insurance makes sense but who in their right mind would prepay the Postage Machine Contract or the Contract Cleaners?

Timing Timing Timing™ That's an excellent question Once again, the Deacon slogan holding true: It's Timing Timing Timing™. <u>Accounting requires the entry to Prepayments, whenever the payment for a product or a service is made for services pertaining to a future period.</u> If the July Contract Cleaners monthly expense is $20,000.00 with the contract specifying the payment must be received by the first of the month. The Postage Machine rental must be paid by the 3rd of the month.

If the entity doesn't utilize <u>a bank transfer</u> that would on the 1st of the month for the Contract cleaners, the 3rd of the month for the Postage Machine, but elects to process a check to reach their place of business, on or before the due date, then these checks must be processed the previous month.

The Accounts Payable or the Checking Account provides the service, so it's credited. The Postage Machine contract and the Contract Cleaners expense accounts can't be debited, as the check is paying for services pertaining to the following month.

On the first day of the following month, Postage Machine rental and the Contract Cleaners accounts, having adjusting entries, comparable to the Fire Insurance premiums that are prepaid a year in advance.

 If the Contract Cleaners permit a five-day grace period, the check can be processed the First of the month. Would automatic payments to their bank account, on the due date or sooner, avoid postings to Prepayments?

 Taking grace periods is common. The Timing rules dictate if the transactions are booked to Prepayments before affecting the expense account.

 Prepayments, Inventory, Fixed Assets are Balance Sheet items. Prepayments don't have permanent residence on the Balance Sheet. Where do they go?

Prepayments are a permanent fixture. It's the transactions that don't have permanent residence.

What I mean by not having permanent residence is, for example The Fire Insurance premiums are spread out over the life of the prepayment. The Prepayment is credited and the expense account is debited over the life of the amortization. See Fig: 4:6

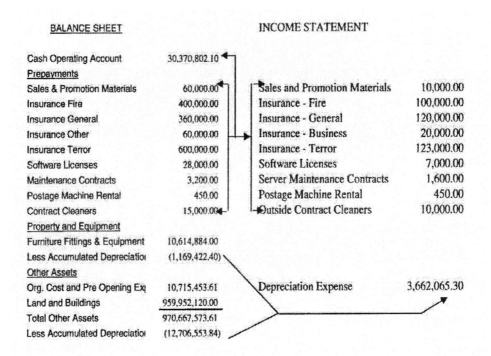

BALANCE SHEET		INCOME STATEMENT	
Cash Operating Account	30,370,802.10		
Prepayments			
Sales & Promotion Materials	60,000.00	Sales and Promotion Materials	10,000.00
Insurance Fire	400,000.00	Insurance - Fire	100,000.00
Insurance General	360,000.00	Insurance - General	120,000.00
Insurance Other	60,000.00	Insurance - Business	20,000.00
Insurance Terror	600,000.00	Insurance - Terror	123,000.00
Software Licenses	28,000.00	Software Licenses	7,000.00
Maintenance Contracts	3,200.00	Server Maintenance Contracts	1,600.00
Postage Machine Rental	450.00	Postage Machine Rental	450.00
Contract Cleaners	15,000.00	Outside Contract Cleaners	10,000.00
Property and Equipment			
Furniture Fittings & Equipment	10,614,884.00		
Less Accumulated Depreciatio	(1,169,422.40)		
Other Assets			
Org. Cost and Pre Opening Ex	10,715,453.61	Depreciation Expense	3,662,065.30
Land and Buildings	959,952,120.00		
Total Other Assets	970,667,573.61		
Less Accumulated Depreciatio	(12,706,553.84)		

Fig 4:6

For the buyer, Prepayments is a Current Asset. For the seller, if the amount is posted to "Deposits Received for future services" Is that a Current Liability for the seller?

The purchaser of the Fire Insurance policy posts the amount paid to the carrier in the Prepayment section. The Insurance Company records the identical amount to Advance Premiums, no different than the hotel or the gym accepting membership payments in advance.

In the Books of the Member using the Spa and Fitness

Dec 15th. Prepayment Spa and Fitness $6,000.00
      Bank Account $6,000.00
   Actual Membership Purchase: January 1st to December 31st 2003 Spa/Fitness Membership

In the books of the Hotel or Fitness Club:

Dec 15th. Bank Account $6,000.00
          Spa Memberships $6,000.00
          Receiving the payment for the membership: January 1st to
          December 31st 2003 Spa/Fitness Membership Mr. Jones

In the books of the Member Purchasing the Services:

Dec 15th. Membership Dues $600.00
          Prepayments $600.00
          One Months amortization of the Prepayment: January 1st
          to January 31st, 2003 Spa/Fitness Membership

Recorded in the Hotel Books:

Dec 15th. Spa Memberships $600.00
          Spa Dues Income $600.00

Just as the buyer amortized one month's membership, the service provider takes one month into Income: January 1st to January 31st 2003 Spa/Fitness Membership.

One party debited the Cash account the other party credited the Cash account. One party booked as Income, the other party booked an expense. It's neat and tidy until Capital Assets, subject to Depreciation are disposed of. Depreciation has its own dedicated chapter.

 Deposits received for future services don't at the time of receipt generate Income to the seller, and the buyer sending the deposit doesn't incur an expense?

 Deposits are NOT Income until the services are rendered, or the product is sold or delivered.

This is applicable to Cash as well as Accrual accounting. Even the Internal Revenue Service acknowledges this as fact!
The IRS requires cash based taxpayers to declare the first and last months rent as income, deposits are not income. Why? The event hasn't occurred to which the deposit is attached.

Bad Debts are included in the chapter on Accounts Receivable. Anything for now?

There are two methods. The Direct Charge off method and the Percentage method. Utilizing the Bad Debt Reserve attempts to match the Bad Debt expense with the Income for the period

Complying with the Matching concept, matching Income with Expenses, The Reserve method attempts to solve this by booking a percentage of the current months sales to Bad Debt expense each month, building up the reserve, which will be utilized when customers default, or when Receivables become worthless. Accrual accounting, through the Reserve method records the Accounts Receivable on the Balance Sheet at the Gross Amount less the Reserve to date. See Fig 4:7

ASSETS

Current Assets
Cash and Cash Equivalents

Cash Equivalents		50,412,684.86
Accounts Receivable	9,231,677.04	
Reserve for Bad Debts	(696,437.05)	8,535,239.99
Other Assets		4,266,650.00
Inventory		1,706,307.46
Total Current Assets		64,920,882.31

The Journal Entry for the month:
May 31st, 2003: Bad Debt Expense $170,539.39
       Reserve for Bad Debts $170,539.39
The Reserve for Bad Debts stands at $696,4270.05 and the Accounts Receivable Net is $8,535,239.99 which should be reasonably accurate to reflect the net worth of the Accounts Receivable at any one time

Fig 4:7

What has to be done so the Bad Debt Expense doesn't get out of hand?

Valid disputes, valid Sales Returns and Adjustments must never be confused with legitimate Bad Debts. Bad Debts happen when the goods and services were delivered according to the terms of the contract.

The customer states they won't, or can't pay. A Legitimate contractual obligation can be transferred to outside collection agencies, or to collection attorneys that might immediately begin litigation.

 Customers delay payments arbitrarily or through legitimate promotions. Accrual accounting books the Income immediately at the time of sale. Is this an interest free loan?

 There is an unstated (imputed) rate of interest. When cash collection is delayed one year or more, then General Accepted Accounting Principles, (GAAP) require an interest earned allocation.

The majority of Accounts Receivable is collected within two to three months after the sales/billing, so in these cases calculating and managing these transactions would be insignificant and too cumbersome.

 Cash accounting doesn't report Bad Debts on the Balance Sheet or Income Statement. How does Accrual accounting treat Bad Debts?

 Accounts Receivable is adjusted downwards with a corresponding entry to Bad Debt Expense, complying with the Matching principle.

 Are Product Costs confined to a manufacturing industry?

 Product costs, Cost of Sales or Cost of Goods Sold are all the same thing, regardless of the nature of the business.

Cost of Goods sold is one of the best examples confirming the Matching principle.

An automobile manufacturer takes parts that might be partially assembled by an outside contractor, or stand-alone parts that their workers assemble are all product costs. The Steakhouse patron orders the soup, fillet with vegetables, salad, desert and coffee supplemented with wine. Those items are Product Costs or Cost of Goods Sold.

Can manufacturing, such as Toyota, Caterpillar, etc accurately track their manufactured products individually?

 This type of manufacturing incurs costs every step of the way, from engine parts to the finished goods. These costs get charged to Inventory (just as the steak is charged to Food Inventory) as Direct Material costs. Part of the manufacturing process is Direct Labor costs and Manufacturing Overhead.

Material and Direct Labor is straightforward. Overhead costs, include anything related to the production of the product, such as Utilities, Property Taxes and Insurance.

Manufacturing entities charge requisitions from the main stores to <u>Work in Process Inventory</u>. Added to that Work in Process Inventory is the Direct Labor and Overhead costs.
Finished Goods Inventory is the value of the final product that's placed in the market for sale.

 What replaces Work in Process Inventory for a service industry?

 The hotel has food and liquor in the storerooms. Imagine, every time customers orders a steak, somebody has go from the kitchen to the main storeroom for a portion of meat? No. Inventory in the kitchens is still Inventory!

If the auto manufacturer at the end of the month has 10,000 automobiles for a combined total of $10 million, sells them for $11 million, the Gross Profit, or Gross Margin is $1 million.

 Cost of Sales is an expense and is always deducted from Gross Income in arriving at the Gross Profit, of Gross Margin. Is the Cost of Sales always affected by Inventory?

No, but usually it is. How does inventory flow? Fig 4:8 show exactly how the transactions flow from the Inventory accounts on the Balance Sheet to the Cost of Sales accounts in the Income Statement.

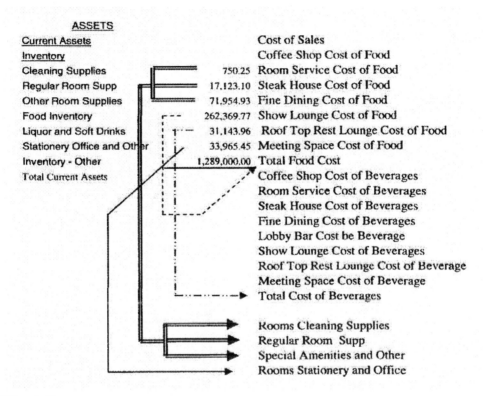

Fig 4:8

When the merchandise is delivered, the Inventory accounts are debited. Accounts Payable is credited. Cost of Sales is an expense, so that is debited, and if the item came from the Inventory, the credit has nowhere else to go accept Inventory.

Take a look at Fig 4:9. On the left side are some expense accounts and liabilities for Sales Taxes collected that must be passed on the government. It takes resources of an Asset to pay down Liabilities. The right hand side is the Balance Sheet Accounts that are affected.

A Sampling (Excluding Payroll)

Rooms Non Inventory Supplies	3,059.06		
Rooms Travel	653.56	Accounts Payable Trade	3,868,182.01
Rooms Printing and Design	7,874.03	Payables Affiliates	4,573,830.67	8,442,012.68
Rooms Laundry	10,677.43	Other	
Rooms Dry Cleaning	520.04	Taxes- Sales & Use	4,935,643.52
Rooms Postage	70.87	Taxes - Income	2,683,702.67
Utilities - Heating	27,830.62	Interest Payable	232,100.87
Utilities - Electricity	33,860.59	Commissions Payable	211,086.94
Utilities - Water	14,926.49	Acc Expenses Payable	310,227.69	8,372,761.69
		Spa Memberships	607,003.50
Management Fee Minimum	112,500.00	Prepaid Customer Rooms	
Management Fee Additional	1,027,651.69	Prepaid Customer Other	458,032.89	1,065,036.39
Trademark and Other	959,197.93	Payroll Liabilities	
		Payroll Signed Gratuities	9,774.85
State Sales Tax	841,030.59	Medical Insurance Payable	
State Hotel Occupancy Tax	480,588.91	Life & Disability Ins.	
City Hotel Occupancy Tax	48,354.16	401k Contributions	
Coffee Shop Sales Tax	51,223.23	Payroll Taxes State	
		Payroll Taxes Federal	
Interest Expense Short Term	3,232,100.87	Payroll Net Payroll Payable	
		Accrued Vacation/Sick	1,325,200.77	1,334,975.62
Coffee Shop Charge Tips	42,579.49		
Taxes- Income Tax Federal	308,176.02		
Taxes Income State and Local	109,688.67		
Taxes - Property	474,308.20		

Fig 4.9

Assets are reduced with credits; Liabilities are reduced with debits. Cost of Sales, or Product Costs use the resources of an Asset, that's typically, Inventory.

Fig 4:10 show definite Cash inflows and definite Cash out-flows. For example: When customers pay all or part of their balances due, this reduces the Accounts Receivable balance by the amount of the payments. The broken line beginning at Accounts Receivable, ending with the arrow at the Cash Operating Account reflects this reality.

Cash flows to the Bank from customers' deposits. Customers use credit cards for making deposits. Then the deposit goes through Accounts Receivable before reaching the Cash Operating account.

CASH USAGE RECEIPTS

ASSETS			LIABILITIES AND CAPITAL	
Current Assets			Current Liabilities	
Cash and Cash Equivalents			Trade and Affiliates	
Cash on Hand	40,000.00		Accounts Payable Trade	3,868,182.01
Cash Operating Account	30,370,802.10		Payables Affiliates	4,573,830.67
Cash Payroll Account	1,882.76		Other	
Cash Certificate of Deposit	20,000,000.00	50,412,684.86	Taxes Payable Sales & Use	4,935,643.52
Accounts Receivable	9,231,677.04		Taxes - Income	2,683,702.67
Reserve for Bad Debts	(696,437.05)	8,535,239.99	Interest Payable	3,232,100.87
Prepayments			Commissions Payable	211,086.94
Sales & Promotion Materials	60,000.00		Accrued Expense Payable	310,227.69
Insurance Fire	400,000.00		Spa Memberships	607,003.50
Insurance General	360,000.00		Prepaid Customer Rooms	
Insurance Other	60,000.00		Prepaid Customer Other	458,032.89
Insurance Terror	600,000.00		Payroll Liabilities	
Software Licenses	28,000.00		Payroll Signed Gratuities	9,774.85
Maintenance Contracts	3,200.00		Medical Insurance Payable	
Postage Machine Rental	450.00		Life and Disability Insurance	
Contract Cleaners	15,000.00		401k Contributions Payable	
Security Deposits			Payroll Taxes State	
Sales Tax	2,300,000.00		Payroll Taxes Federal	
Water and Power	133,000.00		Payroll Net Payroll Payable	
Telephone	57,000.00		Accrued Vacation/Sick	1,325,200.77
Food & Liquor Vendors	250,000.00	4,266,650.00	Tennant Security Deposits	
Inventory			Show Case	90,000.00
Cleaning Supplies	750.25		Lobby Shop	13,800.00
Regular Room Supp	17,123.10		Starbucks	16,800.00
Other Room Supplies	71,954.93		American Express Office	15,000.00
Food Inventory	262,369.77		Garage	700,000.00
Liquor and Soft Drinks	31,143.96		Total Current Liabilities	
Stationery Office and Other	33,965.45		Long Term Liabilities	
Inventory - Other	1,289,000.00	1,706,307.46	Mortgage Payable	644,134,911.29
Total Current Assets		64,920,882.31	Construction Loan	
			Bond Issue 30 year Coupon 7%	
Property and Equipment			Total Long Term Liabilities	
Furniture Fittings & Equipment	10,614,884.00			
Less Accumulated Depreciation	(1,169,422.40)	9,445,461.60	Total Liabilities	
Other Assets			Capital	
Org. Cost and Pre Opening Exp	10,715,453.61		Preferred Stock 7% Interest	
Land and Buildings	959,952,120.00		Preferred Stock 5% Interest	
Total Other Assets	970,667,573.61		Preferred Stock 9% Interest	
Less Accumulated Depreciation	(12,706,553.84)	957,961,019.77	Common Stock $1.00 Par Value	50,000.00
			Additional Paid in Capital	360,621,074.00
			Retained Earnings	
			Treasury Stock	
			Dividends Paid	
			Net Income	4,450,992.01
			Total Capital	
Total Assets		1,032,327,363.68	Total Liabilities and Capital	

– – – – – – – – – Definite Cash Inflows
================ Definite Cash Outflows

Fig 4:10

73

"Accrual or Accrued" is used expensively in accounting. Accruals affect Income and expenses. Please clarify?

 Timing Timing Timing ™ The Matching Principle wouldn't exist if it weren't for the Timing rules. Cash based accounting, (accept for minor aspects, as deposits) cares less about the Matching principle. It's easy to match expenses with Income, if the Income is clear and invoices have been received for all the expenses for the period. In real life this doesn't happen, but the Matching principle cares less about this aspect. For example, hotels, apartment and office buildings incur charges for water usage.

Employees work for a week or two without being paid. Wages earned between payrolls falling at the end of the month gets accrued. Legal Fees, Utilities, Telephone and Commissions are examples that are accruable. There is a chapter on payroll.

The Water Authority sends a bill for $50,000 dated July 21st with a cut off date of July 15th. Cash based accounting books the expense when paid, even a month later. Accrual accounting requires at least an attempt to match expenses to the period of usage.

The water bill covers a few weeks of June including the first two weeks of July. The entity, in accordance with the Matching principle, books an accrual, which is the best estimate for water usage for two weeks of June.

What happens if it's way off the mark? The Accrual is for $35,000.00 the actual bill is $50,000.00. If processing the difference of $15,000.00 is permitted, the computer can only process payment for this amount, which will be incorrect as the bill is for $50,000.00, which is much higher. What happens?

Textbooks make accruals appear uncomplicated. Mechanically, booking the accrual is simple. In real life accruals are provide opportunities for game playing but they provide genuine challenge.

If the buildings have meters these can be read, but the level of technology and the level of sophistication all play a part in how accurately accruals can be done. That's the reason accounting has a procedure (and a requirement) called a Reverse Accrual(s)

Back to water costs. The accrual for $35,000 must be reversed at the beginning of the following month. The Journal Entries are:

Month End June Accrual

June 30th. Water Usage $35,000.00
         Accrued Expenses Payable $35,000.00   Estimated Water Usage June 2003

Reverse Accrual July 1st, 2003:

July 1st. Accrued Expenses Payable $35,000.00
        Water Usage $35,000.00
          Reverse Water Usage Accrual June 2003

 Other than satisfying the Matching principle, what practical use does this have?

 The Deacon 3-Q's™ The quality of the Financial reporting depends on the quality of the input, and the quality of the management of the input.

Some accruals are complex and difficult to reasonably estimate, but some accruals, such as credit card commission on batches submitted but haven't been paid are easy and there is no excuse for being completely out of whack. Accruals are used when the bill for merchandise, or services purchased hasn't arrived, or when the bill does arrive, it covers more than one accounting period.

Outstanding credit card balances are usually part of the Accounts Receivable even if only for a few days. There is a misconception that the moment the merchant swipes the card and closes the sale the funds are automatically in the seller's bank account.

Transactions go into a holding file and remain there until the batch is transferred electronically to the credit card companies or their representatives. The funds can be in the sellers' account three to five business days after they are transmitted. The batches that have been submitted, but are awaiting payment are part of Accounts Receivable.

 How can the credit card commission be booked satisfying the Matching concept?

 For example, if the total of the unpaid batches at the end of the month is $500,000. The fees can be estimated, as it's known from past practice the percentage the merchant has to pay.

If the fee averages 3% then 3% of $00,000.00 is $15,000. This is booked to Commission expense, with the opposite entry going to Accrued Expenses payable. When the payment is received, the accrual is reversed and the proper amount booked.

 Tax Accounting has specific rules and an agenda for Depreciation. How does Financial Accounting differ from Tax Accounting?

 Buildings, Machinery, Computers, Furniture, etc have extended lives. Financial Accounting writes down the asset over their useful life. Tax rules are incompatible with Financial Accounting

 Depreciation's an expense, and it's debited. Which account is credited to complete the double entry requirements? Cash, Bank or Accounts Payable?

Depreciation and Bad Debt expenses are <u>non-cash</u> expenses. For a Bad debt expense, nobody in his or her right mind would process payment through the Bank account to cover that expense. Depreciation expense is debited. <u>Accumulated Depreciation</u> is credited.

I heard a late night estate seminar presenter/ guru promoting real estate, telling the audience that depreciation is a non-cash expense. Depreciation <u>is</u> a non-cash expense that's recognized for both Financial and Tax Accounting.

He roared: "Where can you get a tax benefit without laying out any cash" How many in the target audience had any idea of the mid to long term consequences of making a decision based on a perceived, or otherwise, benefit resulting from tax depreciation.

He didn't tell them there's no depreciation without a capital asset placed in service. Capital assets don't fall out of the trees, instead utilizing all cash up front or triggering credit lines that subsequently consume cash.

 When and where do Adjusting Entries occur?

 Reviewing the monthly closing, which of these are adjusting entries?
The bill for legal fees of $100,000 is booked to Professional Fees and part of the Accounts Payable Trade

 Cost of management attending a conference: Travel and Entertainment, $23,000.00 Corporate agreed to absorb one half reimbursing after the Management entity paid the bill on receipt and submitting proof of payment.

 The Fire Insurance Premiums and Depreciation were not booked. Fire Insurance expense is $10,000 a month.

Prepaid Fire Insurance balance in the Prepayments is $50,000.00. The previous month's Depreciation was booked at $63,000,00 and it should have been $36,000.00.

 The result of a physical food inventory count found a shortage in the food inventory of $100,000.00 Perhaps they forgot to book the transaction?

The legal fees are acceptable. Prior cumulative accruals must be taken into consideration.

The Management entity is responsible for $23,000.00 so crediting Accounts Payable is correct. If the entire $23,000 is booked to Travel, then they must do an Adjusting entry.

These are the Journal Entries when $23,000.00 is booked to Travel and Entertainment:

May 31st, 20 Travel and Entertainment $23,000.00
              Accounts Payable Trade $23,000.00
          Management Conference

If the allocation is made at, preferably, at the time the bills are coded:

May 31st, 20 Travel and Entertainment $11,500.00
           Accounts Receivable Other$11,500.00
              Accounts Payable Trade $23,000.00
          Conference: Home Office portion.

This is what happens when the Travel and Entertainment (and only the home office portion) is billed to the corporate entity, with other standard charges they are obligated for. Management fees: $400,000.00: Trademark Fees $100,000.00. Corporate allows the conference cost to be deducted from the standard obligations.

```
May 31st, 20  Management Fees           $400,000.00
              Trademark Fees            $100,000.00
                    Accounts Payable         $  11,500.00
                    Travel and Entertainment $  11,500.00
                    Accounts Payable Trade   $  23,000.00
                    Accounts Payable Affiliates$500,000.00
```

I dislike that method. I prefer an adjusting entry. If $23,000.00 is originally booked to Travel and Entertainment, the adjustment goes something like this.

```
May 31st Accounts Receivable - Other     $11,500.00
                    Travel and Entertainment $11,500.00
Allocation: Management Conference Travel to Home Office.
```

The Prepaid Fire Insurance and Depreciation expense are both Adjusting entries. Don't adjust the previous months work. Take into account this discrepancy in the current period.

With regards to the discrepancy with the Food Inventory, this shortage must go against Cost of Goods sold. It doesn't matter if the food acquired legs and walked out the door! Accounting wants an answer to: Is it <u>Material</u>?

The concepts <u>Conservatism and Materiality</u> is just as important as the Matching principle. Materiality depends on the circumstances. If the monthly food cost is approximately $1,600,000.00 so $100,000 is minor. If the 150-room generates food revenue of $120,000.00 then $100,000 shortage is a disaster in the making.

(?) Prepayments connect to the Income Statement. Prepayments can also connect to the Bank account. Why?

 Timing Timing Timing™ When vendors refund prepayments, the expense isn't booked. It's a case of the Deacon Slogan: Timing Timing Timing™ The account is debited on receipt of the payment from the vendor refunding the prepayment. Complying with the double entry system, the Prepayment account is credited. (The Prepayment account would have been credited, had it run its course)

Any Balance Sheet Asset, unless acquired for Cash, affects one or more Liability accounts. Period: Income and expenses affect both Assets and Liability accounts. Period: Look at Fig 4:11 Arrows show the flow acquiring the Assets on the left, the Liability accounts on the right hand side.

 Fig 4:10 There is a line from the Client deposits to the Cash Operating account and Accounts Receivable Are deposits taken into income over the length of the contract?

 Fig 4:12 shows the Bank Operating account is debited and Spa Memberships is credited (same applies with Prepaid Customer Other) when the deposit is received. When it's time to take the correct amount into income, Income is credited, and Spa Memberships is debited.

The hotel Spa had a grand opening promotion. From January through May recorded Cash inflows and applied to these Liability accounts is $1,202,006. (See Fig 4:13)

 Timing Timing Timing™ The deposits you made to the health club are recorded as a Prepayment in their books. Membership dues are taken into Income over the life of the membership each month reducing the Liability. Here's an excellent example where cash flow doesn't equal equate into income. Back to Timing Timing Timing™ Fig 4:14 report Total Receipts of $1,202.06.00 and that matches the total Cash from January to May. (See Fig 4:13) The amounts listed for the period, from January through May is the Income booked. The carried forward amounts continue.

ASSETS				LIABILITIES AND CAPITAL	
Current Assets				Current Liabilities	
Cash and Cash Equivalents				Trade and Affiliates	
Cash on Hand	40,000.00			Accounts Payable Trade	3,868,182.01
Cash Operating Account	30,370,802.10			Payables Affiliates	4,573,830.67
Cash Payroll Account	1,882.76			Other	
Cash Certificate of Deposit	20,000,000.00	50,412,684.86		Taxes Payable Sales & Use	4,935,643.52
Accounts Receivable	9,231,677.04			Taxes - Income	2,683,702.67
Reserve for Bad Debts	(696,437.05)	8,535,239.99		Interest Payable	3,232,100.87
Prepayments				Commissions Payable	211,086.94
Sales & Promotion Materials	60,000.00			Accrued Expense Payable	310,227.69
Insurance Fire	400,000.00			Spa Memberships	607,003.50
Insurance General	360,000.00			Prepaid Customer Rooms	
Insurance Other	60,000.00			Prepaid Customer Other	458,032.89
Insurance Terror	600,000.00			Payroll Liabilities	
Software Licenses	28,000.00			Payroll Signed Gratuities	9,774.85
Maintenance Contracts	3,200.00			Medical Insurance Payable	
Postage Machine Rental	450.00			Life and Disability Insurance	
Contract Cleaners	15,000.00			401k Contributions Payable	
Security Deposits				Payroll Taxes State	
Sales Tax	2,300,000.00			Payroll Taxes Federal	
Water and Power	133,000.00			Payroll Net Payroll Payable	
Telephone	57,000.00			Accrued Vacation/Sick	1,325,200.77
Food & Liquor Vendors	250,000.00	4,266,650.00		Tennant Security Deposits	
Inventory				Show Case	90,000.00
Cleaning Supplies	750.25			Lobby Shop	13,800.00
Regular Room Supp	17,123.10			Starbucks	16,800.00
Other Room Supplies	71,954.93			American Express Office	15,000.00
Food Inventory	262,369.77			Garage	700,000.00
Liquor and Soft Drinks	31,143.96			Total Current Liabilities	
Stationery Office and Other	33,965.45			Long Term Liabilities	
Inventory - Other	1,289,000.00	1,706,307.46		Mortgage Payable	644,154,911.29
Total Current Assets		64,920,882.31		Construction Loan	
				Bond Issue 30 year Coupon 7%	
Property and Equipment				Total Long Term Liabilities	
Furniture Fittings & Equipment	10,614,884.00				
Less Accumulated Depreciation	(1,169,422.40)	9,445,461.60		Total Liabilities	
Other Assets				Capital	
Org. Cost and Pre Opening Exp	10,715,453.61			Preferred Stock 7% Interest	
Land and Buildings	959,952,120.00			Preferred Stock 6% Interest	
Total Other Assets	970,667,573.61			Preferred Stock 9% Interest	
Less Accumulated Depreciation	(12,706,553.84)	957,961,019.77		Common Stock $1.00 Par Value	50,000.00
				Additional Paid in Capital	360,621,074.00

Fig 4:11

In the case of health club memberships the Income is taken over more than one accounting period. What happens when a customer sends a deposit for one specific item only?

The customer is billed for $5,000.00 plus taxes. If there is no deposit, here is the Journal entry.

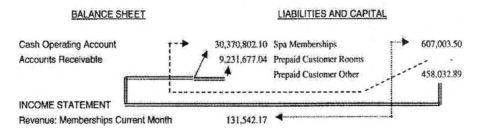

Fig 4:12

Spa Memmberships: Deposits Received

	Six Months	One Year	Total
January	240,000.00	768,006.00	1,008,006.00
February	60,000.00	17,500.00	77,500.00
March	30,000.00	22,500.00	52,500.00
April	15,000.00	10,000.00	25,000.00
May	31,500.00	7,500.00	39,000.00
			1,202,006.00

Fig 4:13

Plan	Receipts	January 2003	February 2003	March 2003	April 2003	May 2003	Carried Forward
6 months	240,000.00	40,000.00	40,000.00	40,000.00	40,000.00	40,000.00	40,000.00
12 months	768,006.00	64,000.50	64,000.50	64,000.50	64,000.50	64,000.50	448,003.50
6 months	60,000.00		10,000.00	10,000.00	10,000.00	10,000.00	20,000.00
12 months	17,500.00		1,458.33	1,458.33	1,458.33	1,458.33	11,666.67
6 months	30,000.00			5,000.00	5,000.00	5,000.00	15,000.00
12 months	22,500.00			1,875.00	1,875.00	1,875.00	16,875.00
6 months	15,000.00				2,500.00	2,500.00	10,000.00
12 months	10,000.00				833.33	833.33	8,333.33
6 months	31,500.00					5,250.00	26,250.00
12 months	7,500.00					625.00	6,875.00
Total	1,202,006.00						603,003.50
Income		40,000.00	50,000.00	55,000.00	57,500.00	62,750.00	
Income		64,000.50	65,458.83	67,333.83	68,167.17	68,792.17	
Total		104,000.50	115,458.83	122,333.83	125,667.17	131,542.17	

Fig 4:14

```
May 31 20    Accounts Receivable      $5,500.00
                    Income                        $5000.00
                    Sales Tax                     $ 500.00
       Jones and Company Better Business Seminars
```

This is what happens when a deposit must be applied: The Accounts Receivable reflects $4,500.00, (Billing of $5,500.00 less $1,000.00 prepaid) and that's the amount the customer is required to pay. Anything less than booking $5,000 to Income isn't acceptable. The $1,000.00 shortfall between what the clients has still to pay, and total Income is the prepaid deposit. Prepaid Deposits account is debited. Debits reduce Liability accounts.

```
May 31st, 20  Accounts Receivable      $4,500.00
              Deposits Customers:       $1,000.00
                    Income                        $5000.00
                    Sales Tax                     $ 500.00
```

 With the exception of the Depreciation expense, does accounting recognize expenses without a formal bill?

 Bank charges, Payroll Processing Fees, Credit Card Commissions are some examples. Imagine the bank sixty days later, hounding you for payment for the monthly bank fees!

Management Fees, Trademark Fees, may be based on revenue with clearly defined contractual terms and conditions governing how the expenses are booked. Realtors sharing commissions is another example.

 How are they recorded?

 Journal Entries. For bank charges the Bank account is credited, an expense account such as Bank Fees is debited. They are part of the monthly Adjusting entries, if they aren't recorded in the current month

 How are outside shared services booked?

The contract specifies terms and conditions. Fig 4:15 records the Total Receipts before any participation. "Forgo" is the amount that is due to the piper.

Participatory or Lease	Total Receipts	Forgo	Net Income
Laundry	88,133.00	74,920.81	13,212.19
Valet and Dry Cleaning	80,580.87	68,493.74	12,087.13
In Room Movies	205,604.20	174,763.57	30,840.63
Parking Overnight Stays	168,163.00	168,163.00	
Revenue Parking - Minimum Rent	84,931.51		84,931.51
Revenue Parking - Participation	370,272.31		370,272.31

Fig 4:15

Can the Total Receipts be booked initially to Income then afterwards allocate the correct amount when actually paying the piper?

You have no business booking the amount under Total Receipts to Income. It is similar to collecting Sales Taxes payable to the government. It isn't your money. Total Receipts should be posted to the Liability account, and when it's time to pay the piper, debit the Liability account and credit the Income accounts for the proper amount earned.

How does accounting deal with major construction contracts?

This is a Long-term Contracts issue. Income is recognized before or after the sale depending on the circumstances

Physical construction, the time for talk are long gone. The project __must__ cover several accounting periods, and there's a customer up front, and there is no doubt the customer has the financial ability to make the payments. Buyer MAY make periodic payments. The contractor can make estimates with reasonable precision to the costs.

Do contractors have a choice in choosing a method with long-term contracts?

 Two methods: The Percentage of Completion and the Completed Contract method, lesser known as the completed sale method. <u>Sometimes</u> a choice isn't an option.

The Percentage of Completion is the most common IF the conditions are fulfilled. Revenue is recognized as work progresses, even if the contract specifically specifies payment is made on completion, as long as a reasonable estimate of the cash that will eventually materialize is made. As revenue is recognized, so are the expenses. This must follow the <u>Accrual</u> method of accounting.

 As the Percentage of Completion Method requires the Accrual method, Cash method taxpayers are forced to use the Completed Contract method. Surely this time round the cash based method would be superior if they were allowed to use it? Expenses can be paid and income deferred for as long as the contract.

 The net Income will be the same under both methods. In this case, NO income or expenses are recognized until the contract is complete, so the Cash based system is in the same boat as the Accrual method.

 The Cash Method rules out selecting the Percentage of Completion Method. Is that the only restriction?

 Even if there's a buyer and there is doubt to the ultimate price the buyer will have to come with ultimately the revenue and cost cannot be accurately determined so this will disqualify the percentage method.

There are restrictions in choosing the Percentage method. Are there restrictions in adopting the Completed method?

 Regardless of the project length, whether or not there is a buyer, whether or not marketing or legal costs can be determined, or if the project is up in the air and for housing projects, they must use the Completed Contract method.

A critical factor even if total costs can be measured at the outset, and should this change at any time during the contract, they cannot measure the percentage of the work completed, the Completed Contract method must be used. General Accepted Accounting Principles (GAAP) require the Percentage method if it qualifies, but the outcome can really be manipulated by recognizing too much in the early years.

 How are Income and Expenses managed for the Forestry, Liquor and Tobacco Industries?

 Product costs must be capitalized until sold or become worthless. Capitalization accumulates all expenses into one asset account then closes them at the appropriate time.

 A requirement for the recognition of income is there must be a binding contract between buyer and seller and the amount must be quantifiable. Are Insurance Companies exempt from this requirement?

 Most recognize income and expenses each period. Cash received is fairly certain which is matched proportionately against future cash flows. As these are estimates, the procedure is similar to setting up the Bad Debt Reserve.

Technically a Life Insurance Company can collect the premiums, and at death pay out the required amount on the policy. The dollar amount of the premiums collected, and the amount paid out is determinable and clear. It's illogical and cumbersome delaying income for this length of time since the final payout consists of premiums and interest earned from those premiums and others. Even going to this length, doesn't indicate whether the company is managed efficiently or otherwise. Actuaries provide reasonably good estimates of its future liabilities through analysis of its current liabilities and policies.

 Franchising is a huge business and it isn't going away. In reality franchisee's can walk away from the business. How does accounting deal with, on the one hand such uncertainty with a start up, to the rock solid big name franchisee?

 If payment can be determined reasonably accurately, revenue must be recognized immediately at the time of sale. If not, the <u>Installment Method</u> must be used, recognizing revenue when payments arrive and booking expenses proportionately.

Cost Recovery First means all receipts go to towards the cost, the excess gets allocated to revenue. GAAP permits the Installment and Cost recovery method only when reasonably certain estimates can't be made.

 Income is Income, expense as an expense isn't real world. They are either Primary or Nonrecurring. How does accounting deal with them?

 Primary Income and Expenses occur during the normal course of business. Nonrecurring aren't normal expenses

If HP Corporation discontinues selling computers it's a nonrecurring transaction. Peripheral would be natural disasters as an earthquake. If HP reported revenues prior to selling the computer division for $4 Billion and the sale of the computer division generated $1 Billion, the $4 Billion remains unchanged. $1 Billion is shown on the income statement under gain or loss from discontinued operations

Chapter 5

Many big name US Corporations changed their accounting methods for Inventories beginning in the mid to late 1960's with that trend continuing for many years. Would earnings be the underlying motive?

 Usually the Inventory changes resulted in a lower Financial and Taxable Income meaning lower tax bills. The first year General Motors changed their accounting for Inventories they reported a tax deferral of $150 million for the current period alone. These changes can carry price tags that come due later on.

 Technically, Inventory is a stack of goods resold in the normal course of business. Stationery and office supplies, soap for the hotel rooms is included in Inventory. The hotel isn't in the soap distribution business yet it's classified as Inventory. What's up?

 The goods consumed from Inventory that are sold in the normal course of business translate directly to Cost of Goods sold. Stationery and office don't have to be in Inventory. They can be purchased piecemeal.

The cost of soap, towels, tablecloths, crockery and cutlery are items that must be counted and controlled. They are used over and over again, and as they are NOT capital assets, they don't quality for Depreciation expense. Why is the Steak a Cost of Goods sold item, and soap placed in the room, not a Cost of Goods sold item? Try serving a steak dinner without steak, but you can rent a room without placing fresh soap in the containers. (For each complaint deduct $2.00 from the room rate)

 Is there an Inventory equation comparable to:
Assets = Liabilities + Shareholders' Equity?

It's Opening Inventory + Inventory Purchases = Total Goods Available for Sale – Closing Inventory = Cost of Goods Sold. There are two unknowns. The Closing Inventory at the end of one month becomes the Opening Inventory for the following month. As this is a legitimate equation it can be:

Beginning Inventory, or Opening Inventory + Purchases = Merchandise Available for Sale. Take withdrawals from the Inventory level, the result is the Closing Inventory. Refer Fig 5:1

Opening Inventory	174,678.09	The starting point is Beginning Inventory or
Add: Inventory Purchases	387,528.43	Opening Inventory. The closing Inventory
Total Available for Sale	562,206.52	becomes he Opening Inventory. Add
Less: Closing Inventory	326,044.02	Inventory Purchases less Closing Inventory
Equals: Cost of Goods Sold	236,162.50	and the result, Cost of Sales.

Opening Inventory	174,678.09	The equation can also be stated this way.
Add: Inventory Purchases	387,528.43	Beginning Inventory, or Opening Inventory
Total Available for Sale	562,206.52	+ Purchases = Merchandise Available for
Less Withdrawals from Inventory	236,162.50	Sale. From that take the withdrawals from
Equals: Closing Inventory	326,044.02	the Inventory level and that comes up with
		Closing Inventory.

Opening Inventory Lbs of Sugar	2000	The Financial statement doesn't show
Add: Deliveries Lbs of Sugar	3000	Inventory as 1000 lbs of sugar. It has a
Total Available for Sale	5000	total dollar value of all, in this case the
Less: Issued. Lbs of Sugar	4000	sugar. This wouldn't create a concern if the
Closing Inventory	1000	prices and units didn't change over the
		period.

Opening Inventory #1Computer	2,500.00	The Total Inventory for Sale is Three
Purchased: Computer # 2	3,000.00	Computers. Total value: Cost $8,800.00. If
Purchased Computer # 3	3,300.00	there were NO computer sales. Inventory
Total Inventory 3 Computers	8,800.00	would be $8,800.00

Fig 5:1

Great, the formula that calculates the Cost of Goods sold eliminates a physical Inventory count?

By definition, this is the Cost of Goods sold for many entities but

For example, the stay at home spouse of a Fortune 100 executive is bored. They go into the cosmetic retail business operating from home.

For convenience, they began in January, and closing the books for the first year in business in December, they determine, all the accounting is complete accept for the calculation for Cost of Goods Sold. After the physical count is complete and valued, Cost of Goods Sold is a calculation.

The volume of Inventory on hand is minute compared to a supermarket or the manufacturing concern, but the principle is identical.

Opening Inventory, (zero in this case) plus all Inventory Purchases = Total Available for Sale. The Final Inventory correctly valued is critical. Deduct this amount from the Total Available and you will get the Cost of Goods Sold.

 Why can't the supplies requisitioned be valued, and this figure be reported for the Cost of Goods sold, avoiding physical Inventory counts?

 Yes and No. Physical inventories can't be completely eliminated. Reports showing the dollar value of items requisitioned from the storerooms do have value.

If there aren't any errors, a physical count of the Inventory SHOULD equal the result applying the Inventory equation. The physical inventory SHOULD match. The word "If" with only two letters, is one of the most powerful words in the English language

There is still no substitute for physical Inventory counts. Technology has reduced the need, depending on the industry, for excessive physical inventory counts.

It's still necessary to open those boxes that can be empty, or contain rocks instead of the merchandise! Barcodes has

Barcodes has helped with Inventory controls, but only a physical inventory count will bring to light the affects of stealing, breakage and mistakes!

 What happens if management isn't willing to identify every single item?

 They must make assumptions. The higher the Cost of Goods sold, the lower the Closing Inventory. The higher the Cost of Goods sold, the higher the expenses affecting gross profit, or loss on sale of the product.

 What costs are included in Purchased Inventory?

 The cost of the product, plus all freight and any other costs in preparing them for resale. For Merchandising, the unpacking, receiving, inspecting, including the clerical recording costs. <u>The Cost Inclusion principle applies to Inventory as well</u>

 When do the Inventory purchases get booked?

 Technically, it's when <u>legal title passes</u> that's governed by the contract of sale. In practice most purchases are booked on delivery and signed for. It's rare when title passes when the goods are still on the high seas.

For some entities, freight and miscellaneous expenses are used for statistical purposes. If so, these items must be accounted for separately, otherwise freight and miscellaneous items are tagged on to the inventory price. An exception is, when buyers take the suppliers discount allowed if payment is made within a specific time. For example 2% if paid within ten days. This can be significant, and almost without exception, this item is segregated.

 Work in Process Inventory ultimately becomes Finished Goods Inventory. Does Inventory comprise of Raw Materials, Freight and Insurance?

Recapping: Inventory valuations start with unit costs. Add to that freight and other items. Manufacturing Inventory in addition, includes Direct Materials, Direct and Indirect Labor, Manufacturing Overhead, Supervisory Labor, Supplies and anything else that relates to the product, gets booked to Work in Process Inventory. This is known as <u>Full Absorption Costing.</u>

 In manufacturing, what happens to marketing and accounting salaries? Are these tagged on the items making up the Finished Goods Inventory?

 NO! Marketing and accounting salaries are non-production wages (I didn't say non productive) No matter the entity these are always period expenses.

 The opposite of Full Absorption Costing is Variable Costing. What's the difference?

 GAAP and the income tax laws require using Full absorption costing, because the total number of units produced relate closely with the total costs related to the product.

The question should be, "GAAP and the tax rules require full absorption costing, should I go to the expense of producing reports based on the Variable Costing methods as well?

Depending on the number of units involved, management at times, wouldn't have made the same decision, had they the information produced under Variable Costing. These reports are for in house use and this is a management accounting issue.

<u>Variable Costing</u> treats fixed manufacturing costs no differently than general and administrative expenses in the period they incurred. All fixed costs are charged out to

revenues for the period. The reasoning behind is, fixed costs are there anyway, even if they didn't produce one item, they still have to be paid. Never mind allocating these costs to products produced during the period. This is another matter for management accounting.

 If the entity forgets to take the discounts, or if Closing Inventory is inaccurate, does this affect one or both of the two unknowns in the Inventory equation?

 You must deal with the mindset you have of "forgetting" The Inventory purchases are the actual deliveries to the entity during the period, and must be booked. Closing Inventory is the total dollar value of the Inventory in the storerooms.

In the real world, outside of accounting textbooks, Inventory deliveries sometimes don't get recorded properly, requisitions don't get extended with their full cost price, and in physical Inventory counts items get omitted, deliberately or by accident.

The Deacon 3-Qs™: The quality of the financial reporting depends on the quality of the input and the quality of the management of the input. An erroneous Payroll Journal entry accrual is serious, but at least the parameters are clearly defined. In my view, there are very few areas in accounting, that are as challenging in arriving at the proper Cost of Goods sold figure, due to number of variables that must be considered.

Technology has reduced Inventory errors tremendously compared to twenty years ago. Figure 5:2 shows when one item in the Inventory formula changes, how the others are affected.

 Do the rules for calculating the Cost of Goods change according to the Inventory system? There are two systems. What are they?

Details	Per Books	Adjusted
Opening Inventory	174,678.09	174,678.09
Add: Inventory Purchases	387,528.43	416,748.07
Total Available for Sale	562,206.52	591,426.16
Less: Closing Inventory	326,044.02	355,263.66
Equals: Cost of Goods Sold	236,162.50	236,162.50
Opening Inventory	174,678.09	174,678.09
Add: Inventory Purchases	387,528.43	416,748.07
Total Available for Sale	562,206.52	591,426.16
Less Withdrawals from Inventory	236,162.50	236,162.50
Equals: Closing Inventory	326,044.02	355,263.66

A adjustment to Inventory Purchases, with no change to the Cost of Goods Sold the effects of this adjustment have no place to go accept Closing Inventory

	Per Books	Adjusted
Opening Inventory	174,678.09	174,678.09
Add: Inventory Purchases	387,528.43	416,748.07
Total Available for Sale	562,206.52	591,426.16
Less: Closing Inventory	326,044.02	326,044.02
Equals: Cost of Goods Sold	236,162.50	265,382.14
Opening Inventory	174,678.09	174,678.09
Add: Inventory Purchases	387,528.43	416,748.07
Total Available for Sale	562,206.52	591,426.16
Less Withdrawals from Inventory	236,162.50	326,044.02
Equals: Closing Inventory	326,044.02	265,382.14

A adjustment to Inventory Purchases, with no change to the Closing Inventory the effects of this adjustment have no place to go accept Cost of Goods Sold.

	Per Books	Adjusted
Opening Inventory	174,678.09	174,678.09
Add: Inventory Purchases	387,528.43	387,528.43
Total Available for Sale	562,206.52	562,206.52
Less: Closing Inventory	326,044.02	238,012.13
Equals: Cost of Goods Sold	236,162.50	324,194.39
Opening Inventory	174,678.09	174,678.09
Add: Inventory Purchases	387,528.43	387,528.43
Total Available for Sale	562,206.52	562,206.52
Less Withdrawals from Inventory	236,162.50	238,012.13
Equals: Closing Inventory	326,044.02	324,194.39

A adjustment to Closing Inventory with no change to Inventory Purchases the effects of this adjustment have no place to go accept Cost of Goods Sold.

Fig 5:2

95

No: There's the Periodic Inventory System and the Perpetual Inventory System. With the Periodic Inventory System, calculating the Cost of Goods sold requires a physical inventory count. The Perpetual Inventory System updates Inventory levels as the products are sold.

To illustrate: A store selling magazines, newspapers, candy, snacks and soda generating nonstop traffic that when the customers pay, the money in placed in a box. Change is given from the same box. If the articles are scanned at the point of sale, that tells me, the amount of the sale and sales taxes collected is recorded, including adjusting, on paper the inventory levels, producing an updated report on the cost of sales for that item.

 Why go to the expense of installing this technology if the owners and management believe it isn't warranted?

 Upgrading, or not upgrading, doesn't automatically make the management guilty under Figures never lie, but sometimes liars figure"

In the first part of the example, Income can't be verified, and if the lease agreement provides for a minimum rent and an override, once a certain amount of gross income is generated during any calendar month, makes doing an audit attempting to verify the income will be futile.

Management might not want the outside owners to upgrade, since revenues can't be verified then "Figures never lie, but sometimes liars figure" could rule the roost. The outside owners might be content with the present system. If full earnings are being declared and verified, this could be an opportunity for them to apply "Figures never lie, but sometimes liars figure" to pocket these earnings tax free, or at the very minimum, under report taxable income.

 In non-manufacturing industries, the withdrawals from the storerooms are automatically Cost of Goods sold?

Didn't we go through this before? I will go into this further.

In a manufacturing entity, fifteen items requisitioned from the storerooms might be part of fifteen distinct items, making up the total Finished Goods Inventory. If a bartender requisitions fifteen bottles of spirits, the items will be removed from the physical storeroom Inventory and recorded as being removed at the cost price of those items. A physical count can confirm the fifteen bottles are no longer part of the physical storeroom Inventory.

If the bartender orders the fifteen bottles on the first of the month, and at the end of the month, the entire fifteen bottles are sold, and that was the entire business for the month, then that's the Cost of Goods Sold for the month. Period!

That's theory, but month end comes around, the bartender has three bottles unopened. If the entire fifteen bottles are reported as the Cost of Goods sold based on the storeroom issues, then the bartender can take the three bottles home, or sell them and keep the money. The solution, the three bottles must be included in the Total Closing Inventory. Total Closing Inventory isn't confined to the physical storerooms. (Recall, Manufacturing has Work in Process Inventory)

The same concept applies to Macy's, Sacks Fifth Avenue etc. The items sold at the store level are requisitioned from the local storerooms, and is comparable to the Inventory at the bar. Replace fifteen bottles of spirits with fifteen winter coats.

There are no coats in the store at the beginning of the month, and if fifteen are requisitioned and sold during the month, then like the bar, this is Cost of Goods Sold. If there are three remaining at the end of the month, these three had better be taken into Inventory. Taking them into

Inventory insures these coats don't acquire legs without being accounted for.

Total Closing Inventory includes inventory from the merchandise on the retail floors, all merchandise in the actual stores storage facilities, including the warehousing that stores the merchandise that supply the retail outlets. Regardless of the method, Periodic or Perpetual, physical Inventory counts can't be eliminated completely.

To recap: Periodic Inventory systems require a physical Inventory count to arrive at Cost of Goods sold. Perpetual inventory system's calculates the Cost of Goods sold when Inventory is issued. The accounting goes like this: One computer for $4,000.00 is sold to a corporate client on credit. Cost of the item is $3,300.00.

May 31st Accounts Receivable	$4,000.00	
Sales Computer		$4,000.00
Cost of Goods Sold	$3,300.00	
Inventory ID #21324		$3,300.00

The reports produce three figures: The Income generated from the sale of that item, the cost of the item sold and according to the report, the actual level of Inventory for those items on hand. The quantity on hand is the number that SHOULD be there. Only a physical count can confirm the SHOULD. Inventory checks MUST be an on going activity. This brings us to: How is Inventory valued?

Acquisition Cost is the price paid. Price changes are not accounted for using this method.
Standard Costs are predetermined estimates of items of what manufactured inventory SHOULD cost, that's determined by past practice and produced for Internal
Management Systems leaving management accounting to reconcile the SHOULD with the ACTUAL

Replacement Cost: Price to replace the inventory item based on the fair market value, and NOT, at a fire sale, based on usual quantities, and not at an extra or at a starvation order level

Net Realizable Value (Exit Cost): This is the price relayed in the normal course of business between a willing buyer and a willing seller. If an item costs $100.00 and that increases to $120.00 at the end of the period the Inventory account is debited for $20.00. The Owners Equity Section can have an account, such as Unrealized Gain on Inventory held until sold. Up to date Inventory valuations may be potentially more helpful, although harder to audit. All of these are for internal use only, as GAAP accepts only the "Lower of Cost or Market"

"Lower of Cost or Market" is the lower of Acquisition Cost or market value. If the market value decreases below the Acquisition Cost on the books, then Inventory is revalued to market value. If market value increases above the acquisition cost, there's no adjustment. (Fig 5:3)

Details	Cost Basis		Lower Cost/Market
Opening Inventory	174,678.09		174,678.09
Add: Inventory Purchases	387,528.43		387,528.43
Total Available for Sale	562,206.52		562,206.52
Less: Closing Inventory	326,044.02	⟶	234,751.69
Equals: Cost of Goods Sold	236,162.50		327,454.83

Fig 5:3

The Closing Inventory under the Lower of Cost or Market is reduced from $326,044.02 to $234,751.69. This $91,292.33 can be booked:

May 31st Market Decline/ Inventory $91,292.33
       Inventory $91,292.33
Revalue Inventory in accordance with Lower of Cost or Market Accounting Rules.

In real life, $91,292.33 is usually buried with the current

month's Cost of Goods sold. The "Lower of Cost or Market" complies with the Conservatism Concept.

The Inventory Turnover ratio measures how fast Inventory turns over. The higher the ratio, the closer the Inventory reflects current costs. Where do you locate the affects of current prices?

Price changes make it is impossible to show current costs on the Income Statement and the Balance Sheet. So long as the Cost of Goods sold and ending Inventory is based on acquisition costs, Financial Statements can only report current cost amounts in the Income Statement or Balance Sheet but NOT both.

It's not enough the Cost of Goods sold and Inventory valuations can be manipulated. GAAP doesn't permit current costs if these costs exceed acquisition costs, and only one of the Financial Statements can closely reflect current valuations. What does one do?

There is NO other way to calculate the cost of goods sold as described earlier in this chapter regardless of the shortcomings. It's put up with it, or shut up.

All you can do is be aware of them and deal with them. Cost flow assumptions MUST be made. There are three major methods available that can be used to calculate the Cost of Goods Sold, ultimately affecting the valuation of the Closing Inventory.

They are: First In. First Out, commonly referred to as FIFO. Then there is Last in Last Out commonly referred to as LIFO. The third one is the Weighted Average Method.

Are the Inventory purchases handled the same no matter FIFO, LIFO or Weighted Average is selected?

The amount of the Inventory purchases for the month is the total merchandise received. The Inventory account is debited Accounts Payable is credited. It doesn't matter what physical items are withdrawn from Inventory

First In and First Out FIFO makes the ASSUMPTION that the Inventory that came in first, goes out first, even in reality the merchandise DIDN'T flow that way. It ASSUMES the Closing Inventory represents the newer items. Last in. First Out, or LIFO, ASSUMES that the Inventory that came in last, goes out first, even if this is far from the real world.

There is a school of thought that LIFO is a clearer indication of current pricing. There is an unofficial term: FISH standing for First In Still Here. Weighted Average uses an average cost for all inventory valuations.

Details	First In First Out	Last In First Out	Weighted Average
Opening Inventory			
Inventory Purchases: 8000 units at $12.00 per unit	96,000.00	96,000.00	96,000.00
Inventory Purchases: 9200 units at $12.75 per unit	117,300.00	117,300.00	117,300.00
Inventory Purchases: 9900 units at $14.00 per unit	138,600.00	138,600.00	138,600.00
Inventory Purchases: 10200 units at $16.75 per unit	170,850.00	170,850.00	170,850.00
Inventory Purchases: 1100 units at $22.00 per unit	24,200.00	24,200.00	24,200.00
Inventory Purchases: 6200 units at $19.34 per unit	119,908.00	119,908.00	119,908.00
Inventory Purchases: 19800 units at $17.15 per unit	339,570.00	339,570.00	339,570.00
Total 64400 Units Available for Sale	1,006,428.00	1,006,428.00	1,006,428.00
Withdrawals: 8000 units at $12.00 per unit	96,000.00		
Withdrawals: 9200 units at $12.75 per unit	117,300.00		
Withdrawals: 9900 units at $14.00 per unit	138,600.00		
Withdrawals: 1100 units at $22.00 per unit		24,200.00	
Withdrawals: 6200 units at $19.34 per unit		119,908.00	
Withdrawals:19800 units at $17.15 per unit		339,570.00	
Withdrawals: 27100 @ $15.63			423,573.00
Closing Inventory	654,528.00	522,750.00	582,855.00
Cost of Sales	351,900.00	483,678.00	423,573.00

Fig 5:4

In Fig 5:4 Opening Inventory is omitted. Inventory

101

purchases are identical for all methods with 64400 units available for sale valued overall at $1,006,428.00. The number of units withdrawn is 27,100 units. Closing Inventory is 37,300 units. The Cost of Sales reported under each method is different, and if proper accounting procedures adhered to, legal

 Two entities selling identical products, in exactly identical quantities and price report different Cost of Sales, affecting gross profit depending on the method chosen. The Closing Inventory of 27100 is the number of units on hand and the Cost of Sales variance is significant. What are the affects on the Balance Sheet?

 FIFO provides Balance Sheet valuations closer to current values, but Cost of Goods might be outdated. LIFO'S Balance Sheet valuations might have costs of items from many years ago, but Cost of Goods sold, should reflect current values. Weighted Average falls between the two. A high inventory turnover mitigates the vast differences between the methods employed.

 With LIFO reporting higher levels of Cost of Goods sold compared with FIFO and Weighted Average, tax wise, why not take advantage of it?

 LIFO compared to FIFO is far easier to manipulate for financial and tax reporting. The cost of goods sold is higher under LIFO, but there's no free lunch as its tax deferral, not a tax break.

If LIFO is elected for income tax purposes, LIFO must be used for Financial Reporting as well. LIFO can defer income taxes, especially in rapidly rising prices. When General Motors first switched from FIFO to LIFO, they sliced $150 million from their current tax bill.

 How much time do they have before the piper sends them a bill?

When Inventory quantities decline, in the year of the decline, and continue until they return to pre decline levels, for lack of a better expression the lower unit costs of prior years become expenses. LIFO provides more opportunity to play with earnings.

When entities dip into LIFO layers Income increases. This MUST be disclosed in the Financial Statements. The SEC goes further, requiring users of LIFO to disclose, in notes to the Financial Statements, the amount that LIFO Inventories would appear, if FIFO had been elected or current costs. By far the majority of entities have elected FIFO or Weighted Average.

The Deacon 3Q's ™ The Quality of the Financial Reports depend on the quality of the input and the quality of the management of that input

Chapter 6

Imaging attending one of my live seminars. I tell the crowd to hold the first thought that comes into their heads on hearing a certain word. You are NOT to change it.

"Depreciation"

Do you relate to any of the following? The loss in value of a luxury sedan acquired a few months ago. Depreciation is major-tax write-offs for the rich and famous. Depreciation is anything that is loosing or has lost value. It's OK if you invest in real estate.

If instead of the word "Depreciation", I told you to think of the word house, a dog, a cat, a bird, a mountain etc. Some have flashbacks from childhood, others might relate to present circumstances, or give me a blank look. The answer I want is: "It depends on the circumstances" In my experience, depreciation falls within the top three areas of the least understood aspects of accounting.

 Are the words Amortize, Amortization and Depreciation interchangeable?

 Amortization is the word that's used to write-down an asset. Depreciation refers to the Amortization of plant assets that includes furniture, fixtures and equipment and the physical structures used in business. (Personal property isn't amortized or depreciated) Depletion is the write down of Wasting Assets.

Wasting Assets are oil, gas. Next time you pull into the gas station, remember gasoline is a wasting asset! <u>Depreciation and Depletion are targeted towards specific categories</u>.

There isn't a given name for the amortization of Goodwill, Trademarks, Patents and Copyrights. These assets can only be amortized if they are <u>acquired through arms length business transactions</u>.

What makes up the total dollar amount of a capital asset that must be depreciated?

 If the acquisition is for land and buildings, add legal fees, transfer taxes, management salaries during the search and negotiations. Fees paid for reports on the structural soundness of the building are allotted to the building only.

Operating expenses for the company automobiles, including depreciation for the automobiles, travel and entertainment during the search, meals and entertainment related to obtaining the land and building <u>should</u> be allotted. In <u>practice</u> it's almost always included in the normal course of business.

 Searches can take a huge amount of management and non-management time and resources. If it's accurately found, due to the time spent they lost $200,000 in business profits. How is this deficiency booked?

 As this is considered an Opportunity Cost, no revenue or expense is allowable.

 What does Capitalization or Capitalizing an asset mean?

 Timing Timing Timing™ It's common to certain industries and circumstances. Others may never capitalize an asset. All the expenses relative to the asset are accumulated. Timing Timing Timing™ determines when Capitalization begins and ends.

 Considering the hotel project, when the Coffee Shop requires major renovation work, but this time they utilize in house personnel to do the job. Does this become an expense in the normal course of business?

106

For self constructed projects, the usual items labor, materials, overhead costs, and interest paid during the construction, MUST be capitalized. GAAP assumes that if the project weren't constructed in the first place, there isn't any need for interest costs!

What interest rates are permitted?

If prior borrowing has taken place, that rate must be used. If debt is taken on for this project, then that's the rate that must be used, to the extent that the interest allocated to the project, cannot exceed the total amount for interest paid for the period.

I have my nose to the ground. This must be an excellent opportunity for "Figures never lie, sometimes liars figure?"

There is the total interest expense for the year, and the total interest expense that must be capitalized for the year. Both must be disclosed as notes to the Financial Statements.

The dictionary refers to Depreciation as something that looses value. What is the accounting definition of depreciation?

Depreciation is the <u>process</u> of writing down the asset; from the time it's <u>placed in service</u>, to the end of <u>its useful life</u>.

It's the cost of the asset less salvage value that's the basis for depreciation: Depreciation allocates the COST of these assets to the period of use. The moment an investment is made in ANY Capital asset, the moment it's placed in service, this triggers Depreciation expense.

For example: Computers, scanners, telephones, and some copy machines placed in service cost $360,000.00 The installment contract requires $10,000.00 each month for 36 months. You mean $10,000 a month is not an expense? These items have devalued 20% within a few hours of installation, is totally ignored by accounting?

 Accounting doesn't consider the monthly payment as expenses. These payments reduce the overall Liability on the Balance Sheet by the amount of each payment less, interest expense.

 Thousands of individuals own rental units that barely break-even each month. Call the late night TV guru what you want, but depreciation has its benefits. Accountants don't dispute this either. So if a non-cash expense isn't a paper loss, then, what do you classify as a paper loss?

 I agree that depreciation is a non-cash event, but that doesn't mean I agree that it's a paper loss. I do agree, it might provide immediate, short- term benefits. When the property appreciates Uncle Sam comes knocking for payback

In the United States, land is NEVER depreciated. The five unit dwelling and land is acquired for $6.5 million, is no different than the Deacon Hotel Property having land and a building valued at almost $960 Billion

For example: A building including the land is acquired for $8,000,000.00; The Land is valued at $1,500,000.00 Depreciable base is $6,500,000.00. There's a mortgage attached to the property of $6,500,000.00; Mortgage payments are $658,207.80 annually. Depreciation doesn't discriminate between Cash and Accrual accounting.

At the year-end, Income before expenses is $778,534.12 Deduct Insurance $24,000.00; Property Taxes $96,000.00;

Mortgage including interest $658,207.80 There's a cash surplus before income taxes of $326.32 for the entire year!

Depreciation may create a net loss, which can, at times be offset against other Income.

Regardless if the property has a mortgage attached, partially owned, owned outright, Depreciation expense is exactly the same. Fig 6:1 the left side includes Depreciation expense, the right side doesn't.

Depreciation is cost recovery, like any legitimate expense, net income will be reduced by the amount of the expense. There is no electing out of the reality that depreciation isn't an option. Depreciation is a requirement.

In my book, if depreciation isn't a paper loss, then what is a paper loss? A stock purchased at $50.00 having declined to $15.00 there is a paper loss of $35.00 per share, so long as the stock hasn't been sold. Stocks are non-depreciable assets subject to the "Lower of Cost or Market" rules, and aren't recoverable through Depreciation expense. (The cost of real property is recoverable through Depreciation expense)

Fig 6.1 reports depreciation expense at $216,667.16, which is far less than the monthly mortgage payments.

 What happens when the property is sold at substantially higher price over the book value of the asset?

 In the absence of prior tax planning, that's when the bill arrives, levying the taxes on the entire gain over the initial contract price. In addition recaptures all or most of the Depreciation expense taken and allowed to date. Both for Financial and Tax accounting, Depreciation is Cost allocation. It isn't a process of evaluation.

How it works Under Accrual			Taxes Excluding Depreciation Expense		
Gross Sales		82,458,000.00	Gross Sales		82,458,000.00
Less Sales Returns		(14,017,860.00)	Less Sales Returns		(14,017,860.00)
Net Sales		68,440,140.00	Net Sales		68,440,140.00
Cost of Sales		(21,216,443.40)	Cost of Sales		(21,216,443.40)
Gross Profit		47,223,696.60	Gross Profit		47,223,696.60
Gross Payroll	5,666,843.59		Gross Payroll	5,666,843.59	
Payroll Taxes	850,026.54		Payroll Taxes	850,026.54	
Advertising	14,842,440.00		Advertising	14,842,440.00	
Telephone	344,674.44		Telephone	344,674.44	
Utilities	328,512.67		Utilities	328,512.67	
Travel/ Entertainment	2,125,066.35	24,157,563.59	Travel/ Entertainment	2,125,066.35	24,157,563.59
Operating Profit or Loss		23,066,133.01	Operating Profit or Loss		23,066,133.01
Insurance	1,000,000.00		Insurance	1,000,000.00	
Interest on Mortgage	382,499.96		Interest on Mortgage	382,499.96	
Management Fees	10,266,021.00		Management Fees	10,266,021.00	
Depreciation	216,666.67	11,865,187.63	Depreciation	-	11,648,520.96
Pre Tax Income or Loss		11,200,945.38	Pre Tax Income or Loss		11,417,612.05
Income Taxes assume 38%		4,256,359.24	Income Taxes assume 38%		4,338,692.58
Net Income (After Tax)		6,944,586.14	Net Income (After Tax)		7,078,919.47

Cost of Building	8,000,000.00
Land	(1,500,000.00)
Basis for Depreciation	6,500,000.00
Length in Years	30
Depreciation Straight Lin	216,666.67

Fig 6:1

Depreciation allocates cost, it cares less if the asset increases in value, remain static or devalues. Historical accounting permits for the return of the cost of the asset, not a dime more, not a dime less.

Cost recovery spans the entire life of the asset, not just the first one or first few, or selected accounting periods. There are two partially offsetting processes. Accounting does NOT recognize the gains in holding the asset. It recognizes the gains on disposition, or sale of the asset. Measured by accounting profits, a return on capital is achieved after all costs have been recovered.

Depreciation is a non-cash expense for both Tax and Financial accounting, so it's a non-cash consideration for the government too. Governments throughout the industrialized

West, regularly use depreciation rate changes to inflate, deflate the economy, or influence certain specific sectors of the economy.

The laws change, but for the year 2004, qualifying business can expense in one shot, in lieu of taking the normal depreciation allowable, a maximum of $100,000 for assets placed in service during the year. Again, depreciation is nothing more than the cost recovery of a capital asset.

It's the estimated life of the asset, not necessarily how long it is kept. Particularly for taxes <u>unless</u> Section 179 is elected, for instance, business automobiles can't be depreciated over a two-year period, even if it's common practice to replace those automobiles within that time frame. There is a specified minimum time that reflects estimated life.

Computers might have an estimated life, on acquisition, of five years, but they're frequently replaced after two years. They work fine. They are far from obsolete, but newer versions take up less space and process faster.

Could you imagine a store not changing their fronts because initially the original version has an economic life of x years, and it has to run its course? Increases in the cost of gasoline, may make some models of automobiles uneconomical to drive. Its reality, at least one manufacturer will step in and produce a vehicle that's appropriate for the times, insuring existing ones will be replaced long before their estimated life.

 The computers that on acquisition had an estimated useful life of five years are replaced after two years stay on the books for the full five years?

 No, No, No! Just as assets acquired cannot begin depreciation until they are placed in service, accounting doesn't permit assets to be on the books that aren't physically present.

There are two conditions before depreciation can be

booked. The first one: An accurate measurement of the primary acquisition cost, plus freight, storage, installation costs etc. Two: An estimation of the salvage value. (Don't confuse this with income taxes as in most cases salvage value is ignored)

Salvage value or otherwise known as the Net Residual Value, are the net proceeds generated when most capital assets are retired. Buildings typically have a zero salvage value, as accounting assumes it costs money to move the remains.

I asked myself the question: In our disposable high tech era, should the requirement that salvage value be calculated be done away with? Computers, copy machines may be worthless, and their value as scrap metal might be appropriate.

The entity using automobiles or delivery vans as part of the normal course of business, might assign a five-year life, one hundred thousand miles on each vehicle. Depending on the make, the response for coming up with salvage value five years from now, might be, scrap, pennies, five percent of the current price, etc.

Car rental companies can't take the same attitude. They only rent cars for a few months after acquisition. They are then sold. Scan the Internet for information on what these vehicles are going for. It might surprise you.

 What do the terms Service Life, Depreciable Life and Useful Life mean? In estimating salvage value for Financial Accounting purposes, is the original estimate written in stone?

 Service life and Depreciable life are interchangeable. Tax legislation, depending on the asset, usually allocate "useful life" that might be way below normal useful life. Taxable income will match pre tax income for Financial accounting purposes.

Accounting works best when it's given specific commands, blunt, with no deviations accepted. Estimating Salvage life depends on so many factors, with the majority completely out of management and the owners' control. Salvage Value is frequently revisited over the life of the Capital Asset.

 What is the rule for characterizing and segregating Depreciable Capital Assets?

 Depreciation SHOULD be computed on an individual asset basis. That's a no brainier for a home business, and even large entities with office furniture, office equipment and possibly vehicles.

Try telling this to one of the traditional telephone providers, that the telephone polls must be depreciated on an individual basis! Even the Deacon property can't depreciate items solely on an individual basis.

Depreciating assets in groups usually work out. Figure 6.2 taking up two pages, takes the assets at the time of the capitalization. This time adds the Acquisition costs, Salvage Value and the Depreciation Expense.

Depreciation Expense is shown for February and March. That's sufficient for our purposes.

 Total valuation for the printers for $15,000.00 can comprise of more than one printer. What can be done to insure Assets, when retired is simultaneously removed from the General Ledger?

Physical counts of the actual Fixed Assets are no less important than physical counts of Inventory. Each printers' serial number can be listed, or an in-house identification number be given. The audit and review of Plant Assets are always part of all good external audits.

Lenders loaning on security of the Inventory are well

Deacon Hotel Depreciation Schedule

Asset Categories	Type	January 2003 Acquisition Cost	Dep. Cost less Salvage Value	February 2003 Depreciation	March 2003 Depreciation
Building Frame, Windows etc Dep Exp.	SL 35yrs	385,330,627.86	416,157,078.09	990,850.19	990,850.19
Boilers	SL 20 Yrs	49,870,000.00	53,859,600.00	224,415.00	224,415.00
Main Electrical Plant	SL 20 Yrs	31,987,000.00	34,545,960.00	143,941.50	143,941.50
Back Up Generators	SL 20 Yrs	3,543,900.00	3,827,412.00	15,947.55	15,947.55
Air Conditioning Plant	SL 20 Yrs	11,000,000.00	11,880,000.00	49,500.00	49,500.00
Fire Sprinkler System	SL 18yrs	3,500,000.00	3,150,000.00	14,583.33	14,583.33
Fire Hose and Fire Alarm System	SL 15 Yrs	1,760,000.00	1,672,000.00	9,288.89	9,288.89
Refrigeration - Main	SL 15 Yrs	12,000,000.00	10,200,000.00	56,666.67	56,666.67
Refrigeration - Seven Smaller Units	SL 15 Yrs	7,000,000.00	5,950,000.00	33,055.56	33,055.56
Elevators - Public Fifteen	SL 25 Yrs	38,000,000.00	32,300,000.00	107,666.67	107,666.67
Elevators - Private - Five	SL 25 Yrs	10,350,000.00	8,797,500.00	29,325.00	29,325.00
Elevators - Freight - Six	SL 25 Yrs	19,490,000.00	16,566,500.00	55,221.67	55,221.67
Elevators - Garage	SL 25 Yrs	6,400,000.00	5,440,000.00	18,133.33	18,133.33
Escalators Lobby and Conference	SL 25 Yrs	8,400,000.00	7,140,000.00	23,800.00	23,800.00
Escalators - Private Four	SL 25 Yrs	2,100,000.00	1,785,000.00	5,950.00	5,950.00
Bathroom- Tubs	SL 15 Yrs	2,790,000.00	2,706,300.00	15,035.00	15,035.00
Bathroom - Showers	SL 15 Yrs	350,987.00	340,457.39	1,891.43	1,891.43
STRUCTURE ESSENTIALS					
Kitchen - Main	SL 25yrs	2,860,113.00	2,802,910.74	9,343.04	9,343.04
Kitchen - Fine Dining	SL 25yrs	261,873.00	256,635.54	855.45	855.45
Kitchen - Steak House	SL 25yrs	254,900.00	249,802.00	832.67	832.67
Kitchen - Conference Meeting Halls	SL 25yrs	543,123.00	532,260.54	1,774.20	1,774.20
Kitchen - Roof Top Restaurant/Lounge	SL 25yrs	321,000.00	314,580.00	1,048.60	1,048.60
Kitchenette - Lobby Bar	SL 25yrs	133,600.00	130,928.00	436.43	436.43
Kitchenette - Room Service	SL 25yrs	211,000.00	206,780.00	689.27	689.27
Indoor Swimming Pool	SL 12yrs	175,000.00	171,500.00	1,190.97	1,190.97
Indoor Squash Courts	SL 12yrs	250,000.00	245,000.00	1,701.39	1,701.39
Marble Flooring - Lobby	SL 25yrs	8,000,000.00	7,840,000.00	26,133.33	26,133.33
Marble Flooring - Bathrooms	SL 25yrs	10,000,000.00	9,800,000.00	32,666.67	32,666.67
Bathroom - Shower Rods	SL 12yrs	300,000.00	294,000.00	2,041.67	2,041.67
Bathroom - Towel Rods	SL 12yrs	430,000.00	421,400.00	2,926.39	2,926.39
Spa - Swimming Pool	SL 12yrs	250,000.00	245,000.00	1,701.39	1,701.39
Spa - Pools	SL 12yrs	160,000.00	156,800.00	1,088.89	1,088.89
Chandeliers	SL 25yrs	1,500,000.00	1,470,000.00	4,900.00	4,900.00
Carpeting	SL 8yrs	5,000,000.00	5,000,000.00	52,083.33	52,083.33
ACTUAL FACILITIES - CONSTRUCTION					
Coffee Shop	DB 200% 15	5,000,000.00	5,000,000.00	55,583.33	55,583.33
Steak House	DB 200% 15	8,000,000.00	8,000,000.00	88,933.33	88,933.33
Fine Dining	DB 200% 15	11,000,000.00	11,000,000.00	122,283.33	122,283.33
Show Lounge	DB 200% 15	30,000,000.00	30,000,000.00	333,500.00	333,500.00
Roof Top Restaurant and Lounge	DB 200% 15	21,000,000.00	21,000,000.00	233,450.00	233,450.00
Meeting and Function Space	DB 200% 15	13,000,000.00	13,000,000.00	144,516.67	144,516.67
200,000 Sq ft Spa and Fitness Center	DB 200% 15	7,000,000.00	7,000,000.00	77,816.67	77,816.67
Business Center	DB 200% 15	1,500,000.00	1,500,000.00	16,675.00	16,675.00
Lobby Shop	DB 200% 15	540,000.00	540,000.00	6,003.00	6,003.00
Garage	DB 200% 15	12,000,000.00	12,000,000.00	133,400.00	133,400.00
Storage Areas	DB 200% 15	500,000.00	500,000.00	5,558.33	5,558.33
Executive, Sales, Accounting Offices	DB 200% 15	2,000,000.00	2,000,000.00	22,233.33	22,233.33
FURNITURE FITTINGS EQUIPMENT					

114

Asset Categories	Type	January 2003 Acquisition Cost	Dep. Cost less Salvage Value	February 2003 Depreciation	March 2003 Depreciation
Rooms - Drapes	DB 200% 7	300,000.00	288,300.00	6,866.35	6,866.35
Rooms - Bed Heads	DB 200% 7	550,000.00	528,550.00	12,588.30	12,588.30
Rooms - Bed Frames	DB 200% 7	300,000.00	288,300.00	6,866.35	6,866.35
Rooms - Rollaway Beds	DB 200% 7	12,000.00	11,532.00	274.65	274.65
Rooms - Bedside Lamps	DB 200% 7	280,000.00	269,080.00	6,408.59	6,408.59
Rooms - Bedside Lamp Shades	DB 200% 7	30,000.00	28,830.00	686.63	686.63
Rooms - Inside Carpeting	DB 200% 7	500,000.00	480,500.00	11,443.91	11,443.91
Rooms - Television	DB 200% 7	400,000.00	384,400.00	9,155.13	9,155.13
Rooms - Safe for Valuables	DB 200% 7	1,000,000.00	961,000.00	22,887.82	22,887.82
Rooms - High Speed Wireless	DB 200% 7	300,000.00	288,300.00	6,866.35	6,866.35
Rooms - Telephones Main Suite	DB 200% 7	300,000.00	288,300.00	6,866.35	6,866.35
Rooms - Telephones Bathrooms	DB 200% 7	100,000.00	96,100.00	2,288.78	2,288.78
Rooms - Refrigerators	DB 200% 7	500,000.00	480,500.00	11,443.91	11,443.91
Rooms - Coffee Makers	DB 200% 7	136,000.00	130,696.00	3,112.74	3,112.74
Coffee Shop - Tables & Chairs	DB 200% 7	58,800.00	56,506.80	1,345.80	1,345.80
Fine Dining - Tables & Chairs	DB 200% 7	73,500.00	70,633.50	1,682.25	1,682.25
Steak House - Tables & Chairs	DB 200% 7	54,096.00	51,986.26	1,238.14	1,238.14
Roof Top Restaurant Tables & Chairs	DB 200% 7	103,488.00	99,451.97	2,368.61	2,368.61
Functions & Catering - Tables & Chairs	DB 200% 7	215,000.00	206,615.00	4,920.88	4,920.88
Functions & Catering - Tele Conference	DB 200% 5	60,000.00	57,660.00	1,922.00	1,922.00
Show Lounge - Tables and Chairs	DB 200% 5	750,000.00	720,750.00	24,025.00	24,025.00
Show Lounge - Performing Stage	DB 200% 5	1,500,000.00	1,441,500.00	48,050.00	48,050.00
Buffet Stands	DB 200% 5	56,000.00	53,816.00	1,793.87	1,793.87
Pianos	DB 200% 5	100,000.00	96,100.00	3,203.33	3,203.33
Dance Floors	DB 200% 5	60,000.00	57,660.00	1,922.00	1,922.00
Bar Stands and Bar Chairs	DB 200% 5	10,000.00	9,610.00	320.33	320.33
Lobby Furniture	DB 200% 5	15,000.00	14,415.00	480.50	480.50
Lobby - Baggage Carts	DB 200% 5	13,000.00	12,493.00	416.43	416.43
Security Television Systems	DB 200% 5	100,000.00	96,100.00	3,203.33	3,203.33
General safe Deposit Boxes	DB 200% 5	20,000.00	19,220.00	640.67	640.67
Telephone - Excluding Rooms	DB 200% 5	30,000.00	28,830.00	961.00	961.00
Telephone - Main Communications Center	DB 200% 5	150,000.00	144,150.00	4,805.00	4,805.00
Internal Security Systems	DB 200% 5	100,000.00	96,100.00	3,203.33	3,203.33
Showcases	DB 200% 5	200,000.00	192,200.00	6,406.67	6,406.67
Garage - Automatic Entry / Departure	DB 200% 5	150,000.00	144,150.00	4,805.00	4,805.00
Satellite and Communications Tower.	DB 200% 5	1,500,000.00	1,441,500.00	48,050.00	48,050.00
Main Safe	DB 200% 5	50,000.00	48,050.00	1,601.67	1,601.67
Office Furniture	DB 200% 5	100,000.00	96,100.00	3,203.33	3,203.33
Printers	DB 200% 5	15,000.00	14,415.00	480.50	480.50
Computer Hardware	DB 200% 5	100,000.00	96,100.00	3,203.33	3,203.33
Scanners	DB 200% 5	16,000.00	15,376.00	512.53	512.53
In House Teleconferencing Equipment	DB 200% 5	7,000.00	6,727.00	224.23	224.23
Copier Machines	DB 200% 5	300,000.00	288,300.00	9,610.00	9,610.00
Dr. Depreciation Expense A/C 32287				3,468,994.06	3,468,994.06
Furniture Fittings & Equipment A/C 10402				3,176,638.46	3,176,638.46
Land and Buildings A/C 10502				292,355.60	292,355.60

Fig 6:2

advised to have representatives physically look over the containers to validate the inventory. If Fixed Assets replace Inventory as security, or contribute a considerable portion of the overall operations of the business, lenders are well advised to require Audited Financial Statements with additional emphasis on Fixed Assets.

 The schedule of the Deacon Hotel has only SL and DB as the methods of depreciation. What do SL and DB stand for, and what other options are available?

 SL stands for Straight Line, and DB stands for Declining Balance. The Straight-line method allows for the traditional Straight-line method, and provides for the option of the Straight-line use method. Declining Balance consists of two Declining Balance rates and the Sum-of-the-years digits.

 Before going into detail on these methods, why do the first five items on the list (Fig 6:2) have Salvage Value in excess of Acquisition Costs?

 Items as the Building Frame, Windows, Boilers, Main Electrical Plant, etc have Residual value at zero or below. Such items will cost substantial sums of money to demolish and remove them.

In these instances, the estimated costs that will be incurred at the end of their useful lives can be added to the Acquisition costs and Depreciated over the life of the Asset. In all other cases, Salvage Values are far less than Acquisition costs.

 The Deacon Hotel Depreciation is identical for each month. Is that normal?

 Yes. As long as Assets are not being added or discarded. For the Hotel project I selected the Declining Balance and Straight Line for convenience in getting the message across.

The Straight-Line Method (Time) takes the economic life of the asset, then pro rates the Depreciation in equal monthly or annual amounts. If an asset costs $1,500,000 with a salvage value of $30,000.00; $1,470.000 is the basis for Depreciation. If that's Straight-line over 25 years, then Depreciation expense is $4,900.00 a month or $58,800.00 a year.

The Straight-Line Use Method, also known as The Production or Use Method. Some entities have all or most of their Income for the first five months of the year, for example, and if it were not for competitive reasons they would close down. The straight-line method might not be in tune with use. Total usage must be estimated for this method to even be considered. If a truck has a Depreciable base, after Salvage Value of $50,000 and it's determined it will provide 200,000 miles of use before "retirement" or "death" Depreciation is 0.25c per mile. In any month the truck is used for 2000 miles, the Depreciation Expense is booked for $500.00

 Why did Deacon Hotels take the minimum Straight-line?

 There is no such thing as the minimum. I wanted to reflect true values as possible. Accelerated depreciation methods, take larger chunks in the early years, and smaller chunks in the later years.

Financial accounting doesn't require accelerated methods of depreciation despite that many Assets loose a large percentage of their values in the early years. No matter the method chosen, annual Depreciation Expense is spread evenly throughout the year!

 No asset can be depreciated lower than Salvage Value, so what happens when Accelerated Depreciation is selected, the Depreciation Expense approaches the Salvage Value long before the end of its useful life.

 Accelerated depreciation isn't complicated. What you see is what you get.

Once Accelerated Depreciation Expense is lower, than what would be under Straight-line, then the amount to be depreciated converts to Straight-line.

Declining Balance became popular when entities realized significant current taxes could be saved, and many are of the opinion it more clearly reflects reality. Accelerated Depreciation evolved into Financial Statements when General Accepted Accounting Principles (GAAP) accepted it. Should the Double-declining Balance be selected for the Financial Statements, usually the 200% wins out over the 150% options. See Fig 6:3

The Depreciable base is $2,706,300. This amount divided by 15 years is $180,420.00 Take $180,420.00 as a Percentage of $2,706,300 and the answer is 6.67%. This percentage is the write-down for this asset, each and every year, for fifteen years under the Straight-line method.

Straight Line

Bathroom Tubs

		Cost	2,790,000.00
		Salvage	83,700.00
		Base	2,706,300.00
		Period years	15
		Annual	180,420.00
		Percentage	6.67%
Year	Amount	Percentage	New Balance
1	2,790,000.00	180,420.00	2,609,580.00
2	2,609,580.00	180,420.00	2,429,160.00
3	2,429,160.00	180,420.00	2,248,740.00
4	2,248,740.00	180,420.00	2,068,320.00
5	2,068,320.00	180,420.00	1,887,900.00
6	1,887,900.00	180,420.00	1,707,480.00
7	1,707,480.00	180,420.00	1,527,060.00
8	1,527,060.00	180,420.00	1,346,640.00
9	1,346,640.00	180,420.00	1,166,220.00
10	1,166,220.00	180,420.00	985,800.00
11	985,800.00	180,420.00	805,380.00
12	805,380.00	180,420.00	624,960.00
13	624,960.00	180,420.00	444,540.00
14	444,540.00	180,420.00	264,120.00
15	264,120.00	180,420.00	83,700.00
Total		2,706,300.00	

Declining Balance

Bathroom Tubs

		Cost	2,790,000.00
		Salvage	83,700.00
		Base	2,706,300.00
		Period years	15
		Annual	
		Percentage	13.33%
Year	Amount	Percentage	New Balance
1	2,790,000.00	372,000.00	2,418,000.00
2	2,418,000.00	322,400.00	2,095,600.00
3	2,095,600.00	279,413.33	1,816,186.67
4	1,816,186.67	242,158.22	1,574,028.44
5	1,574,028.44	209,870.46	1,364,157.99
6	1,364,157.99	181,887.73	1,182,270.25
7	1,182,270.25	157,636.03	1,024,634.22
8	1,024,634.22	117,616.76	907,017.46
9	907,017.46	117,616.78	789,400.68
10	789,400.68	117,616.78	671,783.90
11	671,783.90	117,616.78	554,167.12
12	554,167.12	117,616.78	436,550.34
13	436,550.34	117,616.78	318,933.56
14	318,933.56	117,616.78	201,316.78
15	201,316.78	117,616.78	83,700.00
		2,706,300.00	

Fig 6:3

If you want the 200% Declining Balance for the same period all you have to do is double the straight-line percentage rate. In this instance it's 13.34%. The Double Declining Balance reduces the balance each year by 13.34%, until the Depreciation Expense under this method is lower, than what it would have been if the Straight-line method had been elected in the first place.

When the time arrives, take the outstanding balance, less Salvage Value divided by the remaining number of years, becomes the Depreciation Expense for the remaining life of the asset. (See highlighted area)

Except for the percentage rate, the mechanics are identical for the 200% and 150% Declining Balance. I have never seen in practice is the sum- of- the years digits. I can give you a formula but this will confuse, and this works equally well. Supposing an asset is to be depreciated over five years. Write down like this 1 2 3 4 5

The insert a plus sign (+) in the space between each number It becomes 1+2+3+4+5
Now add them = 15 (one plus two plus three plus four plus five) See Fig 6:4

Year	Base	Depreciation	New Balance	How it Works
1	4,800.00	1,600.00	3,200.00	That is 5/15 of $4,800.00
2	3,200.00	1,280.00	1,920.00	That is 4/15 of $4,800.00
3	1,920.00	960	960	That is 3/15 of $4,800.00
4	960	640	320	That is 2/15 of $4,800.00
5	320	320		That is 1/15 of $4,800.00

Fig 6:4

This is important. Unlike the Straight-line, and the Double Declining Balance methods, year ONE starts with Acquisition Costs, and at the end of the period, the value of the asset on the books is the Salvage Value. Sum-of- the-years digits begin with the amount to be depreciated. Cost minus Salvage value.

To recap: Financial Accounting requires Salvage Value. Tax legislation, for the most part, has eliminated Salvage Values. Financial statement net Income hardly ever agrees with Taxable Income?

 They both agree Depreciation isn't a loss in value. It is the Cost Recovery of a business asset, as of the date it's placed in service.

Financial and Tax Accounting both book the gain in excess of book value, when the asset is disposed of or sold. The idea the business should pay the least amount of tax now and as late as possible, in accounting is known as the Least and Latest Rule.

Many individuals, never in their wildest dreams, would have thought they would ever need an accountant, have invested in rental Income property. To make sure they are not short-changed, I am going back over some vital real world aspects of depreciation.

An example: Rental apartments, including land, is sold for $8,000,000.00 Land is never depreciated, so it's the building and the other assets at $6,500,000.00 qualifies for depreciation. For simplicity, its $6,500,000 divided by 30 years straight-line making the Depreciation Expense at $216,666.67 per year.

The building is sold after ten years. For convenience, here, there are no Capital Improvements, so the Depreciation Expense is constant for the full ten years. Book value is Acquisition Cost less Accumulated Depreciation to date)

The book value at the end of ten years is the original $8,000,000.00 (ignoring capital improvements) less Accumulated Depreciation to date of $2,166,667.coming in at $5,833,333. It's sold for $16,000,000 before selling and other miscellaneous expenses.

It doesn't matter the owners might have borrowed against

the equity. Financial and Tax accounting permit, from $16,000,000 the selling price, to deduct approved selling expenses. Selling and miscellaneous expenses is $1,000,000 reporting the amount realized of $15,000,000.

The difference between $15,000,000 and the book value of $5,833,333.00 is taxed. Depending on the tax code, it might be Capital Gain, or a combination of Capital Gains and Ordinary Income. To reiterate: Financial Accounting recognizes this gain as well

 Why doesn't Financial Accounting adopt the income tax code for depreciation and have done with it?

 Financial Reporting attempts to report the status of the Assets on the Balance Sheet in the most accurate way possible.

There's no agreement among accountants if Financial Accounting achieves this, or if doesn't come close.

For Inventory, if LIFO is elected for tax purposes, it MUST use LIFO for Financial Statement purposes too. The affects of LIFO, compared to FIFO, must be disclosed in the notes to the Financial Statements. Depreciation doesn't have this restriction.

Most publicly held companies use the straight-line method for Financial Accounting reporting purposes, but elect the most liberal depreciation methods for tax purposes the law allows.

As businesses constantly acquire and retire assets, (Selling them before or after their useful life, donating to charity, or the trash can) over all it doesn't make a lot of difference. So long as Financial Accounting refuses to allow anything close to the depreciation allowed under the tax code, it isn't a big deal. What's more important to me is, insuring all the retired assets have been removed from the books, and Depreciation Expense reconciled and properly booked.

The Deacon Hotel booked in excess of $3 million of Depreciation Expense per month, and that isn't petty cash. What happens if the Salvage Values are way off the mark? Hopefully this will be determined early in the depreciation cycle?

 Management makes decisions on their best estimate at the time. Best estimates can be an opportunity for "Figures never lie, but sometimes liars figure"

The estimates made at the time, are no different in principle, than estimates for the Bad Debt Reserve, or providing for Warranty expense under the past usage procedures.

For example, if for years and years' Bad Debt expense remained steady at 5% of sales and then in one unexplained month, the Bad Debt percentage increased. If during the life of the asset it turns out to be much longer, or much shorter, then Salvage Value may change.

 Does accounting go back and restate all the prior periods and reissue the Financial Statements?

 That would be chaotic. Accounting can't do that, but when a revaluation is a must, determine the book value of the asset, then make a decision whether to immediately slow down, or accelerate the Depreciation expense

For example, when the asset was placed in service the best estimate was a fifteen-year life, depreciating it using the Straight-line method. If the base for depreciation is $1,500,000 over fifteen years, Depreciation expense is $100,000 a year.

After five years, $500,000 of Depreciation expense has been taken on the asset, reducing book value to $1,000,000: After five years in service, the estimated life is now reduced from fifteen years to ten years. Shortening the useful life from fifteen years to ten years means depreciation has to be made up or accelerated.

This asset now has five years to reach salvage value, assuming there was no change in the dollar salvage value. The $1,000,000 book value divided by the number of years to go, which is now five years, requires $200,000.00 of Depreciation expense each year compared with $100,000.00 a year currently being booked. It can also go the other way.

If the best estimate at the time of the asset being placed in service is ten years. At the end of five years, and no change in actual dollar Salvage Value, the revised estimated life is now fifteen years. (Increases in Salvage Value slows down the Depreciation expense, decreases will accelerate the Depreciation expense)

A depreciable base of $1,500,000.00 at the original ten year estimated life requires Depreciation expense of $150,000.00. After five years $750,000.00 Depreciation expense reduces the book value to $750,000.00.

In this case, the asset is given an extra five years of life! Effective immediately, Depreciation expense reflects this reality by taking $750,000.00 over ten years, reducing the Depreciation expense from $150,000.00 per year to $75,000.00 per year.

 Half way through the estimated service life of the boilers the investment program underway substantially increases their life, or at least insure they maintain peak performance through their original estimated life. If $100,000.00 is spent, under what conditions is it a capital improvement? Capital improvements increase the book value of the asset. What about the Depreciation expense?

 It's a given that all Capital Assets require repairs and maintenance. It's also a given, all Capital Assets will ultimately be disposed. It isn't a given the asset will undergo expenditure to improve it.

Technically repairs maintain the asset in its expected operating condition. Maintenance includes cost of cleaning and adjusting. Both contribute zero to increasing the assets value. In today's market place, these definitions overlap so extensively, so thankfully accounting books both of these costs as repairs in the current period.

Improvements also known, as "Betterments" The more common term is capital expenditure that makes the asset perform better. These investments are treated as separate assets, causing an increase in the Depreciation expense, requiring immediate answers whether or not the estimated life of the asset has increased, and if the salvage value has changed.

 If $300,000.00 is characterized as repairs, the expense is booked in the current year reducing income. It's over with and the benefit immediate. If it's characterized as a capital expense, and allowable over five years, $60,000.00 goes to the Income Statement each year. That isn't as clear-cut as $300,000.00 in one shot. Could part of the $300,000.00 be classified as both repairs and capital expenses?

 Absolutely. Projects can have both characteristics. For example, a roof is destroyed by water, but this time round they purposely reinforce the roof to handle stronger air conditioning units, as well as the strength to handle water damage.

It's a judgment call determining just how much of this is a capital expense, or period expense. Because of Conservatism, accounting usually books the expenditure as a repair over a capital expense.

 Accounting goes on the side of booking expenses in the current period where there is reasonable doubt. Whenever judgment calls rule the roost, does this provide opportunities for "Figures never lie, but sometimes liars figure?"

This area brought down WorldCom. I want to use a real life situation that can happen under your very noses and not get noticed.

I'm in charge of a condominium or a residential co-operative association. (I wish!) The association spent huge sums of money on the boilers, heating, air conditioning and fire sprinklers. The reserve more than adequately covered the payment of those expenses, but I have decided to retire from the board within the next few years, and I want to leave on a wave of popularity and sound management. I know too well that what see is not always what you get.

I know for sure major work still has to be done on the plumbing, electrical systems, swimming pools, indoor garage, physical structure, the roof and the lobby. This capital outlay will make the all the previous capital expenditures look like petty cash. My cash forecasts, no matter how they are done, require the reserves to be built up aggressively insuring funding is adequate when these projects are put out to tender.

The city recently increased property taxes. If the association demands the needed increase in the monthly maintenance, this affects property values, but more important, I will be extremely unpopular, and I cannot handle at this time the political fall out. I have to make sure the Financial Statements look healthy, and convince the outside auditors they are healthy, and make sure they sign off insuring at least the perception, of a financially sound and well managed association.

Corporations need a healthy bottom line and a healthy Capital and Retained Earnings. I must have a healthy association surplus. The nature of a condominium association is that I am extremely limited what I can maneuver on the Income side. I asked two questions. What reduces a surplus? The answer is a no-brainer. Increase expenses! What will increase a surplus? Again, that's a no-brainer. Decrease expenses!

The association has never been stingy or asked questions when it came to repairs. They are approved in the millions at the drop of a hat, but this year, I have an advantage. Not only did we complete a massive renovation, but repairs excluding the Capital Expenditures for this year so far, and we are nowhere close to the end of the year, have the highest dollar value in the condominium associations' history! Ah!

Now I become a liar that begins to do some figuring and put into practice, what I have been preaching to each one you what to be on the look out for. "Figures never lie, sometimes liars figure"

I must reduce the expenses as reported on the Income Statement, but the association reports under the Accrual method, so I can't defer expenses by delaying paying the bills. The association has an excellent credit rating, and I am not about to give that up.

In any case, I want to do something now, that won't come up for years. I don't want to have to micro managed this for the rest of my stay here. I also need to get it through the external audit, in one shot, so they won't revisit this the following year.

Figures never lie, but liars sometimes figure" I did some figuring. The legitimate capital expenses stay as they are, but the amount spent on repairs this year is so huge, that I can reallocate half of that amount, without the blink of an eyelid to capital improvements, and that won't even raise an eyebrow to the uninitiated for at least six years. The affects will begin to hit home with a vengeance after five years. I am out of there. I might be invited back for a hefty retainer, to bring the association back to solvency!

As I created this fiasco, again it's a no-brainer to consult and perform miracles when the time comes. I need to plan now for my replacement to take over. I need to make sure I am replaced by a "yes" person and having nowhere near the qualifications, experience or inquiring mind that I am blessed with having.

 For Inventory, the lower of "Cost or Market" is the accepted method. Does this principle apply to Capital Assets?

 If the test results show, the then book value exceeds the sum of the undiscounted cash flow, asset Impairment has occurred. Then they must write-down the assets to fair market value.

 For Inventory if the book value is higher than Market Value, write it down to Market Value. If the book value is lower than Market Value leave it alone. What about Impairment?

 The FASB uses the word Impairment, when the book value exceeds the sum of the undiscounted future Cash flows. When the undiscounted Cash flows exceed the current book value, but a smaller decline in the asset value is recorded, then the technical term of Impairment is replaced by a mere economic loss!

This is best explained by an example:

Original intentions

Apartment Building Costs $20 million; Accumulated Depreciation $5 Million; Book Value $15 Million: Estimated
Rental Income over 30 years $50 Million
Anticipated selling Price of building $8 Million
Construction of a sports arena changed the original forecast:

Revised Rental 15 years: Discounted Rate 12%
It now expects to collect $1.35 Million per year for the next fifteen years, and expects to sell the building for $5 million at the end of the fifteen-year term. Discounted at 12% per year, this comes to $10.1 Million.

The building has a market value of $10 million. There is no impairment.

The undiscounted future cash flows $1.35 Million x 15 years + $5 Million selling price is $25.25 Million. The $25.25 million exceed the current book value of $15 Million, so no impairment, but it has suffered an economic loss, but will not recognize any loss in its accounts

In this case, expected rentals $600,000 per year for 15 years, sell the building after 15 years for $3 million. The current value of the building has a present value today at $4.6 Million. Building Market value today is $4 million, so There's impairment. The book value today at $15 Million exceeds the undiscounted cash flows of $12 Million. (600,000X15+3)

As there is impairment, the first step is to remove the existing valuation from the books and access a new valuation. The then current value, market value, can be determined with reasonable accuracy.

 If computers originally booked having a useful life of five years are retired before their useful life, how do you eliminate these computers from the books?

 All of the following must be known before any asset can be removed from the books. 1. The Book value of the asset, that's acquisition cost less accumulated Depreciation taken to date. 2. Salvage value. 3. When did the sale take place? The middle of the year or the end of the year or is it anywhere in between? 4. The selling price, or how much did you get for the asset?

Bring Depreciation expense up to date if it hasn't been done. If Depreciation expense is booked monthly, it doesn't matter when the sale takes place. We are bringing back the set of facts we used in 6:3, retiring the asset that originally having an estimated useful life of fifteen years, retiring that asset during the eleventh year. See Fig 6:5

Bath Tubs - Straight-Line Method

		Cost	2,790,000.00
		Salvage	83,700.00
		Base	2,706,300.00
		Period years	15
		Annual	180,420.00
		Percentage	6.67%

Year	Amount	Percentage	New Balance	Book Value
1	2,790,000.00	180,420.00	2,609,580.00	2,609,580.00
2	2,609,580.00	180,420.00	2,429,160.00	2,429,160.00
3	2,429,160.00	180,420.00	2,248,740.00	2,248,740.00
4	2,248,740.00	180,420.00	2,068,320.00	2,068,320.00
5	2,068,320.00	180,420.00	1,887,900.00	1,887,900.00
6	1,887,900.00	180,420.00	1,707,480.00	1,707,480.00
7	1,707,480.00	180,420.00	1,527,060.00	1,527,060.00
8	1,527,060.00	180,420.00	1,346,640.00	1,346,640.00
9	1,346,640.00	180,420.00	1,166,220.00	1,166,220.00
10	1,166,220.00	180,420.00	985,800.00	985,800.00
Depreciation end of Tenth Year		1,804,200.00		

Building up Depreciation Expense in the year of Retirement

January Year 11	985,800.00	15,035.00	970,765.00	970,765.00
February Year 11	970,765.00	15,035.00	955,730.00	955,730.00
March Year 11	955,730.00	15,035.00	940,695.00	940,695.00
April Year 11	940,695.00	15,035.00	925,660.00	925,660.00
May Year 11	925,660.00	15,035.00	910,625.00	910,625.00
June Year 11	910,625.00	15,035.00	895,590.00	895,590.00
Total Building Up Depreciation		90,210.00		
Total Accumulated Depreciation		1,894,410.00		

Fig 6:5

If the Depreciation Expense has to be updated:

June 30th, Depreciation Expense $90,210.00
          Accumulated Depreciation $90,210.00
Update Depreciation Expense for Retirement of Asset (Named)

We assume, for convenience, this is the only Asset on the Balance Sheet.

Furniture Fittings/Equipment: $2,790,000.00
Less Depreciation $1,894,410.00 $895,590.00

Get rid of the Asset on the Books. If retired for Cash, debit Cash, if retired by some other method debit Accounts Receivable

If retired at Book Value

July 1st, Cash $ 895,590.00
  Acc. Depreciation: $1,894,410.00
    Furniture Fittings/Equipment $2,790,000.00
Receipt of Cash on Retirement of Asset retired at book value.

This is one area of accounting that it's legitimate to plug. The account having the acquisition cost of the asset, must be adjusted by the original acquisition cost of the asset been retired.

All Accumulated Depreciation for that asset being retired must be removed. The account that receives the proceeds of the asset being liquidated gets debited. There is only one or the other, a profit, a loss or break even on the retirement of the asset.

If retired at a price higher than Book Value:

July 1st, Cash $1,000,000.00
  Acc. Depreciation: $1,894,410.00
    Gain on Sale of Assets $ 204.410.00
    Furniture Fittings/Equipment $2,790,000.00
Receipt of Cash: Retirement of Asset retired for $1,000,000.00

If retired at a price lower than Book Value:

July 1st, Cash $ 1000,000.00
  Acc. Depreciation: $1,894,410.00
  Loss Retirement $ 795,590.00
    Furniture Fittings / Equipment 2,790,000.00
Receipt of Cash on Retirement of Asset retired at $1,00,000.00

 This is a long way from autos, hotels, dry cleaners and supermarkets. Suppose oil is found in the ground underneath your property. How is this liquid gold accounted for?

 I am not qualified to offer advice on what to do in this enviable position. Oil companies have to ask this question consistently.

Should all exploration the costs be capitalized or only the costs of the known successful ones? GAAP permits one of two methods, <u>Full Costing or Successful Efforts Costing.</u>

Full Costing capitalizes all costs, as long as successful operations will more than support the costs of all operations. Successful efforts Costing, segregates the successful operations compared with the unsuccessful operations. All costs are capitalized the moment it becomes clear which ventures are proved unsuccessful then the unsuccessful ones become booked as a legitimate charge in the period it's determined it will not bear fruit.

 What happens when the oil company has a well and oil is flowing?

 Amortization of Wasting Assets is specifically called Depletion. The most common method elected is Units-of-production Depletion method.

If an oil company spends $4.5 million to discover an oil field, which contains an estimated 1.5 million barrels of oil, then this oil field is "Depleted" at the cost, divided by the number of barrels $4.5/1.5$ and comes out $3.00 per barrel of oil

 A decade or so ago during a seminar the speaker told the audience that the company's Intangible Assets could be more valuable than the entities real estate. Has accounting caught up with these modern times?

 That era from the mid nineties to the end of the year 2000, in my evaluation contained more hype and paper profits than any other time in modern history. When Time merged with Ted Turner's CNN Network, long before the merger of America on Line, this was the first multi million-dollar merger with almost no real estate.

The point I am making is that Microsoft Windows®, Travelers Insurance umbrella Trademarks came into being

long before this era of hype and paper. Many of the patents and copyrights Microsoft obtained in the 1980's laid the foundation for their incredible growth in years later. The point being, Intangible assets, have always been, and always will be vital.

 What is the definition of Intangible Assets?

 Typical examples, Research Costs, Patents, Trademarks, Trade secrets, Know-how and Copyrights. The most common Amortization method is the Straight-line method.

R&D, which stands for Research and Development. General Accepted Accounting Principles (GAAP) requires immediate expensing under the accounting principal known, as "Conservative" that R&D is too uncertain to forecast.

Some accountants are adamant there must be a future benefit often using Microsoft, Pfizer and others as a reference. Some analysts, especially the non-accountant types find it unbelievable these major assets don't appear on the balance sheet. If a pen manufacturer spends research and development funds on manufacturing a pen that stays upright in the pocket of a shirt or suit without having a clip! Eventually a patent is granted. The patent doesn't show up on the Balance Sheet although five million pens are produced and sold, and they license the rights to other companies. What happens if the company is sold? That's another story.

If patents are acquired from another entity, the cost is amortized, over the shorter of the patent's remaining legal life, or the estimated economic life. If developed internally the research and development rules are enforced.

 Under what circumstances does accounting capitalize advertising? What about Goodwill?

 Training Training Training ™ Advertising, NEVER! Even if the benefits of advertising extend over multiple accounting periods, the FASB require immediate expensing of advertising expense. Three reasons are provided. It satisfies the Conservative concept and Timing, Timing Timing™ It's almost impossible to quantify the future benefits of advertising, and if costs remain fairly stable over the years, the bottom line is, it makes no difference whether they are capitalized or otherwise.

Goodwill kicks at when the business, or an operating arm is sold, and the buyer pays a certain price for the business and gets a basket of assets for that price. That's the reason it's referred to as a Basket Purchase. The amount paid over the total fair market revaluation of the Assets and Liabilities is often booked as goodwill. Work in Process Technology, or Work in Process R&D, must be written off by the new business, unless the assets have already proven their worth.

 Transferring the business to the new owners trigger one or both of two things, Goodwill and possibly, Work in Process R&D. How do they differ?

 As far as the quality of earnings is concerned, high recurring earnings are preferable than one-shot earnings. If something happens, a huge one-shot hit is preferable than spreading the costs over a period of time. Work in Process R&D, unless certain quantifiable benefits are there, these costs MUST be written off in one shot regardless of the amount. Goodwill is written off over time!

Consider the assets transferred have a fair market value of $10 million compared to $15 million paid for those assets. The excess, if it's reported as Goodwill the $5 million is written off over a specified number of years. Goodwill is extremely subjective. Assuming out of $5 million, $4 million can be allocated to work in process R&D, only $1 million will be written off to Goodwill over time, and $4 million will hit the Income Statement immediately. This will create a higher quality of earnings, as there will be less to explain when business conditions might change for the worse.

Chapter 7

Payroll – and Accruals: Few words generate such powerful emotions Total Payroll include Payroll Taxes and Employee benefits. Payroll frequently is the largest single expense.

 Inventory has LIFO FIFO Depreciation has two main methods, one of the Straight-Line or one of the accelerated methods. There is only ONE method for Payroll.

The moment that any common law employee comes on board, specific accounting entries are done for as long as that common law employee is on the books. Does the company provide medical and other paid benefits to this employee? The answer is a yes or a no, or not right now! Does the employee participate in the cost of these benefits? Again, it's a yes or a no or not right now. In ninety nine percent of the times for payroll the answer is: Yes or No.

Payroll taxes and benefits might add fifteen to twenty percent to the basic payroll. There are businesses out there that manage paperclips with more concentrated effort than their payroll. They wonder why thy have liquidity issues, or heading for bankruptcy.

 How about Independent Contractors? Hiring them can save on Payroll Taxes and Employee Benefits?

 Independent contractors must pay their own taxes and medical contributions. The law won't permit Deacon hiring employees as Independent Contractors, but the law does allow sub contracting out certain functions, such as the night cleaning function. They will hire those people as statutory employees. Why?

Certain tests have to be met. Here are few of them. If the entity dictates how to do the work, instruct the exact hours to arrive and depart, provide tools to do the job, or insist on using their tools and the list goes on, then they aren't

legally Independent Contractors. Even industries hiring Independent Contractors as a way of life, such as Realtors,
must be up to date with the laws, and have contractors sign
valid engagement letters.

I am not an attorney, but if the entity is planning, or already on the Independent Contractor route on a long term
or permanent basis, make sure the attorney has provided
you proper council. Hiring Independent Contractors, that
the law might reclassify as statutory employees can be
costly.

 Deacon Hotel has a host of Departments. How
about selecting one Department for the workings
of Payroll, Taxes and Employee Benefits?

Rooms Gross Payroll	$590,536.28
Rooms Employer Payroll Taxes	$ 62,115.56
Rooms Vacation and Sick	$ 53,148.26
Rooms Employer Medical	$ 26,625.00
Rooms Employer Life Disability	$ 1,775.00
Rooms Employer 401k	$ 12,401.17
Grand Total	$746,601.27

 Payroll Expense for the Rooms Department is
$746,601.27. Are payroll Taxes, Vacation, Sick,
Employer Medical, Life and Disability and 401k
pulled out of thin air?

 Accounting accrues four hours a month per employee for this benefit. If the employee doesn't have
the time in their account, employers can enforce
the rules and the days that aren't worked will not
be paid.

For example, if the company policy dictates that for all employees, paid Sick, Vacation and Personal days are forfeited
if they aren't taken by the end of the year. If an employee
that hasn't called in sick for the prior year, gets legitimately

ill for three days in February of the following year, technically the employee hasn't accrued three days of benefits. Does management pay the employee the Sick benefit or do they deduct the time?

This employee could have worked ten years straight without ever calling in sick. Management must decide whether or not to pay this employee. All it takes for a union employee to file a grievance in the name of fairness, the Director of Human Resources might have an official visit from the union official claiming what is good for one is good for all. Deacon's business philosophy is, and it's in line with the majority of forward thinking enterprises, non-union labor might command a slighter higher rate, but you are far better off keeping it non-union.

For those that control their own businesses, don't count on management to be as committed as you. Ten years time, when the unions have you by your neck, management that violated all the policies you so conscientiously worked on, have long left voluntarily, or being fired and moved on.

 Accounting Accrues the expense for Vacations and Sick as is occurs. How does accounting prevent an employee getting paid for those days they are not entitled to?

 The Deacon 3 Q's™ The quality of the financial reports depends on the quality of the input and the management of that input. The more hourly employees, the more critical it is to make sure the hours worked and hours paid are controlled and verified.

Gross Payroll will be the number of hours worked at regular and overtime hours multiplied by the employee base rate. Salaries are quoted in dollars per year, or dollars per hour.

If quoted per annum, take that amount and divide it by 52 weeks in the year. The result of that, divide by the hours of the workweek, which is usually 40 hours. That's the employee's hourly rate. If the standard rate isn't forty hours that is the number of hours used.

The difference between the Gross and the take home pay is the amount of the deductions for taxes and any other voluntary deductions for medical, 401k contributions, savings etc.

FICA stands for Federal Insurance Contributions Act. This act administers the Social Security contributions that caps at certain level of compensation. After the limitation on Medicare contributions was raised, the Medicare portion of 1.25% levy is usually reported separately. For the vast majority of statutory (W2) employees, for 2005 the combination of the two is 0.0765% of Gross Income.

Deacon's Payroll Taxes for the Rooms Department is $62,115.56. That's the total of the employee's Social Security contributions plus the employer's matching of Social Security contributions, and Federal and State Unemployment taxes.

 What about paid Vacations and Sick? Are they pulled out of a hat?

 Employees genuinely get sick, but that doesn't mean sick pay doesn't have to be managed. Depending on the industry, when employees call in sick, the work still has to be done by others making up for it.

Deacon Management tells the room attendants that that are to service a minimum of fourteen rooms per day or the highway. They think they get can revenge by calling in sick the next day. Again, that might be unpredictable and this might cost overtime. Employees taking off sick days when they play games cost them as well, especially when they haven't got the time in "their account"

 Is in "their account" another Deacon special?

With the exception the Independent Contractors, all hired staff triggers Payroll Taxes. The cost of funding State and Federal unemployment taxes is petty cash compared to the cost of matching the employee's FICA (Social Security contributions) State Unemployment contributions max out, depending on the State to approximately to the first $7000.00 of employee compensation, multiplied by a percentage.

If the paid sick and paid vacations days are based on a forty-hour week, and the employee is entitled to three weeks paid vacation days per year, the employee accrues ten hours of paid vacation per month. The same formula applies for paid sick and personal days.

Accounting books ten hours per month. If corporate policy forbids taking paid vacation time before it is earned, or having a minimum length of time on the job, employees can't demand two weeks paid vacation after three months of service. In my experience, if these benefits haven't been taken at the end of the calendar year, they are usually forfeited.

 How did you come up with ten hours a month for the paid Vacation benefit for one employee?

 If the entity provides six paid days a year (some provide zero, others provide seven or eight or anything in between) for vacation, multiply six days by eight hours a day, and that equals forty-eight hours a year. Forty-eight hours divided by twelve months for a year is four hours per month.

That's a management accounting issue. Did your hourly employees arrive in the building two hours early, clock in, and as management wasn't around, proceed to the employee cafeteria? Did they complete their shift and then return to the cafeteria for another hour, then clock out. Did the employee get paid for the time in the cafeteria while management wasn't on the look out? While the cat's away the mouse will play.

The bulk of Employer Payroll Taxes is the matching of the employee's social security contributions currently at 0.765% of Gross Pay up to a certain limit. The Rooms Department Payroll for May 2003 reports $590,536.28, and payroll taxes for $62,115.56. In this case Payroll Taxes is 10.52% of Gross Payroll. Factor in State Unemployment Insurance contributions, that's a far cry from 8% that matches the FICA contributions. What happened?

 Paid Vacation, Personal and Sick days are considered regular compensation, subject to the employer matching of Social Security. Add to Gross Payroll amount this benefit, the percentage reduces from 10.52% to 9.65%.

 The Closing Inventory for the month is the Opening Inventory for the following month. Does the payroll ending date, become the opening date for the following payroll? Do salaried employees have the same schedule as hourly employees?

 Regardless, if it's a Twenty-four hour operation, or seasonal, almost without exception, the pay period consists of a specified number of days. Salaried employees are not required to have the same pay schedule as the hourly employees.

 Cash accounting recognizes expenses when paid, so the employees that haven't cashed their checks for a week, under the Cash method allow payroll expenses to be deferred one week for those employees?

 You wish! Employees pay Social Security and Income Taxes on a pay as you go method. The W2 at the end of the year, reports Gross Pay, regardless when and if the checks are cashed, or how the entity paying the employee recognizes the expense.

For example: Employees receive their last paychecks for the year on December 23rd The last week is usually accrued by the entity as Payroll Expense even though the employees receive that weeks earnings the following year. Employees are deemed to report on the Cash method. Their W2's report the actual amounts paid to them during the calendar year.

 Independent Contractors defer Income by reporting under the Cash method for tax purposes, by holding on to their checks until the following year, thereby deferring Income?

 You wish! Independent Contractors may organize their work life as a sole proprietor, or an incorporated entity. Holding a check, that they could have cashed doesn't defer Income.

 Employee benefits, as paid Sick and Vacation are expenses under Accrual accounting in the month they are earned, regardless if, and when they are used. How many employee hours and the base pay contributed to approximately $600,000 worth of payroll for one department for one month?

 A non-accounting goal of this chapter is to bring awareness, just how much payroll costs contribute to the overall expenses of operating a business.

Accounting accrues four hours a month per employee for this benefit. If the employee doesn't have the time in their account, employers can enforce the rules and the days that aren't worked will not be paid.

The bottom line, these items add, in this example 8.08% to the hourly rate of pay the moment employees are hired. It makes no difference whether the employee contract provides for payment hourly, or the employee is on a salary quoted at a certain amount per annum.

Referring to Fig 7:1, the far left column, are the hours

Type of Ben	# Daily Hours	# Days Week	# Weeks Year	Benefit Days	Benefit # Hours	Salary Pre Benefit	Hourly Rate	Annual Costs	Employee Cost	Cost %
Paid										
Personal	8	5	52	5	40	37,440.00	18.00	720.00		
Sick	8	5	52	6	48	37,440.00	18.00	864.00	3,024.00	8.08%
Vacation	8	5	52	10	80	37,440.00	18.00	1,440.00		

Fig 7:1

expected from the employees each workday. To the right, enter the number of workdays in the week. The next column specifies the number of weeks in the year, that's 52. The benefit hours are the number of days the employee receives as a paid benefit. (Five personal days a year equals five times eight hours a day) To the right of the number of benefit hours, is the employee gross salary. Convert the annual salary to the hourly rate, and actual costs are the benefit hours multiplied by this hourly rate. Employees having the base salary of $18.00 an hour, or $37,440.00 a year, adds $3,024.00 a year based on the benefits shown here.

If the hourly rate is $18.00 an hour or $37,440 a year, add the mandatory matching of Social Security, Unemployment, Sick, Vacation for two weeks, and Personal translates into Payroll expense of $43,559.50

Take the $37,440.00 + $3,024.00 + $3, 095.50(FICA) = $43,559.50. There are 2080 standard working hours during the year. The $18.00 an hour increases to $20.94 an hour. It will be much higher when Medical, Life Insurance, 401k matching and Pension contributions are added.

Timing Timing Timing [TM] The April payroll ended on April 25th. The next payroll ended May 9th with the final payroll for May ending on May 25th. The period April 25th through April 30th had to be accrued as well as the payroll for the last week of May in complying with the Timing Rules. Fig 7:2 reported

Fig 7:2 reported $114,418.29 being for the payroll that had to be accrued for the last week in April.

Month	Day		# Occupied	# Required	# Hours	Rate	Gross Daily
April	Saturday	26	994	71	18	18.00	23,004.00
April	Sunday	27	970	69	18	18.00	22,448.57
April	Monday	28	992	71	18	18.00	22,957.71
April	Tuesday	29	993	71	18	18.00	22,980.86
April	Wednesday	30	995	71	18	18.00	23,027.14
Total Accrual			4944	353			114,418.29

Fig 7:2

Is the Gross Payroll the only actual payroll cost that is accrued? How are accruals booked?

Paid Vacation, Personal and Sick, including 401k contributions must be accrued. In practice the Journal Entry usually include all the items, but for now, we'll focus on Gross Payroll.

April 30th: Gross Payroll $114,418.29
        Accrued Payroll, Vacations, Sick $114,418.29
Accrual Gross Payroll for the period April 26th through April 30th,

Regardless the dollar amounts accrued, be it from one percent to one hundred percent accurate; it must be automatically reversed the first day of the following month.

Here is the entry reversing the accrual for April 30th,

May 1st   Accrued Payroll, Vacations $114,418.29
            Gross Payroll $114,418.29
Reverse Accrual for Payroll for the period April 26th through April 30th,

So much went into Accruing Payroll Expense for the period only to be reversed at the stroke of a pen. Why bother?

Reversals are done effective the first day of the following month. Figure 7:3 shows the actual payroll expenses for the last week of April 20. Now compare that with the actual amount accrued!

Month	Day		# Occupied	# Required	# Hours	Rate	Gross Daily
April	Saturday	26	994	71	18	18.00	23,004.00
April	Sunday	27	970	81	18	18.00	26,190.00
April	Monday	28	992	99	18	18.00	32,140.80
April	Tuesday	29	993	110	18	18.00	35,748.00
April	Wednesday	30	995	71	18	18.00	23,027.14
Total Accrual			4944	432			140,109.94

Fig 7:3

Thanks to the estimated accrual being off more than 20%, April's payroll was greatly understated.

 The Accrual might just as well not have been reversed?

 What! Accruals, for lack of a better term are NEVER EVER NOT reversed the following month. Reversing the accrual at the beginning of the month, allows the Payroll account to be credited with the exact amount of the accrual from the previous month, and replacing that with the actual costs for the period.

Note the accrual was off by 20% compared to the actual Payroll cost for the period.

Accruals can be a little off the mark. This area is prime property for "Figures never lie, liars sometimes figure"

Never underestimate the difficulties in estimating accruals, as Utilities, Telephone, Legal and Payroll, if the support and paper systems don't do the job. The Financial Statements didn't include a column for Budgets. The accrual at the end of April is understated by at least 20%. Is it possible that the Payroll Budget for the month had already been met or substantially gone over budget even before the accrual? You bet! Management is faced with incredible temptation to understate the accrual based on best estimates, to carry themselves over to live another month!

 Does the entity have some flexibility for Medical, Life and Disability costs?

 Paid Vacations, Personal and Sick days are at the discretion of the employer. If the industry standard pays five paid sick days a year, the entity doesn't; have to provide the benefit, not alone match it.

It's a piece of cake calculating the premiums. All employees, covered under the carrier costs a certain amount, regardless of the hours worked. If the plan requires employees to pay into system, their contribution is petty cash compared to the employer contribution

A characteristic of 401k plans is that employees must fund them. Employers have the option, but not the obligation, to match all, or part of the employee's contributions.

For example, the employer matches 50% of the employees' contribution, up to a maximum of 6% of Gross Compensation: The employee's gross salary is $40,000.00 a year with the employee contributing 6% of gross. That's $2,400.00 a year. The entity matches 50% of the employee contribution. If the employee pays 10%, that's $4,000.00 a year. The employer matches $2,400.00. This time the employee pays in 2 % of gross salary, that's $800.00 with the employer matching 50% of that which is $400.00.

 Total Receipts include Sales Taxes collected. The employee Tax Withholding is another example of government legislating, and one of the benefits of this legislation is they get unpaid help?

There's Tax Withholding, Medical Insurance, Life/Disability, Pension etc. Employer contributions are all legitimate expenses. The employee portion can be compared with the principle of collecting Sales Taxes and passing those on the government.

These are the Payroll Journal Entries, excluding Accruals.

Dr. Gross Payroll	$1,728,884.91	
Dr Payroll Taxes	$ 181,852.76	
Dr. Vacation and Sick	$ 155,599.64	
Dr Employer Medical	$ 84,475.00	
Dr Employer Life and Disability	$ 7,247.00	
Employer 401k Matching	$ 36,306.58	
Medical Insurance Payable		$ 91,045.82
Life and Disability Payable		$ 7,247.00
401k Contributions Payable		$102,868.65
Payroll Taxes/Employee Withholding		$224,755.04
Payroll Taxes/Employee Withholding		$677,178.29
Accrued Vacation and Payroll		$155,599.64
Net Payroll		$937,671.45

The employer Medical expense for $86,475.00 is the portion the employer contributes towards the medical premiums. The difference between the Medical Insurance Payable of $91,045.00 (that's the total amount due to the carrier) is the employee's contribution deducted from their salaries. The Payroll Tax and Deductions, State and Federal combined less employer Payroll Taxes is the withholding by the employees.

 The Deacon slogan Timing, Timing, Timing™ require expensing paid Vacations and Sick in the month it's earned. Its one matter accruing expenses, to comply with the Timing rules, but this can go on for eternity if it isn't stopped.

Timing Timing Timing ™ Deacon slogan, Timing, Timing, Timing™ gives power to the Matching principle that revenue and expenses are booked in the month they occur. Paid Vacations and Sick are booked at the time they are earned, and not if and when they are taken by the employee. As these benefits are used up this account is adjusted. Rather than confuse with verbiage, Fig 7:5 shows one employee utilizing a paid Sick day. The Sick day expense is included in the Total Payroll for the week, but it's allocated to Benefits instead of Regular Pay.

Day	Hours Scheduled	Hours Worked	Payment Approved	# of Hours	Hourly Rate	Total Cost	Regular Pay	Paid Sick Personal
Monday	8	8	Yes	8	18.00	144.00	144.00	
Tuesday	8	8	Yes	8	18.00	144.00	144.00	
Wednesday	8	8	Yes	8	18.00	144.00	144.00	
Thursday	8	Sick	Yes	8	18.00	144.00	144.00	
Friday	8	Sick	Yes	8	18.00	144.00	144.00	
Saturday	OFF	OFF	No					
Sunday	OFF	OFF	No					
Monday	8	Sick	Yes	8	18.00	144.00		144.00
Tuesday	8	Sick	Yes	8	18.00	144.00		144.00
Wednesday	8	Sick	No		18.00			
Thursday	8	8	Yes	8	18.00	144.00	144.00	
Friday	8	8	Yes	8	18.00	144.00	144.00	
Saturday	OFF	OFF	No					
Sunday	OFF	OFF	No					
Total Cost						1,296.00	1,008.00	288.00

Fig 7:5

The Journal Entry: in absence of any Adjusting Entries:

Gross Payroll $1008.00
Payroll Taxes $ 80.64
Accrued Vacation/Sick $ 288.00
     Federal Income Tax Withheld $300.00
     State Income Tax Withheld $150.00
     FICA $105.31
     Payroll Account (Net Pay, Whatever) $821.33

The debit of $288.00 reduces the Accrued Vacation and Sick Account

 OK the employee is paid for a Sick Day and isn't entitled to it? How does that show up?

 If these accounts aren't reconciled regularly there will be problems. They experience heavy traffic

The Deacon 3Q's™ the quality of the financial reporting, depends on the quality of the input, and the quality of the management of the input. You don't leave the bank statement unbalanced for months, so learn to keep track of these Liability accounts too!

 Are all Accruals booked the same way?

 Are Accruals done differently for Payroll than for Utilities? If heating costs for the month is estimated at $35,433.00 that's the correct amount to be accrued. Make sure it's reversed the beginning of the following month, just like Payroll.

Property Taxes are one of the easiest to Accrue. Beginning the first month, take the prior years Property Tax expense of $3,600.000 making $300,000.00 to be accrued each month. If partial payment is due on March 31st for $927,000.00 the Journal Entries are as follows:

Jan 31st,   Property Tax Expense $300,000.00
                    Accrued Expenses $300,000.00
         Property Tax Accrual for the month of January

Feb 28th,   Property Tax Expense $300,000.00
                    Accrued Expenses $300,000.00
         Property Tax Accrual for the month of February

Mar 31st,   Property Tax Expense $300,000.00
                    Accrued Expenses $300,000.00
         Property Tax Expense for the month of March

 Why hasn't the Accrual been adjusted for the increase in Property Taxes in the month of March?

 The billing arrived in April. The accrual was done at the end of March. Property owners can access their account on the Internet. By April 2nd or April 3rd they could have known exactly how much they will be paying for previous three months Property taxes.

OK they are not up to your standards. Unfortunately, most people will act when the bill comes in the month of April. How is it dealt with?

 Had they bothered to go off automatic pilot for a moment, realizing this information is on the Internet, before closing the books for March, they could book the correct Property Tax Expense, eliminating the accrual. As their productivity is pretty standard, here are the Journal Entries booking the expense, with the bill arriving in April for $927,000.00.

April 15th, 20 Property Tax Expense $ 27,000.00
            Accrued Expenses $900,000.00
                Accounts Payable/Bank $927,000.00
        Payment of Actual Property Taxes for the period January
        2003 through March

Management must decide whether or not they should increase the monthly accrual from $300,000.00. The question is: Will this be permanent, or is it a one-time assessment?

 In that instance, the amount due is higher than the Accrual. Had the Accrual been higher than the billing, what would have happened?

 Given Government's thirst for increased revenue, this seldom happens for Property Taxes, but that cannot be said for most other expenses. The concept of Materiality triggers. What is the reason for the variance?

Figures never lie, sometimes liars figure. Figures don't desert us or back us up later. When we were under the gun and made decisions at the time we managed the input, we thought were acting in the best interest of the organization. Life didn't go as we planned. It's easy to look at those figures with the benefit of hindsight and accuse the individuals, as we cannot accuse the figures, of being liars, which may be the furthest from the truth that you can get.

Chapter 8

So Liquidity is measured by dividing Current Assets by Current Liabilities?

It's known as the Quick, or Acid Test Ratio. Fig 8:1 shows Current Assets and Current Liabilities for Deacon Hotels at the end of July 2003.

Balance Sheet for Deacon Management Corporation
For the Period Ending July 31st, 2003

Current Assets			Current Liabilities	
Cash and Cash Equivalents			Accounts Payable Trade	12,258,411.82
Cash Equivalents		59,842,336.89	Payables Affiliates	10,035,953.31
Accounts Receivable	23,842,383.02		Taxes & Accrued Expenses	17,498,095.86
Reserve for Bad Debts	-1,051,705.01	22,790,678.01	Payroll Liabilities	1,917,247.33
Other Assets		3,787,450.00	Trade & Security Deposits	1,328,242.61
Inventory		2,238,583.96	Total Current Liabilities	
Total Current Assets		88,659,048.86		43,037,950.93

Fig 8:1

So this entity is in excellent financial health?

Current Assets and Current Liabilities need breaking down and analyzed. Other Assets comprise of the Prepayments and Non-Food and Beverage Inventory. The question must be answered: If the Inventory must be liquidated at a fire sale, what would it realize? All Current Liabilities must be paid. Total Current Assets are $86,659,048.86. From that deduct Other Assets and Inventory. The new total for consideration is $82,633,014.90. Take a look at the Cash Equivalents.

Out of $59,842,336.89 the Certificate of Deposit contributes $20,000,000.00. Payroll has $496.42, and House Bank of $40,000.00 the Bank Operating Account is $39,801,840.37. If the Certificate of Deposit is restricted, then Current Assets for our purposes, is reduced from $82,633,041.90 to $62,633,014.90

Go over to the Current Liabilities. Trade and Security

Deposits aren't likely to be called in this month. From Taxes and Accrued Expenses of $17,498,095.86 Sales Taxes are $9,172,082.12, the remaining are Income Taxes and Interest Payable. Complying with the conservative concept, I am not adjusting the Current Liabilities. How did I know how much the Sales Taxes contributed to the total amount? Investigate or ask.

 The Accounts Receivable can be sold or pledged?

This amount is outrageous! Sales and customer service persons usually react with awe when they realize that Finance or Accounting will be holding customers to their signed contracts, calling in all the accounts in default, or past due status.

They usually go on automatic pilot complaining that sales and customer service will suffer. Accounting has to do the job

Some contracts permit payments to be spread over three to four months. The longer customers are allowed to delay payment, in absence of a promotion or contract, the more difficult it is to collect on overdue accounts. The cash comes in through your front door via Accounts Receivable. The cash goes out through your back door via Accounts Payable. Unless you charge interest, the longer you allow customers to delay paying the bills, the more it's coming out of your pocket extending to them interest free loans.

Pledging Accounts Receivable usually commands high interest rates. For some this is the only source of financing available, but Deacon Balance Sheet shows the entity can easily cover short-term liabilities. For Accounts Receivable the question is: How do you know, how much of the total Accounts Receivable is actual junk.

The Accounts Receivable Ageing lists all the customers that have balances outstanding, including how old they are. In other words, how long they have remained unpaid. The word ageing is no coincidence) See Fig 8.2. This is the Accounts Receivable Ageing that we will be working from. All the customers are consolidated under Corporate Accounts, which wouldn't happen in practice.

Deacon Management Corporation
Accounts Receivable Ageing As of July 31st, 2003

Customer	0-30	31-60	61-90	91-120	121+	Amount Due
AR AMERICAN EXPRESS	2,983,241.51	151,176.17	603,609.07	176,424.17	61,106.32	3,975,557.24
AR CORPORATE ACCOUNTS	4,884,478.48	3,605,446.32	1,496,807.48	1,053,923.49	2,773,994.02	13,814,649.79
AR DINERS CLUB	331,257.65	7,127.39	23,466.05	8,270.08	26,054.65	396,175.82
AR DISCOVER	117,501.65	14,296.52	36,147.19	18,468.14	19,145.24	205,558.74
AR MASTERCARD AND VISA	1,288,236.95	1,382,276.16	400,781.55	164,993.25	328,611.07	3,564,898.98
AR RENTALS & GARAGE	482,225.86	449,140.54	477,767.61	476,408.44		1,885,542.45
TOTAL	10,086,942.10	5,609,463.10	3,038,578.95	1,898,487.57	3,208,911.30	23,842,383.02
Performance	42.31%	23.53%	12.74%	7.96%	13.46%	100.00%

Fig 8:2

 If the credit card companies pay so promptly, why are there amounts outstanding in the 121+ day column? Rentals and Garage close to $2 million is more than a collection problem?

 The issuers of Credit and Charge cards place some responsibility on the seller at the time of sale. Examples are: Swipe the card, at the bare minimum there must be an imprint of the card.

The signature at the back of the card must match he signature on the sales draft at the time of sale.

 Comply and the entity can say Good Bye to Credit Card losses?

 I wish, I wish! A cardholder authorizes in writing the expenses for somebody else, and on receiving the bill, conveniently forgets about the explicit authorization. Calling the 800 Number is effortless and free. It's easier than going through paperwork, locating the record or taking the effort to think. Dispute the charge!

153

These claims must be backed up within a specified time or they receive a "chargeback" In real life this takes an enormous amount of resources.

I guarantee, for those cardholders that casually dispute these charges, and if they turn out to be valid, if they are levied a minimum amount of $100.00 that's passed on to the merchant that incurred unnecessary expense in backing up these claims, might think before picking up the phone.

 The Bad Debt Reserve is $1,051,705.01. (Refer Fig 8:1) 120 days + is more than $3,000,000.00: Where does one locate the write off policy? How is the Bad Debt expense booked?

 In pure theory, the moment the Receivable becomes worthless, or if collection is in doubt, it must be written off, or at the very least be written down.

Deacon adopted the requirement that all outstanding Accounts Receivables at 120 days+ MUST be written off against the reserve. That doesn't mean collection stops. That requirement enforced religiously, insures Accounts Receivables are primarily Accounts Receivables and NOT Accounts Deceivable! The Reserve must be positive at all times.

Financial Accounting recognizes two methods. These are the Reserve Method and the Direct Charge off Method. The Internal Revenue Service doesn't recognize the Reserve Method.

When customers' accounts become Bad Debts, the entire balance is written off against the reserve. If it's later collected, the proceeds are booked against the Reserve.

The Direct Charge Off Method takes each determinable worthless account at the time it becomes worthless and books it to Bad Debt expense. The Reserve method takes a percentage of sales each month, and charges this amount to Bad Debt expense. More on this later

 Determining worthlessness can be a judgment call? How are decisions made on what qualifies as a worthless receivable?

 A Donald Trump imposter checks into a hotel past 1:00am, refusing to pay as his personal assistant sent authorization to bill all charges to The Trump Organization. The clerk doesn't protect the assets by getting an imprint of a credit card, or cash, or make a copy of any identification, assigns the most lavish suite available.

The imposter has an early morning meal. 8:00 o'clock in the morning, the imposter is out and there is no way he can be located.

Does this stupidity happen? Yes. This is a worthless receivable! In instances where clients have paid for years and are now falling on tough times, for the first time payment looks doubtful, management is still faced with a decision, and it might not be as clear cut as the imposter.

Sometimes management is more concerned about looking good, and delaying the consequences for another day, or passing on the problem for somebody else to make the decision for as long as possible into the future. By the time heads roll, the real culprit has resigned or promoted. That's the reason the 120+ day requirement is key. More entities should adopt this requirement, and enforce it religiously.

 Hotels, Car Rentals, Doctors levy "No Show" charges if clients don't cancel within a certain time frame. If over 1000 customers dispute $500.00 of these charges, and the seller hasn't responded, then $500,000.00 is part of the Accounts Receivable. They won't go away without a Journal Entry booking this junk to Bad Debt expense, or adjusting Income, if appropriate.

That's the reason you must identify and remove the junk that's hidden in the overall Accounts Receivable. There's a vast difference between a legitimate bad debt and a legitimate adjustment to revenue.

A debt is a legal obligation that can be litigated. Adjustments to income occur when customers' are overcharged, or discounts later extended.

I asked you this earlier, and you didn't answer the question. How does the Reserve method work in practice?

Examples and Journal Entries work best here. The Sales are $12,000,000 annually. (For convenience, each month generates $1,000,000) Past experience shows 4% of Gross Sales become worthless, $40,000.00 a month, is booked to the Bad Debt expense.

July 31st, Bad Debt Expense $40,000.00
            Reserve for Doubtful Accounts $40,000.00
            Bad Debt Reserve Increase for July 2003)

Although $40,000.00 is written off to Bad Debt expense under the Reserve method, assume, after reviewing the Accounts Receivable Ageing there are worthless Receivables and a few Accounts "Deceivable" you find these are valued at $12,000.00. The Journal Entries are:

July 31stReserve for Doubtful Accounts $12,000.00
            Accounts Receivable $12,000.00
        Actual Specific Bad Debts for the month of July 2003

The Accounts Receivable is credited removing them from the overall Accounts Receivable balance outstanding. The debit entry goes against the Reserve.

If the Direct Charge Off Method is elected the Journal

Entry is as Follows:

July 31st, Bad Debt Expense $12,000.00
     Accounts Receivable $12,000.00
    Actual Specific Bad Debts for the Month

 How do you account for those Receivables collected after they have been written off?

 Take the money! If $10,000.00 is received after being written off, without incurring outside collection agency fees. Debit the bank account in the ledger, and credit the Reserve by building it up by the amount collected. Receivables that have been written off to Bad Debt expense, and later collected, is called a "Bad Debt Recovery"

Oct 31st Cash Operating Account $10,000.00
   Reserve for Doubtful Accounts $10,0000.00
  Recovery of Bad Debts written off in July 2003

 If previously written off receivables are collected by an outside collection agency, assuming the collection fee is 50% of the amount collected, how does this get booked?

 If the customer paid the Collection Agency directly, usually they deduct their fees and submit the net amount due.

Nov 30th Cash   Operating Account $5,000.00
    Collection Fees $5,000.00
     Reserve for Doubtful A/C $10,000.00
    Recovery of Bad Debts July 2003

I prefer this method. The Reserve gets the full credit. Collection Fees expenses are more easily tracked and controlled.

 If the collection agency succeeds in collecting, but fails to deduct the fees. The agency sends a bill for the services rendered. How is this recorded?

Nov 30th, 20 Cash Operating Account $10,000.00
              Collection Fees $ 5,000.00
                  Reserve for Doubtful A/C $10,000.00
                  Accounts Payable or Bank $ 5,000.00
        Recovery of Bad Debts July 2003. Fees to Outside Agency

The collection fees are $5,000.00. Accounts Payable is credited. In real life, if the debtor sends payment to the entity, it's a while later before the Agency sends an invoice, so an Accrual should be done at this time.

 The Direct Write Off Method provides more choices, when and if they write off certain Receivables?

 Good Management doesn't wait 120 days+ to write off junk and deteriorated receivables. It requires a specific policy and procedure insuring heads will if this isn't complied with to the letter of the law! If the Direct Write off method is chosen, the actual receivables chosen for the month are then the actual Bad Debt expense for the month.

But it isn't a bed of roses under the Reserve method either. Why? When we booked $40,000.00 to Bad Debt expense, and simultaneously credited the Reserve with the same amount, that didn't prevent the build up of Junk Receivables, or "Accounts Deceivable"

The Reserve Method requires a build up of the reserve, then the actual bad debts from the Accounts Receivable for the month must be booked against the reserve.

I have seen in practice, the Reserve been build up to astronomic heights, and absolutely no Bad Debt Receivables booked against it. Why? Management didn't want to look bad and write off those Junk Receivables, as it isn't the Bad Debt Expense they have to account for, it's the Receivables (or Deceivable) that they book against the Reserve, that must be accounted for.

Especially at year end, if the Accounts Receivable isn't

158

physically reviewed, management easily can conclude the Reserve has become bloated and decide to reduce it. Debiting the Reserve account and crediting Bad Debt expense accomplishes this task.

This is an opportunity for "Figures never lie, sometimes liars figure" as reducing Bad Debt expense increases the profit margins, and if bonuses are attached to this performance, beware! I have witnessed in practice, the Reserve reduced in one year, only to find worthless Receivables, and an enormous quantity of "Accounts Deceivable" going back years.

In the year this surfaces usually there isn't sufficient amount in the reserve to cover anywhere close to absorb this disaster. Bad Debt expense for that year is astronomical and it isn't due to a major bankruptcy.

In many cases, the decision makers approving reductions in the Reserve without physically examining the Accounts Receivable have received and spent their bonuses, and likely, have moved on to bigger and better things and will continue to do this until they are they come across management that know how to manage the Accounts Receivable.

 What happens when the Reserve becomes too big for its' own good?

 The Reserve must be monitored. The percentage can be changed upwards or downwards. Under both the Reserve and the Direct Write off methods, prior to year end, the entire Accounts Receivable must be scrutinized for doubtful and worthless Receivables, not to mention, the "Accounts Deceivable" and either booked to Bad Debts or charged off against the Reserve. The Reserve requirements for the following year must be reviewed as well.

The 120+-day-old account write off requirement helps, as these accounts aren't part of the Accounts Receivable,

Corporate and the local office can keep an eye on them. They know how much of these are "Accounts Deceivable" so there is no point in wasting time and energy going after them. They aren't easily buried, as they would be with thousands of active Accounts Receivable clients.

 Early August, it's found, the past four months payments for the Garage lease have been paid by direct deposit. As the Bank account hadn't been reconciled, is it acceptable to book these payments via Journal Entry?

 Yes as long as the payments are in the Bank account by July 31st, 2003. If the checks are located in the drawer, they are out of luck. They will have to wait until the checks are deposited.

 Ah I caught you! That's Cash accounting?

 No. The revenue was booked. (Income accounts are credited, Accounts Receivable is debited) It takes booking a bad Debt Expense, bank charges or the actual payment from the client for an Accounts Receivable account to "go away"

 What happens if the client sent the payments, but, in the books, they were not recognized? For example, the Garage is leased under Deacon Hotel, but the lessee operates under ICF LLC.

 Don't laugh, this happens all the time. Just ignore these transactions, and reconciling the bank account will be a nightmare. Accounts Receivable must include a temporary holding account, where these transactions are posted temporarily, and then reconciled.

If that's the case, for the Garage, Space Rentals, etc. the total Accounts Receivable doesn't change, only the allocations do. The holding account in the Accounts Receivable is debited and the outstanding Garage amounts are credited.

It's the first day of the new month. All cash deposits, except for the last day have been recorded. What happens with this deposit?

Send it to Deacon. No! No! No! The last day's Sales activity for July 31st, 20 is $309,794.58. Out of this $109,794.58 is cash, $200,000.00 in credit cards billings. This transaction is booked for July

July 31stCash Operating Account $109,794.58
    Accounts Receivable $200,000.00
         Income $309,794.58
Income for July 31st, 2003

What happens if the $109,794.58 cash is never deposited?

The Deacon 3Q'sä: The quality of the financial reporting depends on the quality of the input and the management of that input. The input quality is excellent, management, insures the money is deposited and the bank accounts reconciled. The Bank Balances on the Balance Sheet are <u>book balances.</u> The actual bank statement reports a different picture.

Does reconciling the bank account under Accrual differ from the Cash method?

Regardless of the accounting method, the aim is to insure the balance shown on the bank statements, agree with the Cash account balances in the General Ledger. Fig 8:3 Typically this is bank reconciliation under Accrual accounting.

Begin with the closing balance on the Bank statement. Add all the deposits sent to the bank from the statement date, to the end of the month, that the bank hasn't yet credited the account. Why? The cash is debited for the deposit amounts. At times it takes a while for the banks to credit the account

Bank Account Reconciliation

Balance Bank Statement		45,202,908.32
Add: Deposits in Transit		
Deposit July 28th, 2003	602,134.17	
Deposit July 29th, 2003	123,210.58	
Deposit July 30th, 2003	113,716.48	
Deposit July 31st, 2003	108,794.58	947,855.81
Add: Standing Monthly Payments not on Books		
Standing Order Vendor A	39,305.37	
Standing Order Vendor B	60,184.72	
Standing Order Vendor C	39,243.27	
Standing Order Vendor D	35,362.90	174,096.25
Add: Returned Items	765.90	
Less: Bank Fees	50.00	
Less: Incoming Wire Transfer Fees	45.00	860.90
Less: Outstanding Checks		
(See Attached Listing)		6,288,777.61
Less: Incoming Wire Transfers on Statement: not on Books		
Customer A	24,976.68	
Customer B	43,941.71	
Customer C	41,614.23	
Customer D	28,524.52	
Customer E	27,211.41	
Customer F	41,666.34	
Customer G	27,168.42	235,103.30
Balance Per Books July 31st, 2003		39,801,840.37

Fig 8:3

account. The goal is to get the bank balance to agree with the book balances, the bank balances would have reflected these deposits had they credited the account.

 The deposit in transit for July 31st, 2003 is $108,794.58. What happens if $108,000 reaches the bank?

 It takes human beings to count cash and prepare deposit slips, and get the cash to the bank. Accounting must compare the amount that should be in the bank compared with what did get to the bank and make a lot of noise if it doesn't match.

Supposing only $108,000.00 reached the bank? Then

162

make an Adjusting Entry regardless of the reason it never got there. Adjusting entries for shortages, credit the Bank Operating Account with the shortage, and debit an expense account, such as Cash over and short. The accounting concept of **Consistency** applied here.

This concept states, accounts handle certain functions, then be consistent in its use. If Cash over and short is used for cash shortages, and there's a Miscellaneous over and short to handle other shortages, don't mix them. Make a decision and be consistent.

 Add standing Monthly Payments not on the books. The monthly bills have been paid. Why? It's over and done with?

 What's the task at hand? As long as the standing order payments aren't booked, the funds SHOULD still be in the bank account. Are they? No! The vendors are paid with standing orders. The book bank account and the expense categories must be updated.

 It's easy to monitor bank charges and check up on Incoming Wire transfers and other ACH payments by logging on to your account on the Internet. Book those transactions during the month, and don't wait for the paper statement to arrive by snail mail.

 Ideally, that's how it should be. Yes, go on line and take care of the accounting before they get out of hand, book the transactions in the month incurred complying with the Matching principle.

July 10th, 2003   Bank Fees $50.00
                        Cash Operating Account $50.00
                    Incoming Wire Transfer Fees

Outstanding checks are those checks that haven't cleared the bank account. What about those checks that have been prepared and awaiting signature, or have been signed, and have been on the "Financial Controllers'" desk for the past month?

 Under Accrual accounting, the moment the check is processed, it's an outstanding check, regardless if it's mailed, or is on somebody's desk for a year! Processing, Accounts Payable is debited, which reduces the vendor balances outstanding on the books, the Bank account is credited, which reduces the Bank account in the books.

We all know it takes cash to pay vendors, but the Accounts Payable Ageing can report prompt payments. Look at the balance showing for the outstanding checks. You might be in for a surprise.

 Did you create the outrageous $23 Million Accounts Receivable for illustration purposes only?

 This can easily occur in real life. It doesn't take a genius to accumulate a bunch of junk Accounts Receivables, with or without "Accounts Deceivable"

 As Julie Andrews sang in The Sound of Music: "Let's start at the very beginning. A very good place to start" In tackling this outrageous $23 million fiasco, where is the beginning?

If the Accounts Receivable has never been respectable, then the answer is a no brainier. Deacon Hotel had respectable receivables. When did it begin to change for the worse? These are the Ageing results back to January (Following Page)

 The downward cycle began in May. Do you begin with specific past due categories?

Before jumping in and analyzing one account one line at a time, look for immediate bottlenecks in the system. Taking care of these bottlenecks immediately, prevents the situation from deteriorating further, and providing opportunities to implement damage control.

Month	Amount	30+	60	90	121+
January	$ 4,668,330.50				
February	$ 6,774,718.05	16.5%			
March	$ 6,629,501.48	30.9%	12.2%		
April	$ 6,903,495.30	29.8%	20.0%	5.6%	
May	$ 9,231,672.04	25.3%	19.9%	14.8%	3.64%
June	$16,849,329.46	18.86%	13.8%	10.9%	10.1%
July	$23,842,388.02	23.50%	12.7%	8.0%	13.5%

They had eleven days backlog in transferring the credit card batches contributing $4,700,000 towards this fiasco. The Corporate billings for June went out in July. Not one bill for July had gone out. This added $8,500,000.00 to the fiasco. The pre junk Accounts Receivable is about $10,600,000.00.

(?) What Adjustments go against Income?

In the real world, it's time consuming and wont' be this clear-cut. When adjustments to Income are a must, complying with the Matching Principle, accruals are done. These are the results:

Revenue Adjustments:	$4,192,657.32
Sales Tax Adjustments	$ 599,043.75
Bad Debt to Reserve:	$2,370,941.67
Unapplied Vendor Payments	$1,403,316.59

Unapplied client payments are Contra Asset category transactions. It's the transfer from the Bank account to the

the Accounts Receivable, as long as the funds are in the bank account.

The Bad Debt Reserve is $1,051,705.01, which is insufficient to absorb the Bad Debts of 2,370,941.67. The shortfall of $1,319,236.66 must be immediately booked to Bad Debt Expense.

 Deacon's requirement that all outstanding Accounts Receivables upon reaching 121+ days, including all known bad debts, even a day old must be transferred to the Reserve, and the Reserve must reflect reality. Do Bad Debt Reserves have to be built up this fast in real life?

 To repeat: Write off policies and procedures MUST reflect the nature of the business, and the credit terms extended by contract to the client. If the contract provides that no payments need me made for one year, and they haven't sold the receivable, its pointless writing off those receivables at 121+ days.

The Conservative accounting principle considers the industry. The quality of the Receivable deteriorates in value the longer it remains unpaid due to the greater chance of the customer defaulting.

The integrity of the Financial Statements is the key. There are limits to the quantity of junk in the Accounts Receivable.

 Increasing Bad Debt reserves in real life is easier when losses have incurred from a major bankruptcy or a shift in the economy?

 When it comes to the pubic and shareholders attention there's an chance a major borrower is on the brink of default, some financial institutions will rush to book write offs, and make that public.

It sends a message the financial conditions are solid, and the Financial Statements have integrity

Are you guilty, as charged for controlling paper clips, staplers, pencils, pens, and adding machine tapes to the extreme that the employees spend half the day moving from desk to desk like beggars, taking whatever they need to accomplish their tasks, but carry thousands of dollars of Receivables, with no interest and penalties, have no idea how many "Accounts Deceivable" there may be included, but wont' take control of those customers that are using you as a bank, for if you tighten credit and collections, customers will go to the competitor? Perhaps your competitor is more than you are, because they enforce payment within a tight credit and collection policy.

 What do the Receivables look like now after the junk has been removed?

 The un-submitted credit card batches and the corporate bills didn't go out so that is the best picture. See Fig 8: 4. Compare this with Fig 8:2

Deacon Management Corporation
Accounts Receivable Ageing As of July 31st, 2003

Customer	0-30	31-60	61-90	91-120	121+	Amount Due
AR AMERICAN EXPRESS	2,841,173.11	142,367.24	465.28			2,984,005.63
AR CORPORATE ACCOUNTS	4,651,961.39	3,393,120.84	648,733.86	140,993.10		8,834,809.19
AR DINERS CLUB	315,726.06	6,823.63				322,549.69
AR DISCOVER	112,019.91	13,385.25				125,405.16
AR MASTERCARD AND VISA	1,227,024.20	1,300,869.54				2,527,893.74
AR RENTALS & GARAGE	482,225.86					482,225.86
TOTAL	9,630,130.53	4,856,566.50	649,199.14	140,993.10		15,276,889.27
Performance	63.04%	31.79%	4.25%	0.92%	0.00%	100.00%

Fig 8:4

 Does the Accounts Payable Ageing have the amounts that are due to vendors?

167

Fig 8:5 This is an example of the Accounts Payable Ageing. The 91-120 day column indicates how long the business is holding out before paying the vendors. The Accounts Receivable Ageing 91-120 day column indicates how long your clients are holding out and getting interest free loans from you.

 If the overall Budgeted Departmental expenses is $10,000,000.00 comprising of a few expense categories. Actual expenses are $9,000,000.00. Does management takes this as $1,000,000.00 under budget? Who cares if they have over spent in some categories, and under spent in other categories?

 If the overall Budgeted Departmental expenses is $10,000,000.00 comprising of a few expense categories. Actual expenses are $9,000,000.00. Does management takes this as $1,000,000.00 under budget? Who cares if they have over spent in some categories, and under spent in other categories?

This happens, and depending on the corporate culture the divisions may adopt "What the eyes don't see, the heart will never grieve over"

The problem is this, if the budget isn't properly prepared, it needs at least one year of no monkey business to set the groundwork for a proper and realistic budget.

Advertising can consist of print, media or the Internet. Public relations expense might be allocated it's own account. Print, media or Internet advertising might be detailed further. If the overall sales expenses are below budget, but if one of the categories are over budget, corporate will usually demand an explanation. If the mentality sets in, "What the eyes don't see, the heart will never grieve over" then it might become common practice to reallocate from the surplus to the shortage.

Vendor	0-30	31-60	61-90	91-120	121+	Total Amount
401K PROVIDER	107,002.23	106,277.72	102,868.65			316,148.60
MEDIA ADVERTISING	65,417.67	25,732.31	14,173.26	46,291.10		151,614.34
PRINT ADVERTISING	11,134.98	41,362.23	10,236.24	61,765.79		124,499.24
AMERICAN EXPRESS CORPORATE	34,053.16	85,421.59				119,474.75
AUDIO VISUAL	32,913.02	197,191.50	24,097.91			254,202.43
CELLULAR CALLS	5,319.10	5,244.10				10,563.20
SERVER MAIN CONTRACTS	48,000.00					48,000.00
CONTRACT CLEANERS	15,000.00					15,000.00
COPY MACHINE SUPPLIES	6,569.61	4,311.05				10,880.66
DECORATING	9,298.26	10,890.14				20,188.40
ELECTRICTY	62,567.21	63,803.27				126,370.48
EMPLOYEE MISCELLANEOUS	8,215.67					8,215.67
EMPLOYEE TRAVEL	3,635.51					3,635.51
NAME ENTERTAINMENT	40,665.77	18,021.24	12,289.94			70,976.95
GARAGE	182,570.70	177,187.78	162,540.80	181,111.62		703,410.90
GIFTS GIVEAWAYS	16,529.38	36,662.63	6,002.37			59,194.38
HEATING	51,392.22	52,441.04				103,833.26
SOFT DRINKS		123,119.48				123,119.48
HOTEL & CATERING OTHER	63,179.30					63,179.30
ROOM CLEANING SUPP	28,402.03	38,327.30				66,729.33
CANNED FRUIT, PEANUTS	48,209.50	62,103.87				110,313.37
ENGINEERING SUPPLIES	13,868.47	608,333.01	103,045.80			725,247.28
SPIRITS WINE AND BEER	578,946.52	641,400.36				1,220,346.88
MEAT FISH AND FROZEN FOODS		3,113,403.43				3,113,403.43
ROOM REG SUPPLIES		167,171.30	49,662.62			216,833.92
STATIONERY OFFICE / OTHER		147,693.77	68,915.33			216,609.10
IN ROOM MOVIES CONTRACTOR	151,410.94	146,291.94				297,702.88
INSURANCE TERROR	150,000.00					150,000.00
WORKERS COMP	1,284.31	21,311.03	6,181.10			28,776.44
LAUNDRY	36,296.61	37,037.36	33,366.99			106,700.96
LAUNDRY PARTNER	75,305.37	73,636.50	74,868.89			223,810.76
GROUP LIFE INSURANCE PREM	7,247.00	7,247.00	7,247.00			21,741.00
GROUP MEDICAL INSURANCE	91,043.82	91,043.82	91,045.82			273,137.46
IN HOUSE ROOM MOVIES			146,430.22			146,430.22
NON INVENTORY SUPPLIES	11,402.69	17,763.41	12,907.61			42,073.71
POSTAGE MACHINE CONTRACT	586.65					586.65
POSTAGE STAMPS	856.54					856.54
PRINTING AND DESIGN		30,134.03	29,808.25			59,942.28
OUTSIDE CONSULTING	856.54	27,531.55				28,388.09
LEGAL	122,656.11	125,159.29	93,171.04			340,986.44
AUDITING	1,970.04	29,061.08	26,181.15			57,212.27
SALES & PROMOTION MATERIALS			60,000.00			60,000.00
SIGNAGE	8,051.57	7,328.62				15,380.19
CD'S FOR SALE	560.18					560.18
SPA PRODUCTS	642.40					642.40
VIDEOS FOR SALE		591.01				591.01
STAFF ADVERTISING	1,852.30	25,992.14	6,299.22			34,143.66
INTERNAL REVENUE SERVICE	704,389.39	699,619.95				1,404,009.34
STATE OF NEW YOIRK FINANCE	233,786.39	232,203.41				465,989.80
LOCAL CALL PROVIDER	28,265.72	28,842.57				57,108.29
LONG DISTANCE CALL PROVIDER	36,831.09	37,582.76				74,413.84
TRADE PROMOTIONS	33,586.35	34,067.70	21,682.62			89,336.67
UNIFORM CLEANING	5,660.46	5,775.98	5,203.58			16,640.02
HOTEL UNIFORM SUPPLIES		66,382.35				66,382.35
VALET AND DRYCLEAING PARTNER	67,239.68	69,948.59				137,188.27
WATER	27,563.36	28,125.88				55,689.24
TOTAL	3,232,237.82	7,568,779.08	1,168,226.41	289,168.51		12,258,411.82
Performance	26.37%	61.74%	9.53%	2.36%	0.00%	100.00%

Fig 8:5

Don't ever loose sight of the overall goal. If budgets are properly prepared, and certain dollar amounts are budgeted for utilities, and due to a bitterly cold winter and heating costs go through the roof, management hasn't a problem in explaining this, but if the travel and entertainment budget goes through the roof, and nothing can be shown for it, they can be tempted to bury this overage some place else.

Management makes non-financial decisions based on these results. Had they been apprised of the change in climate, how would the following year's budget been planned? Corporate can't allow a happy go lucky don't care if you go over or under the budget, but they must encourage their divisions to freely communicate changes, so future business decisions can be made using better financial reports.

 What has this got to do with Accounts Payable?

Expenses are realized through the Accounts Payable and cash flow requirements start at this level.

 What about legitimate Employee Reimbursements?

If the employee has legitimate travel expenses comprising of airfares, hotel accommodations, travel to and from the airports, meals, phone calls, laundry and miscellaneous items, etc dumping them on the Financial Controllers' desk asking for a check won't work.

An in-house designed Time and Expense report having columns for each expense, the amount spent, the reasons for the expenditure. The employee must complete and attach all the original receipts too.

When complete, depending on company policy and procedures, an Accounts Payable processed check, or preferably processed through payroll for reimbursement.

 Can the same format work for Petty Cash expenses?

Petty cash receipts, in themselves don't book the expense category. Petty Cash is not an expense. Petty Cash is cash on hand, and from this cash on hand expenses are incurred, not the other way round.

If the entire petty cash float for $1000.00 is booked to Office Expenses, when it's time for replenishing the fund, the receipts add up: $100.00 for Taxi's, $100.00 Luncheons for employees that couldn't leave the office, $300.00 Plumbing, $200.00 Toner and Cartridges, $200.00 Postage and finally $100.00 for Virus Protection Software.

Taxi's and Luncheons are Travel and Entertainment. Meals are 50% allowable expenses for tax purposes. Repairing the leak is Repairs and Maintenance. Toner and Cartridges is Printing and Stationery, Postage is another category, and Virus Protection is Software!

Setting up the system isn't complex. If the petty cash float is $1200.00. The Journal Entry debits Petty Cash $1200.00, and credits the Bank Account for $1200.00. Complete an in house designed form, similar to the Employee Reimbursement expense requisition. The Journal Entries go like this:

July 31st,	Travel	$	100.00
	Meals and Entertainment	$	100.00
	Repairs	$	300.00
	Printing and Stationery	$	200.00
	Postage Stamps	$	200.00
	Software	$	100.00
	Bank Operating		$1,000.00

Replenishing the Petty Cash fund to $1,200.00

The expenses are properly booked. Attached to this in house report is the paperwork.

 What is the breakeven point?

In practice there is more to it than what meets the eye.

Wage earners must take home a certain dollar amount each month, to provide the cost of the roof over their heads and essential food and miscellaneous items, before considering the non-essentials. If monthly expenses require $10,000.00 a month, this is the dollar amount they must bring home after taxes, without dipping into savings, or going into debt. Any amount over and above is surplus that can be assigned to savings or acquisition of assets.

For example: Wage earner, Opportunity Seeker sells Deacon's books. The difference between the prices Deacon sells the book to them, and whatever they can get for it up to the recommended retail selling price is profit.

Opportunity Seeker orders the maximum of one hundred books for storage in the garage. Technically the space utilized in the garage should be allocated and given a value, but before he took his chance with Deacon, that space housed junk that his son asked him to store in 1964 and never returned for them, so there were no tears, when the books arrived, those items were thrown in the nearest dumpster, so Opportunity Seeker didn't allocate a dollar value to that space at this time.

Deacon sold him two thousand books on a non-refundable basis. Opportunity Seeker sold one hundred books a week, so at the rate it takes twenty weeks to deplete this inventory.

If he can get these books at a lower price, some or all of the price advantage can be passed on and the breakeven will remain the same or the change will be hardly noticeable, BUT this is too basic.

Let's extend this, how is the breakeven calculated if he left his full time job and allocated fair market value for storage, used garage space is $200.00 a month

If the following is allocated to the sale of Deacon's Books:

Telephone	$ 90.00	A Month
Utilities	$ 40.00	A Month
Miscellaneous	$ 90.00	A Month
Salary	$ 4,000.00	A Month
Rent	$ 200.00	A Month

The price determined by the quantity placed and paid for at the following rates:

# Books	Price
100	$56.00
1000	$48.00
1500	$44.00
2000	$40.00
5000	$32.00

How many books can Opportunity Seeker purchase at any one time, and what is the most desirable quantity? Its one thing if the books are delivered personally, but most likely the books are shipped requiring proper packaging and incurring shipping charges. In practice this should be factored in, but the overall message will still get across.

Unless Opportunity Seeker is willing to finance his salary and other expenses with borrowed money or savings, the monthly expenses of $4,420.00 a month, excluding the cost of the books, which is a variable, must be matched by book sales.

If Opportunity Seeker has 100 delivered per week (and sells them) then the cost is $5,600.00 per week, times four weeks making the required average monthly Inventory outlays of $22,400.00.

Add the standard $4,240.00, the breakeven now is $26,640.00. Divide that by 400 books, on average. It's determined that no book can be sold for less than $66.60. If Opportunity Seeker discounts the book 15% from the Suggested Retail Price of $80.00, the selling price from

Opportunity Seeker is $68.00. This is extremely close to the breakeven price of $66.60.

Now it changes. Opportunity Seeker has 1000 Books delivered. He stores them and sells 100 per week. Based on 4.5 weeks per month and selling100 books a week, over two months, 900 books would be sold. That's close enough for our purposes:

2 months Standard Costs @ $4,420.00	$ 8,840.00
1000 Books @ $48.00 per Book	$48,000.00

Take $56,840.00 divided by 1000 books, the breakeven becomes $56.84 compared to $66.60. Allowing 20% discount from the Suggested Retail Price prices the book at $64.00. Now Opportunity Seeker generates about $8.00 per book over the breakeven point.

How about purchasing 5000 books? If Opportunity Seeker is working at a maximum capacity of 100 a week, considering Deacon won't take back unsold inventory, and if Deacon comes out with a newer version, the books mightn't have the monetary value they now command. Look at the product and the terms.

Every business has fixed costs, whether they sell no units, one unit or ten thousand units. Take an apartment complex. Is each apartment occupier responsible for his or her utilities based on usage? Or is the total cost for utilities for the entire complex paid by the owners? Even if the occupants pay each apartment's share of direct usage separately, there are the hallways and outside lighting!

Compared with Opportunity Seeker selling books, a software company launching a new product, the Insurance agency hiring independent contractors, the number of units in the apartment complex is fixed, so total Income is limited. (Opportunity Seeker attends a convention and gets confirmed orders for 3000 books. The apartment owner at the convention doesn't get to rent an extra 30 apartments on a building that has 100 units that are fully occupied)

An apartment building has 100 units. If the vacancy rate is 10% then on average 10 units are vacant at all times. In this case standard recurring costs no matter what are $100,000.00 a month translating to $1,200,000.00 on an annual basis.

The apartments have 30 units under rent controls generating $500.00 a month contributing $15,000.00 to the break-even. The remaining 60 units must generate on average $1,417.00 a month must to absorb the remaining $85,000.00. The question is, will the market bear this price?

If the real estate agency won't allow their Independent Contractors to use their office space and other facilities, and if an agent takes six months to close a deal, that generates $10,000.00 in fees to the agency, who cares? The contractor looses out if they need to spend so much time with clients that may, or may never purchase a property.

As long as the real estate agent hasn't provided much guidance and desk space, they shouldn't care less. The one thousand-room Deacon Hotel, like the apartment building, is limited to one thousand units BUT the occupants consistently come and go, paying a nightly fee far exceeding the equivalent apartment revenue taking into account labor and supplies.

So if the apartment rents for $500.00 a month compared to the hotel room that rents for $50.00 a night for twenty nights will generate $1,000.00. BUT there is no free lunch. Rooms have to be serviced.

The hotel compares to the airline industry, rooms vacant for one night, or a vacant seat on an airplane can't be sold at discount the following day. The supermarket can discount extremely ripe peaches, at least getting a few pennies before discarding them.

Fig 8:6 show the basic formula in coming up with the breakeven for a Deacon style hotel operation.

In reality there are many more items. The dollar amounts will differ, but the concepts won't change. The essentials consume $90 Million. Beyond that, it's all profit.
It takes $90+ million to keep the doors open. The hotel has a fixed number of rooms and facilities. At 1000 rooms at 365 days a year, the maximum number, over a year, is 365,000 room nights. Based on the expenses (and that includes a mortgage) and if every room was occupied every single night of the year, they would have to charge $248.47 to cover these essential expenses.

If the market supports an <u>average rate</u> of $325.00, they have to fill 765 rooms per night 365 days a year.

 Sales and Marketing personnel face sometimes undue pressure insuring the product isn't given away" Why not sell the article at cost, or even below cost to move the product? Fill both the airplane and the hotel room!

 Know the industry. A high-end pen stationer might dispose Inventory at cost to make room for new items, generating cash to pay employees and other overhead. If the hotel can't attract sufficient number of customers willing to pay the rate, consider closing down a few floors, reassign the labor or send them on vacation.

Timing Timing Timing ™

The Matching Principle would not exist without the Timing Rules which plays a no small role in accounting. It is an area ripe for both graduates and interns looking to put into practice: "Figures never lie, sometimes liars figure"

Break Even for Deacon Hotels

Payroll Including Payroll Taxes and Benefits	24,000,000.00	
Mortgage Including Interest	36,000,000.00	
Property Taxes	3,600,000.00	
Utilities - Heating	630,000.00	
Utilities - Electricity	750,000.00	
Utilities - Water	335,000.00	
Repairs and Maintenance Building	270,000.00	
Repairs and Maintenance Equipment	170,000.00	
Repairs and Maintenance Electrical	140,000.00	
Insurance Fire	1,200,000.00	
Insurance General	1,200,000.00	
Insurance Business	230,000.00	
Insurance Terror	2,400,000.00	
Insurance Workers Compensation	16,000.00	
Telephone	600,000.00	
Operating Supplies	2,000,000.00	73,541,000.00
Sub Total		
Food and Beverage Cost	2,400,000.00	2,400,000.00
Promotional Expenses	1,200,000.00	
Professional Fees Audit and Legal	250,000.00	
Management Fees Minimum	1,300,000.00	
Minimum Royalty/Franchise Fees	12,000,000.00	14,750,000.00
Grand Total Annual		90,691,000.00
Average Monthly Layout		7,557,583.33
Maximum Number of Rooms		365000
Number of Rooms available for Rent		365000
Cost Per Room if Occupied 365 days a year		248.47
Market Room Rate Per Night (Average)	325.00	
Cost per Room	248.47	
Gross Profit Margin	76.53	
Total Expenses Contributing Break Even	90,691,000.00	
Market Rate Per Room	325.00	
Number of Rooms Contributing	279049.2308	
Maximum Number of Rooms	365000	
% Occupancy to Make Minimum Break Even	76.45%	

Fig 8:6

177

Chapter 9

Long-term Liabilities – Including Bonds

Corporate Income Taxes

Interest Rates

Warranties

Introduction to Off Balance Sheet Financing

Leasing: Operating and Capital Leases

Mortgages attached to the building are Long-term Liabilities. What other items make up Long-term Liabilities?

 Both Short-term and Long-term Liabilities are contractual obligations. These are recognized to the fullest extent of the contract.

Mortgages, Bonds, Notes and Leases require interest payments at regular intervals during the entire life of the long-term liability. Sometimes agreements require setting aside funds for retiring Long-term obligations.

Accounting doesn't recognize non-executed contracts, despite both parties having obligations and haven't dispensed any cash. Financial Institutions, extending open-ended credit lines book the actual amounts their clients have drawn on. The Financial Statements must disclose potential loss from lawsuits unused credit lines must also be disclosed.

There are Potential Liabilities and Constructive Liabilities. Potential liabilities happen when tobacco companies have to defend multi million-dollar lawsuits. The FASB rules that the loss has to be "probable" before accounting recognizes the Liability. In practice probability is 80%

Traditional textbooks might tell you that such losses are debited to an expense account "Loss from Damages Claim Account" but in but in practice, even if it existed, it would likely be buried somewhere else.

Dr. Loss from Damage Claim   1,000,000
    Cr. Estimated Liability for Damages   1,000,000

Contingency or Contingent Liabilities are disclosed in the notes to the Financial Statements. This happens when potential liabilities arise, due to government regulations or claims pending. The amounts can't be determined at year-end. Hopefully, the outcomes won't have a material affect on the entities financial position

Constructive Liabilities arise out of intent, rather than obligation. Let's look at plant closure. It's a given there will additional payroll and other directly related expenses. Even if the amount isn't known at this time, however a restructuring charge can be booked.

Dr. Restructuring Charges $23,000,000.00
     Cr Liability: Severance Pay $23,000,000.00

When the employees are discharged, payments are booked to the Liability for Severance Pay to Employees. This does provide opportunities for Figures never lie, but liars sometimes figure"

The "Conservative accounting" approach is commendable. That still doesn't prevent expenses being grossly exaggerated, or massively shortchanged. Too little reduces current year expenses insuring the shortfalls are booked the following year. If it's exaggerated, corrections are required the following year, resulting in a massive surplus. Manipulation can be very real.

 Can we finally get to Income Taxes?

 Corporations, if they qualify can elect Sub Chapter S to avoid the Corporate Income Taxes. Sub Chapter S status place the corporation on a par with Partnerships and Sole Proprietorships for tax purposes. These are "pass through" entities

They take the Net Income or Net Loss, plus some other items, and allocate these amounts, pro rata to the individuals, who then pick up those items up on their individual tax returns. The LLC, which stands for Limited Liability Company. This can be taxed as a partnership or it can take steps permitting it to be taxed as a corporation.

Corporations must estimate their tax liability during the year, and make estimated payments based on that estimate adjusted during the year for unexpected occurrences.

```
Dr. Income Tax Expense              100,000
        Cr. Income Taxes Payable             100,000
            To accrue Quarterly payment

Dr. Income Taxes Payable            100,000
        Cr. Cash                             100,000
```

GAAP requires, computation of income taxes for the Financial Statements must be based on Financial Statement results, not taxable income. For example: Based on the Financial Statements, the income taxes that should be paid is $1,000,000.00, but under the tax legislation the amount they have to pay is $800,000.00 thereby creating differences:

There are Permanent and Temporary differences to account for. Permanent differences are tax-exempt interest income. Temporary differences are Depreciation differences, Bad Debts and Warranties etc. How are these booked?

```
Dr. Income Tax Expense        $1,000,000.00
        Cr. Deferred Income Taxes        $200,000.00
        Cr. Income Taxes Payable         $800,000.00
```

 Does Deferred Income Taxes Payable ever close out to zero?

 Yes, in the perfect world of textbooks. If deferred Income Taxes are there due to Depreciation and Warranty differences, and if no further Capital Assets are acquired for the life of the Assets on the books, then they will reduce to zero. But in my experience, this isn't the real world.

Temporary differences, depending on the Timing rules might create Deferred Tax Assets. GAAP requires, to recognize a Deferred Tax Asset Valuation account, the balances reduced must be based on expected future tax savings

 In reality the Income Tax Liability account most likely won't revert to zero. How does one protect from "Figures never lie, sometimes liars figure"?

The notes to the Financial Statements must disclose the minimum components comprising of Income before Income Taxes, segregating domestic from international operations. The same must be done with Taxable Income, highlighting the Temporary differences, the deferred, and allocations between taxes paid to the US Government and foreign governments. What is the effective tax rate?

This is the percentage of the total tax paid, divided by the total income. The statutory rate of tax is the rate specified in the law.

 What about Warranties after the sale?

 Warranty provided for service, or repairs after the sale, is similar to estimating the Bad Debt reserve. Past experience determines the average percentage of sales that will generate repairs under warranty.

Dr. Accounts Receivable	$280,000	
Dr. Warranty Expense	$11,200	
Cr. Sales		$280,0000
Cr. Estimated Warranty Liability		$11,2000

Past experience can't be discarded. The FASB ruled "Accounting for Contingencies" requires the accrual of the expense, and the related warranty liability, when they can "reasonably estimate" the amount. If the estimated service and repairs for the period is:

Dr. Estimated Warranty Liability	$1,750.00
Cr. Cash or other assets	$1,750.00

 How is the Interest expense booked each month? How is the Interest Rate determined?

 There is a process: "Finding the Internal rate of return" This rate discounts future cash flows to its present values.

Deacon borrows $12,500,000.00 at 7% interest, covering ten accounting periods. See Fig 9:1. Each period equals one month. The Interest expense for the first month is $72,916.67: the second month is $65,814.37 and so on. Interest expense for the first month is higher compared with the second month and so on. Don't divide the total Interest expense for the year by twelve equal installments.

#	Initial Amount	Interest Expense	Sub Total	Payment	New Balance	Mortgage Reduction
1	12,500,000.00	72,916.67	12,572,916.67	1,290,454.04	11,282,462.63	1,217,537.37
2	11,282,462.63	65,814.37	11,348,276.99	1,290,454.04	10,057,822.95	1,224,639.67
3	10,057,822.95	58,670.63	10,116,493.59	1,290,454.04	8,826,039.55	1,231,783.41
4	8,826,039.55	51,485.23	8,877,524.78	1,290,454.04	7,587,070.74	1,238,968.81
5	7,587,070.74	44,257.91	7,631,328.65	1,290,454.04	6,340,874.61	1,246,196.13
6	6,340,874.61	36,988.44	6,377,863.04	1,290,454.04	5,087,409.00	1,253,465.60
7	5,087,409.00	29,676.55	5,117,085.56	1,290,454.04	3,826,631.52	1,260,777.49
8	3,826,631.52	22,322.02	3,848,953.53	1,290,454.04	2,558,499.49	1,268,132.02
9	2,558,499.49	14,924.58	2,573,424.07	1,290,454.04	1,282,970.03	1,275,529.46
10	1,282,970.03	7,483.99	1,290,454.03	1,290,454.03	0.00	1,282,970.04

Fig 9:1

$12, 500,000.00 equals the present value of 10 monthly cash payments of $1,290,454.04 each discounted at 7%. $12,500,000.00 today at 7% can be compared with collecting $1,290,454.03 for ten months providing $12,904,540.39. See Fig 9:2

#	Initial Amount	Interest Income	Sub Total	Receipts	New Balance
1	1,290,454.03	7,527.65	1,297,981.68		1,297,981.68
2	1,297,981.68	7,571.56	1,305,553.24	1,290,454.03	2,596,007.27
3	2,596,007.27	15,143.38	2,611,150.64	1,290,454.03	3,901,604.67
4	3,901,604.67	22,759.36	3,924,364.03	1,290,454.03	5,214,818.06
5	5,214,818.06	30,419.77	5,245,237.84	1,290,454.03	6,535,691.87
6	6,535,691.87	38,124.87	6,573,816.74	1,290,454.03	7,864,270.77
7	7,864,270.77	45,874.91	7,910,145.68	1,290,454.03	9,200,599.71
8	9,200,599.71	53,670.16	9,254,269.87	1,290,454.03	10,544,723.90
9	10,544,723.90	61,510.89	10,606,234.79	1,290,454.03	11,896,688.82
10	11,896,688.82	69,397.35	11,966,086.17	1,290,454.03	13,256,540.20
		351,999.90		11,614,086.27	
				1,290,454.03	
		351,999.90		12,904,540.30	13,256,540.20

Fig 9:2

183

<u>The Initial Journal Entry booking the $12,500,000.00 is:</u>

Dr Cash $12,500,000.00
      Cr. Mortgage Payable $12,500,000.00
              To Record Loan

 Usually the financing of Long-term assets has a clearly stated interest rate, but at times contracts specify the total overall payments at specific dollar amounts each month. How is the interest calculated?

 GAAP doesn't provide exceptions for contracts having a stipulated rate of interest, or those that have an implicit rate of interest. Long-term contracts must be on the Balance Sheet at the present value of all future cash payments. Historical accounting takes the rate when the Long-term liability came into existence.

Deacon Hotels acquired equipment that if paid in cash would be $2,500,000.00. Deacon exercised the option to delay payment for three years, then paying $2,544,005.70.

The Equipment is booked at the contact price of $2,500,000.00.

Dr. Equipment $2,500,000.00
      Cr. Note Payable $2,500,000.00
      To record Equipment at the known Cash price

<u>For the first year Interest Expense</u>

Dr. Interest Expense $14,583.33
      Cr. Note Payable $14,583.33

<u>Entry made one year after issuance of Note</u>

Dr. Interest Expense $14,668.40
      Cr. Note Payable $14,668.40

<u>Entry made the second year after issuance of the Note:</u>

Dr. Interest Expense $14,753.97
  Cr. Note Payable $14,753.97
The Note Payable balance is $2,544,005.70. That's the amount
due in one lump sum.

Dr. Note Payable $2,544,005.70
  Cr. Bank $2,544,005.70
Note Paid at Maturity.

 Does accounting discriminate between recording the Interest Expense for new and used equipment?

 GAAP requires the current rates on the open market. Once determined, the Journal Entries are identical.

 Accounts Payable transactions in the books of the buyer, is Accounts Receivable transaction in the sellers' books. What about long-tern liabilities?

 The borrower's Long-term Note Payable is a long-term Note Receivable in the lenders books.

Pure accounting theory states both entities should have identical interest rates, but the real world, buyers and sellers have different viewpoints towards credit risks. Borrowers' book Interest expense, the sellers' book Interest Income.

 What's the difference between Common Stock and Bonds? Can Bonds be liquidated overnight on the major exchanges?

 Bonds represent debt. Stock represents ownership. Bondholders' have liens on the Assets. Common stockholders have rights on the Corporate Assets in liquidation or bankruptcy after all salaries and wages, bondholders and vendors have been paid.

Bondholders have tremendous power. If the entity issuing the bonds default on one payment, that alone can trigger a management reshuffle or an overthrow. Stocks and Bonds can be publicly traded, and if so, the prices will fluctuate according to the market forces.

There are three primary types of bonds. Mortgage bonds carry mortgages on real estate with specific properties encumbered. The typical corporate bond, excluding railroad and public utilities, is the debenture bond, carrying only the general credit of the entity. Convertible bonds permit the holders' within a specific time frame, to convert them into a certain predetermined number of shares of common stock.

 How do the bonds get to market? Where are the conditions found binding both the entity and bondholders?

 The Bond Indenture, likely the most important document, is the written agreement between the entity and the investment bankers. It stipulates the terms, conditions, rights and duties of the borrower, and lists all the limitations to declaring dividends and to make other distributions.

The Investment Banking or syndicate usually bear the interest rate risks and turbulence during that period they are initially being offered to the public. They usually reap the gain, or suffer the losses during this period. The Bond Indenture indicates the par value of the bond.

There isn't "one size fits all either" It's best illustrated by examples: Deacon Ocean Liner Condominiums Corporation issues $650 million 10% interest every six months for the next twenty years. This is the key. <u>The Indenture stipulates $32.5million</u> every six months. At the end of twenty years the entire $650 million is repaid.

Deacon Properties issue $180 million of 15-year bonds. The Indenture stipulates payment of $13.1 Million every six months for 15 years. This compares with the home mortgage. Each payment is part interest payment and part reduction in the principal amount. These are Serial bonds

Deacon Media issues $950 million worth of bonds, promising repayment at the end of fifteen years. No payments until maturity. This is a Zero-coupon bond.

 Does the entity receive in cash the total number of bonds, at the price, and rate, specified on the Indenture?

 Issuing price depends on the future cash outlays stipulated in the Indenture, and the discount rate the market allocates, taking into account the risk of the borrower and the general interest of the market. Technically the price equals the present value of the required cash flows discounted at the appropriate market rate.

The issue price almost always differs from the par value on the certificate, as the moment the bonds are floated market forces determine the rate. If the coupon rate is 7%, and the market currently demands 10%, these bonds will be sold at a discount. The opposite applies, if the coupon rate is 10% and the market demands 7% then the bonds will be sold at a premium.

 Are bonds ever floated at Par?

 As far as I know, only in the perfect world of textbooks. Just in case it has happened, or might occur, these are the Journal entries for a $100 million bond issue, repayable at the end of 15 years, 5% interest payable semi annually.

The Bond Sale:

Dr. Cash $100,000,000
      Cr. Debenture Bonds Payable $100,000,000
Record $100,000,000 5% 15 year Bonds issued at Par

Interest expenses must be recorded too. The interest expense for one year ($100 million at 5% pa) is $5,000,000.

Both the expense and liability accounts are identical in dollar terms.

Recording the Interest:

Dr. Interest Expense $5,000,000.00
   Cr. Interest Payable $5,000,000.00
     Record the Interest Expense

 Bondholders often sell the bonds between the Interest payments. Does the buyer get a windfall?

 When the bonds are sold between Interest payments, interest is factored in, so buyer and seller isn't shortchanged.

 If bonds are issued at Discount or a Premium, how does the entity book the appropriate Interest payments? The amount received doesn't equal the amount stated in the Indenture.

 If the Bonds issued have overall, Par value of $100 million obligating Interest payments of $5,000,000 every year, that's the amount they pay out regardless of the amount received, or how the market treats the bonds now, or any time in the future.

The entity receives what the market deems the bonds are worth. If its $90 million then Journal entry debits Cash for $90 million, credits Bonds Payable for $90 million. The actual Interest payments are based on $100 million, at the rate provided for in the Indenture.

 Surely the Discount or the Premium is recorded in the books?

 Sometimes. It resembles the Accounts Receivable Balance less Reserve for Bad Debts: (See following page)

Bonds Payable	$100,000,000.00
Less Discount	$ 593,000.00
Bonds Payable: Net Book Value	$ 94,407,000.00

Bonds Payable	$100,000,000.00
Plus: Premium on Bonds	$ 593,000.00
Bonds Payable: Net Book Value	$100,593,000.00

 What's the difference between callable bonds and retiring bonds before maturity?

 All Callable Bonds have common provisions, often providing for the <u>right</u>, but not the <u>obligation</u>, to retire portions of the issue before maturity. The price will be stipulated in the Indenture.

The Callable price decreases as the maturity date comes closer. If the bonds, at the time of issue are 7%, and interest rates rise to 10%, the market price drops. The Call price stipulates a much higher value over par, its senseless calling in the bonds. The solution is, buy back the bonds on the open market, and retire them. The gains are classified as extraordinary, and aren't included within the operating income category

 Do all the bonds sold within the particular issue become due on the same date?

 Bond Indentures sometimes provide for early retirement. Serial bonds can provide for payment of portions of the principal on one or more maturity dates.

Sinking Fund Bonds sometimes require the entity to accumulate a fund of cash, or other assets, that will be sufficient to pay the bondholders on the maturity date, or if the bonds are retired before due date.

Trustees normally administer these funds. They are located

in the Non-Current Investment section of the Balance Sheet. This is the absolute minimum you have to be aware of at this level.

 What is "Off Balance Sheet Financing"?

"What you see is what you get" This achieves the aim of keeping Liabilities (debts) off the Balance Sheet. If the business has restrictions imposed on how much it can borrow, or if certain ratios must be maintained, look for "Off Balance Sheet Financing" It might not stand out so clearly as most accounting textbooks make it out to be.

Sometimes businesses go into ventures, assuming investors and lenders don't have the knowledge to identify and deal with these issues, and they are surprised when they find out otherwise.

Accounting does NOT recognize executory contracts and contingent liabilities. Promises to pay amounts in the future, without events having occurred or occurring aren't recognized as legitimate transactions. Off Balance Sheet Financing may achieve what accounting won't legitimately recognize.

The Financial Accounting Standards Board (FASB) has dealt with cases individually, and the general theme coming out of all these, if the party requiring the financing controls both who receives the benefits and those bearing the risks, then the liability is booked to the party controlling the events. The debts don't appear on the Balance Sheet of the entity requiring the financing.

An airline requiring additional aircraft can purchase the aircraft with borrowed funds. In this case they have to book the Liability on the Balance Sheet. The alternative, pay the owners of the aircraft a definite amount for twelve years. The aircraft are financed without creating a Liability on the Balance Sheet.

Now it changes. The airline signs a lease for twenty years. The leased aircraft have a useful life of twenty years, the lease payments compensate for the cost of the aircraft and a reasonable amount for the level of risk. The airline has almost all the economic benefits of the aircraft, as if they owned them outright. They will book the lease commitment as a Liability.

If the lease covers a period, substantially less than useful life, and by contract, the aircraft must be sold, or transferred to another airline, the owner has full control and therefore incurs the benefits and risks. In this case the airline won't report this Liability on the Balance Sheet.

Deacon Publishing and Commerce Clearing House Publishing require reliable storage and printing presses. A joint venture is created, agreeing each company can utilize one half of the plant capacity each year for the following twenty years and pay all operating and debt servicing. Deacon Publishing and Commerce Clearing House, both assign the purchasing commitments for the construction and financing of the plant. This is an executory contract, so no Liabilities are booked on the Balance Sheets for either of the entities involved. The bankers will probably require Deacon to guarantee the loans.

Commerce Clearing House later has issues. They can't or won't pay their share, even if they use plant, so Deacon bears the economic risk. Deacon must book the Liability on the Balance Sheet.

If the bank approved the loan on the assets of the plant, without any guarantees from Deacon or Commerce Clearing House, the Liability is recorded on the books of the Joint Venture.

Sold outright, Accounts Receivables aren't recorded on the Balance Sheet, but if they are assigned as collateral, the Liability must be booked.

Now, the Receivables are sold to a financial institution. Deacon agrees to collect the monthly outstanding Receivables for a fee, remitting the cash received immediately to the financial institutions. Deacon treats this as a sale. No Liabilities are recorded on the Balance Sheet.

If the financial institutions require additional security for the items they think are poor credit risks, or some of those Receivables are destined for the Bad Debt categories, then Deacon's risk level is higher. The Receivables transfer is considered a loan and is booked as a Liability on the Balance Sheet. If the financial institution bears all the risks, the Receivables are considered as being sold.

 Leasing is big business and it isn't going away. Lease payments might be more complex than booking the payment to an expense account. Are you serious, when you referred to the airline leasing aircraft, they can be responsible as if they owned the asset?

 No, I am the majority stockholder in a paper-processing outfit! Of course I am dead serious. There's the Operating lease method, and the Capital lease methods.

Operating leases occur, when the owners provide rights to use the property for a specific length of time. The assets then revert to the owners. Car rentals are an excellent example. Should Deacon lease computers and if at any time I can stop paying and return them, this is an executory contract and it's an Operating lease. If I can't walk away from the lease, it's an executed contract. It's a form of borrowing. How are the computers booked?

At the signing of the lease there can be a simultaneous acquisition of an asset, and a lease payment, resulting in creating an Asset and a Liability recorded at the present value

Dr. Computer Leaseholds $600,000.00
     Cr. Lease Obligations $600,000.00

By the end of the year, there are two distinct separate entries. One Amortizing the asset, and the other taking into account the annual payment. The annual payment for the computers is $202,337.86 per year for three years with a total outlay of $603,013.57.

What's the interest rate?

The rate is 7% per annum. See Fig 9.3 Delivery is the first day of the year. For simplicity entries are recorded at the last day of the year. The real world requires it to be done on a monthly basis.

#	Initial Amount	Interest Expense	Sub Total	Payment	New Balance
1	600,000.00	3,500.00	603,500.00	202,337.86	401,162.14
2	401,162.14	2,340.11	403,502.25	202,337.86	201,164.39
3	201,164.39	1,173.46	202,337.85	202,337.85	0.00
Total		7,013.57		607,013.57	

Fig 9:3

The Asset is Amortized over the three-year lease period. How would the Journal entries be done, assuming the Straight-line method?

Dr. Amortization Expense
   (Computer leasehold) $200,000.000
         Cr. Computer Leasehold $200,000.00

The interest portion is booked:

Dr. Interest Expense $ 3,500.00
Dr. Computer lease Obligations. $ 198,837.86
      Cr. Bank Account $202.337.86
Recognizing Lease Payment including Interest and Principal reduction for Year 1

Dr. Interest Expense $ 2,340.11
Dr. Computer lease Obligations. $199,997.75
      Cr. Bank Account $202.337.86

Recognizing Lease Payment including Interest and Principal reduction for Year 2

Dr. Interest Expense $ 1,173.46
Dr. Computer lease Obligations. $201,164.39
            Cr. Bank Account $202.337.85
Recognizing Lease Payment including Interest and Principal reduction for Year 3

 Deacon, I thought you would have been smarter and chosen the Operating Lease method. Then the lease expense is debited with the full monthly payment?

 You failed to take into consideration the Amortization of the asset ($600,000.00 divided by 3 years) is $200,000.00 a year. So long the payments and Interest rates are identical the overall cost of the asset is identical.

It all comes down to "Timing, Timing Timing™ If ownership transfers at the end of the lease by contract, or even if its probable ownership will change due to bargain purchase clauses, the Capital Lease method is mandatory. If that isn't enough, if the lease extends for a minimum of 75% of the life of the asset, and the present value of the minimum lease payments equals or exceeds 90% of the market value of the asset at the time the lease is signed, then the Capital Lease method MUST be used

 OK Circumvent those conditions?

 The fourth one is the killer. If the present value of the monthly payments has characteristics of an Installment, the FASB goes further. If the purchase price exceeds 90% of the assets value, then the lessee has effectively purchased the equipment.

 Do the lease providers) care less if the lessee is an Operating or a Capital lease?

You bet they do. Aircraft manufacturers of corporate jets might not want exposure to many of the risks common to the airline business, so they require the signing of long-term and non-cancelable leases. Computer manufacturers don't want to lease assets, where they have more than 10% of the original market value to loose, and at those values, must find another customer at the end of the lease.

They want the fourth condition to be part of the package. If the product leased is an Operating lease in the books of the buyer, it's an Operating lease in the seller's books.

 So where are all these tax benefits of leasing over purchasing?

 There MAY be benefits to leasing. Leasing companies buy computers, airplanes, and office furniture etc from the manufacturers and lease them.

Depreciating an asset is meaningless, if there isn't sufficient taxable income to offset these deductions, or the taxpayer is consistently in the lower tax rates deductions might be almost worthless. Operating leases generate an immediate expense, independent of the income tax brackets.

Remember: No matter if the enterprise is headquartered at 1130 GAAP Road, Apartment Number 245 Location, living room table, or one of the largest organizations in the world and the net profit for the year is anything from ten cents to billions of dollars, pounds or yen, etc, whether the ledgers are done by hand or with the latest cutting edge technology available, the Deacon 3Q's™ apply. The Quality of the financial reports depends on the quality of the input and the quality of the management of that input. It's the management of that input where "Figures never lie, sometimes liars figure"

Chapter 10

Are the dividends paid a legitimate expense to the corporate entity?

 No, No, No! Dividends are NOT expenses. Within a controlled corporate group, corporations can receive a portion of the Total Dividends tax free in view of the double taxation consequences.

 You spoke about Retained earnings. Should more time be spent evaluating them?

 Retained earnings are the total lifetime Earnings from day one, less lifetime Dividends and Distributions. Earnings increase Retained Earnings. Losses decrease Retained Earnings, including Dividends.

The Board of Directors declares the dividend, and declaring dividends triggers legal considerations. Generally, the dividends cannot be paid out of Capital. They can be paid out of surplus after considering any restrictions the Bondholders have placed on the corporation. The Board of Directors usually declares dividends below the legal maximum.

 Are they always paid out in cash?

Dividends can be paid in Cash, Other Assets or shares of Common Stock. If the Dividends are Cash Dividends, the Journal Entry is as follows:

July 15th, 2003   Retained Earnings $459,000.00
                   Dividends Payable $459,000.00

When the Cash Dividend is paid out, the Cash account is credited and Dividends Payable is debited. If the dividend is in the form of an Asset, instead of crediting the Cash account, the actual Assets are credited. Retention of earnings over the years, allows the corporation to pay a Stock Dividend. The Retained Earnings account is still debited, but as there is no cash outlay, the Contributed Capital Accounts are credited.

What? Considering that the Shareholders Equity is made up of the Capital accounts and the Retained Earnings, isn't the net affect a big fat zero?

GAAP, Generally Accepted Accounting Principles, require newly issued shares be based on the market value of the shares. Supposing If Deacon declares a stock dividend of $500,000.00 the journal entry is as follows:

Dr. Retained Earnings $500,000.00
    Cr Common Stock $1.00 Par $240,000.00
    Cr Additional Paid in Capital $260,000.00

This reduces, what would have been available for dividends and increases the Capital Contributed. Stock Dividends are declared along the lines, for example, for each share of stock the holder receives an additional two shares. The beauty of Stock Dividends is, they don't consume cash, and as the stockholder gets more paper, but usually they have little economic substance.

Isn't the Stock Dividend another word for a Stock Split?

No. They are similar. Stock splits reduce the par value of the stock within a specified category of stock rights across the board. If Deacon has 50,000 shares at $1.00 par, a split makes it 100,000 shares at $0.50 per share. (If that's a two for one split)

Stock splits usually occur when the share price has risen substantially, and management is of the opinion the price has got too high. After a stock split the corporation has more shares on the market, and although the price on the market will decline, they are more affordable.

What about Earnings Per Share?

.

Listed companies MUST report earnings per share. This topic goes beyond the scope of this book, but the most basic calculation is, take the Net Earnings, less Preferred Stock Dividends, then divide that figure by the <u>average</u> number of Common Shares outstanding during the accounting period.

If the corporation has more than four categories of stock, each category must be reported separately. All changes in Shareholders' Equity must be explained. The Statement of Earnings and Retained Earnings can be found separately.

 The third statement within the hierarchy of the Financial Statements is the Statement of Cash Flows. Isn't it time it was introduced?

 Yes, it is. The Statement of Cash Flows does NOT convert the Financial Statements to the Cash method of accounting. It's easy to go from Accrual to Cash based Financial Statements, but not the other way round. Accrual accounting requires the Statement of Cash Flows.

This report shows how cash came in, and how it's consumed. From the Brown family to the worldwide conglomerate Cash flows don't equal Net Income. Financial Accounting Income doesn't equate with Taxable Income. Even the highly profitable entities can fold if cash flow isn't managed. The Statement of Cash Flows is a vital tool.

This important Financial Statement can only be prepared after the Income Statement and Balance Sheet have been completed. To be taken seriously, this Financial Statement must be the final version. See Fig 10:1 The Statement of Cash Flows begins at the Net Profit figure, then adds and subtracts amounts

The Statement of Cash Flows here gives the basic idea of this complex Financial Statement. They are ALWAYS segregated into Operating, Investing and Financing sections.

Deacon Management Corporation
Statement of Cash Flow for the Twelve Months
January through December 2003

Items	Current Month	Year to Date
Cash Flows from operating activities		
Net Income	508,848.18	3,743,051.93
Add Back:		
Accumulated Depreciation	3,176,638.46	34,943,023.06
Preopening and Organization Costs	292,355.60	3,215,911.60
Accounts Receivable	1,690,164.09	<4,994,202.30>
Reserve for Bad Debts	<207,554.03>	<73,023.24>
Prepayments & Security Deposit		
Prepay-Sales & Promotion Mat	25,000.00	<25,000.00>
Prepay-Insurance Fire	90,000.00	<90,000.00>
Prepay-Insurance General	120,000.00	<120,000.00>
Prepay-Insurance Other	23,200.00	<23,200.00>
Prepay-Insurance Terror	150,000.00	0.00
Prepay-Software Licenses	7,000.00	<7,000.00>
Prepay-Server Maint Contracts	4,000.00	<28,000.00>
Prepay-Postage Machine Rental	450.00	<450.00>
Prepay-Contract Cleaners	18,000.00	<18,000.00>
Security Deposits Sales Taxes		<2,300,000.00>
Security Dep - Water and Power		<133,000.00>
Security Dep - Telephone		<57,000.00>
Security Dep - Food Liquor Ven		<250,000.00>
Inventories:		
Cleaning Supplies	8,710.88	<9,732.31>
Regular Room Supp	861.82	<15,017.84>
Other Room Supplies	197,225.98	<24,041.72>
Food Inventory	117,068.80	<36,818.23>
Liquor and Soft Drinks	34,418.07	<70,828.47>
Stationery Office and Other	<1,615.28>	<28,071.88>
Inventory - Other	<401,782.76>	<1,753,962.06>
Current Liabilitites		
Accounts Payable Trade	2,753,425.12	8,581,406.32
Payables - Affiliates	<142,176.71>	2,323,428.85
Taxes Payable Sales and Use	<2,726,628.80>	1,798,101.14
Taxes - Income Federal & State	370,751.10	1,548,445.65
Interest Payable	<11,905.55>	3,138,498.59
Commissions Payable	<13,192.49>	93,869.41
Accrued Expense Payable	391,818.48	1,028,614.88
Spa Memberships	<41,167.17>	211,499.99
Deposits - Customers Rooms		
Deposits - Customers Other		27,119.36
Security Deposits-Show Case		90,000.00
Security Deposits-Lobby Shop		13,800.00
Security Deposits-Starbucks		16,800.00

Deacon Management Corporation
Statement of Cash Flow for the Twelve Months
January through December 2003

Items	Current Month	Year to Date
Security Deposits-Amex Office		15,000.00
Security Deposits-Garage		700,000.00
Accrued Vacation Personal Sick	<904,666.36>	1,222,580.12
Total Adjustments	5,020,399.25	48,910,750.92
Net Cash provided by Operations	5,529,247.43	52,653,802.85
Cash Flows from investing activities		
Furniture Fittings & Equipment	<61,120.00>	<10,676,004.00>
Org Cost & Pre Opening Exp	0.00	<10,965,320.19>
Land and Buildings		
Net cash used in investing	<61,120.00>	<21,641,324.19>
Cash Flows from financing activities		
Proceeds From		
Mortgage Payable	0.00	653,250,000.00
Mortgage Payable	<2,469,203.60>	<25,522,530.47>
Construction Loan		<600,000,000.00>
Additional Paid in Capital	<30,200,000.00>	<30,200,000.00>
Treasury Stock		
Dividends Paid		
Net cash used in financing	<32,669,203.60>	<2,472,530.47>
Net increase <decrease> in cash	<27,201,076.17>	28,539,948.19
Summary		
Cash Balance at End of Period	30,860,267.45	30,860,267.45
Cash Balance at Beg of Period	<57,868,272.38>	<100,000.00>
Net Increase <Decrease> in Cash	<27,008,004.93>	30,760,267.45

Fig 10.1

Start with beginning balances and the ending balances of
Cash and Cash Equivalents. The accounting period is usually twelve months, with Current Assets and Current Liabilities reverting to the Cash position within twelve
months, but the Statement of Cash Flows, Cash Equivalents that convert back to Cash within three months or less
can only be considered.

Accrual accounting assumes the entity is an ongoing concern the auditors must take seriously in performing an audit. What is the assumption for the Statement of Cash Flows?

 The work papers assume Cash increases with Net Income. So the net Income for the month of December is $508,848.00 Add back Depreciation and Amortization Expense.

 Deacon books Depreciation and Amortization in one shot. In manufacturing, can't part of the Finished Goods Inventory include Depreciation expense for the items used in the manufacture of those items?

 Absolutely, Depreciation can be part of the Cost of Goods Sold making up the Work in Process Inventory. That why Operations, Investing and Financing are affected.

We didn't cover the complexities for Marketable Securities, but under certain conditions when these have lost value they must be written down. As the securities haven't been sold, the Income Tax laws won't recognize the loss, but Financial Accounting does book this as an unrealized loss. Losses reduce Net Income, but these losses don't consume cash, and as the securities haven't been sold, no cash has come in either.

What happens? Add it back to the Net Income amount. Deferred Income Taxes originally reduced Net Income. Had the government received cash for those deferred taxes, they wouldn't exist on the Balance Sheet.

Twining Twining Twining ™ The entity paid the insurance carrier $1,200,000.00 on October 1st This payment consumed Cash, even though it's a Prepayment. When Prepayments are amortized, expenses are increased by the amount of the amortization, but not one of those expenses consumed cash. Once again, add it back!

This is getting boring. Increases in the Accounts Payable represent expenses that have been booked, but haven't consumed cash. The assumption, expenses consume cash hasn't happened here. Increases in customer advances increased cash initially. Revenue isn't recognized until legally earned, so another adjustment.

An increase to Accounts Receivable relates to Sales. Net profit is the net effect of Income less expenses. The assumption, Sales generate cash didn't happen, so this must be adjusted by the portion of the Income for the period that contributed to an increase in Accounts Receivable that didn't translate into Cash during the accounting period.

Increases in Accounts Receivable don't give benefit to the Cash position, but decreases in Accounts Receivable will boost the Cash position. Why? Customers begin paying off their outstanding balances.

Increases or decreases in Warranties affect the Income Statement, but haven't consumed a dime of Cash. Depreciation was added back, increases or decreases in the Bad Debt Reserve hasn't increased or decreased the Cash position either.

Finally I am posting the Balance Sheet for the year in two formats, and the Income Statement in a couple of different formats too, to impress upon you, that there's more to accounting than a few line items some owners of businesses are receiving from their outside accountants.

On the other hand, if the listed companies were to report their entire detailed Financial Statements, they would intimidate some people, confuse others and in some cases, they would get a barrage of questions they wouldn't be able handle it.

Balance Sheet for Deacon Management Corporation
As At December 31st, 2003

ASSETS			LIABILITIES AND CAPITAL		
Current Assets			Current Liabilities		
Cash and Cash Equivalents			Accounts Payable Trade	8,581,406.32	
Cash Equivalents		30,860,267.45	Payables Affiliates	2,323,428.85	
Accounts Receivable	4,994,202.30		Taxes & Accrued Expenses	7,607,529.67	
Reserve for Bad Debts	73,023.24	5,067,225.54	Payroll Liabilities	1,222,580.12	
Other Assets		3,051,650.00	Trade & Security Deposits	1,074,219.35	
Inventory		1,938,472.51	Total Current Liabilities		20,809,164.31
Total Current Assets		40,917,615.50			
Property and Equipment			Long Term Liabilities		
Furniture Fittings/Equipment	10,676,004.00		Mortgage Payable	627,727,469.53	
Accumulated Depreciation	(3,215,911.60)	7,460,092.40	Construction Loan		
Other Assets			Bond Issue 7% Coupon		
Org Costs & Pre Opening	9,363,954.93		Total Long Term Liabilities		627,727,469.53
Land and Buildings	959,952,120.00				
Total Other Assets	969,316,074.93		Total Liabilities		648,536,633.84
Accumulated Depreciation	(34,943,023.06)	934,373,051.87			
Total Other Assets		941,833,144.27	Capital		
			Preferred Stock 7%		
			Preferred Stock 5%		
			Preferred Stock 9%		
			Common Stock $1 Par	50,000.00	
			Additional Paid in Capital	330,421,074.00	
			Retained Earnings		
			Treasury Stock		
			Dividends Paid		
			Net Income	3,743,051.93	
			Total Capital		334,214,125.93
Total Assets		982,750,759.77	Total Liabilities and Capital		982,750,759.77

Fig 10:2

As a business owner or a manager on the day-to-day challenges of operating a business, how can the short Financial Statement method be sufficient, and in my view, it can't be used in introducing Financial Accounting at this level.

Figure 10:2 is the Balance Sheet for the year ending December 31st, 2003. That's what I call a short format. Fig 10:3 this is the Balance Sheet in much more detail. Small to medium size businesses may opt to continuously report on the second format but due to the numerous items it may be inappropriate, but they will have to have supporting

Balance Sheet for Deacon Management Corporation
As at May 31st, 2003

ASSETS

Current Assets		
Cash and Cash Equivalents		
Cash on Hand	40,000.00	
Cash Operating Account	22,982,137.88	
Cash Payroll Account	38,129.57	
Cash Certificate of Deposit	7,800,000.00	30,860,267.45
Accounts Receivable	4,994,202.30	
Reserve for Bad Debts	73,023.24	5,067,225.54
Prepayments		
Sales & Promotion Materials	25,000.00	
Insurance Fire	90,000.00	
Insurance General	120,000.00	
Insurance Other	23,200.00	
Insurance Terror		
Software Licenses	7,000.00	
Maintenance Contracts	28,000.00	
Postage Machine Rental	450.00	
Contract Cleaners	18,000.00	
Security Deposits		
Sales Tax	2,300,000.00	
Water and Power	133,000.00	
Telephone	57,000.00	
Food & Liquor Vendors	250,000.00	3,051,650.00
Inventory		
Cleaning Supplies	9,732.31	
Regular Room Supp	15,017.84	
Other Room Supplies	24,041.72	
Food Inventory	36,818.23	
Liquor and Soft Drinks	70,828.47	
Stationery Office and Other	28,071.88	
Inventory - Other	1,753,962.06	1,938,472.51
Total Current Assets		40,917,815.50
Property and Equipment		
Furniture Fittings & Equipment	10,676,004.00	
Less Accumulated Depreciation	(3,213,911.60)	7,400,092.40
Other Assets		
Org. Cost and Pre Opening Exp	9,363,954.93	
Land and Buildings	959,952,120.00	
Total Other Assets	969,316,074.93	
Less Accumulated Depreciation	(34,943,023.06)	934,373,051.87
Total Assets		**982,750,759.77**

LIABILITIES AND CAPITAL

Current Liabilities		
Trade and Affiliates		
Accounts Payable Trade	8,581,406.32	
Payables Affiliates	2,323,428.85	10,904,835.17
Other		
Taxes Payable Sales & Use	1,798,101.14	
Taxes - Income	1,548,445.65	
Interest Payable	3,138,498.59	
Commissions Payable	93,869.41	
Accrued Expense Payable	1,028,614.88	7,607,529.67
Spa Memberships	211,499.99	
Prepaid Customer Rooms		
Prepaid Customer Other	27,119.36	238,619.35
Payroll Liabilities		
Payroll Signed Gratuities		
Medical Insurance Payable		
Life and Disability Insurance		
401k Contributions Payable		
Payroll Taxes State		
Payroll Taxes Federal		
Payroll Net Payroll Payable		
Accrued Vacation/Sick	1,222,580.12	1,222,580.12
Tennant Security Deposits		
Show Case	90,000.00	
Lobby Shop	13,800.00	
Starbucks	16,800.00	
American Express Office	15,000.00	
Garage	700,000.00	835,600.00
Total Current Liabilities		20,809,164.31
Long Term Liabilities		
Mortgage Payable	627,727,469.53	
Construction Loan		
Bond Issue 30 year Coupon 7%		
Total Long Term Liabilities		627,727,469.53
Total Liabilities		648,536,633.84
Capital		
Preferred Stock 7% Interest		
Preferred Stock 5% Interest		
Preferred Stock 9% Interest		
Common Stock $1.00 Par Value	50,000.00	
Additional Paid in Capital	330,421,074.00	
Retained Earnings		
Treasury Stock		
Dividends Paid		
Net Income	3,743,051.93	
Total Capital		334,214,125.93
Total Liabilities and Capital		**982,750,759.77**

Fig 10:3

schedules and subsidiary ledgers with more details. What I call the Consolidated Income Statement, that's the shortest of all the Income Statements, providing a general overall picture of the financial position. If I invested in an entity that's performing exceptionally well, and I am not interested

Income Statement for Deacon Management Corporation
For the Month Ending December 31st, 2003

Revenues	Current Month	Percent	Year to Date	Percent
Room Revenue	9,386,931.20	51.18%	106,533,962.75	55.32%
Revenue Spa and Fitness	321,388.82	1.75%	3,106,117.53	1.61%
Revenue Rooms Generated Phone	209,438.02	1.14%	2,274,053.74	1.18%
Revenue Business Center	57,772.87	0.31%	431,815.05	0.22%
Revenue Other	57,525.98	0.31%	703,022.72	0.37%
Space Rental and Garage	506,054.12	2.76%	5,356,842.66	2.78%
Revenue Food and Beverage	7,802,218.47	42.54%	74,179,659.62	38.52%
Total Revenue	18,341,329.48	100.00%	192,585,474.07	100.00%
Rooms Department Expense	1,178,790.15	6.43%	11,728,380.35	6.09%
Food and Beverage	3,516,160.91	19.17%	34,251,025.91	
Spa and Fitness	95,453.37	0.52%	1,030,775.70	0.54%
Telephone Department	60,735.06	0.33%	1,211,857.09	0.63%
Business Center	60,057.70	0.33%	780,843.01	0.41%
Front of the House	135,443.08	0.74%	1,382,459.23	0.72%
Doormen and Other	71,073.62	0.39%	799,269.22	0.42%
Repairs and Maintenance	437,514.20	2.39%	3,646,358.19	1.89%
Security	72,924.17	0.40%	815,394.78	0.42%
Human Resources	40,132.10	0.22%	584,904.19	0.30%
Sales and Marketing	385,346.90	2.10%	3,321,867.56	1.72%
General and Administrative	1,124,979.70	6.13%	11,192,683.74	5.81%
Excutive Offices	487,157.89	2.66%	2,205,882.55	1.15%
Total Non Food & Bev Non Operating Expenses	7,665,768.85	41.80%	72,951,701.52	37.88%
Net Operating Income or Loss	10,675,560.63	58.20%	119,633,772.55	62.12%
Non Operating Expenses				
Insurance	383,200.00	2.09%	4,982,939.71	2.59%
Management and Trademark Fees	2,275,291.91	12.41%	24,928,244.86	12.94%
Interest Expense	3,150,404.14	17.18%	38,562,614.28	20.02%
Property Taxes	325,000.00	1.77%	4,587,982.20	2.38%
Depreciation and Amortization	3,662,065.30	19.97%	40,379,253.92	20.97%
Excise and Other Taxes	-	0.00%	-	0.00%
Gain or Loss Dispos of Assets	-	0.00%	-	0.00%
Gain or Loss Other	-	0.00%	-	0.00%
Total Non Operating Expenses	9,795,961.35	53.41%	113,441,034.97	58.90%
Profit or Loss before Income Taxes	879,599.28	4.80%	6,192,737.58	3.22%
Income Taxes Federal and State	370,751.10	2.02%	2,449,685.65	1.27%
Net Profit or Loss	508,848.18	2.77%	3,743,051.93	1.94%

Fig 10:4

in the workings of the entity, that might suit my needs, but if I have a major stake, or control in a privately owed business and my life's savings depended on it, you bet, I want to know much more than the basics. Fig 10:4

Income Statement for Deacon Management Corporation
For the Month Ending December 31st, 2003

Revenues	Current Month	Percent	Year to Date	Percent
Revenue Coffee Shop Food	577,468.95	7.40%	6,125,090.72	8.26%
Revenue Room Service Food	28,025.79	0.36%	304,400.88	0.41%
Revenue Steak House Food	777,360.34	9.96%	11,170,992.89	15.06%
Revenue Fine Dining Food	1,147,424.49	14.71%	13,869,059.10	18.70%
Revenue Show Lounge Food	64,419.28	0.83%	733,614.49	0.99%
Revenue Roof Top Rest Lounge Food	1,415,656.46	18.14%	11,073,551.90	14.93%
Revenue Meeting Space Food	487,250.83	6.25%	3,131,617.87	4.22%
Revenue Total Food	4,497,606.14	57.65%	46,408,327.85	62.56%
Revenue Coffee Shop Beverage	49,345.08	0.63%	370,198.60	0.50%
Revenue Room Service Beverage	13,055.31	0.17%	69,321.91	0.09%
Revenue Steak House Beverage	43,398.31	0.56%	875,721.15	1.18%
Revenue Fine Dining Beverage	319,171.52	4.09%	1,128,859.35	1.52%
Revenue Lobby Bar Beverage	787,138.15	10.09%	7,278,759.02	9.81%
Revenue Show Lounge Beverage	24,046.24	0.31%	132,408.91	0.18%
Revenue Roof Top Rest Lounge Bev	948,648.94	12.16%	8,128,458.82	10.96%
Revenue Meeting Space Beverage	105,811.75	1.36%	575,036.88	0.78%
Revenue Total Beverages	2,290,615.30	29.36%	18,558,764.64	25.02%
Total Food and Beverage Income	6,788,221.44		64,967,092.49	
Food and Beverage Other				
Revenue Room Service Delivery Ch	5,029.31	0.06%	45,886.65	0.06%
Revenue Show Lounge Entertainment	666,710.00	8.55%	5,706,210.00	7.69%
Revenue Roof Top Bar Entertainment	128,290.05	1.64%	1,062,967.74	1.43%
Revenue Meeting Space Room Rent	202,675.00	2.60%	2,189,088.10	2.95%
Revenue Meeting Space Audio Visual	11,292.67	0.14%	208,414.64	0.20%
Total Food and Beverage Other	1,013,997.03	13.00%	9,212,567.13	12.42%
Total Revenue Food and Beverage	7,802,218.47	100.00%	74,179,659.62	100.00%
Cost of Sales				
Coffee Shop Cost of Food	236,762.77	41.00%	2,286,654.88	9.81%
Room Service Cost of Food	10,009.28	36.00%	118,530.88	0.51%
Steak House Cost of Food	279,849.72	36.00%	4,031,086.44	17.29%
Fine Dining Cost of Food	458,969.80	40.00%	5,505,001.62	23.61%
Show Lounge Cost of Food	21,258.36	33.00%	259,069.84	1.11%
Roof Top Rest Lounge Cost of Food	481,323.03	34.00%	4,116,380.71	17.65%
Meeting Space Cost of Food	121,812.71	25.00%	990,351.77	4.25%
Total Food Cost	1,610,065.67	35.80%	17,307,076.14	74.23%
Coffee Shop Cost of Beverages	17,764.23	36.00%	117,710.67	0.50%
Room Service Cost of Beverages	4,308.25	33.00%	29,370.99	0.13%
Steak House Cost of Beverages	12,585.51	29.00%	253,498.43	1.09%
Fine Dining Cost of Beverages	73,409.45	23.00%	349,941.16	1.50%
Lobby Bar Cost be Beverage	291,241.12	37.00%	2,542,278.47	10.90%
Show Lounge Cost of Beverages	5,530.64	23.00%	40,154.52	0.17%

Fig 10:5 Part 1

Income Statement for Deacon Management Corporation For the Month Ending December 31st, 2003				
Revenues	Current Month	Percent	Year to Date	Percent
Roof Top Rest Lounge Cost of Beverage	284,594.18	30.00%	2,519,598.12	10.81%
Meeting Space Cost of Beverage	22,220.47	21.00%	156,906.12	0.67%
Total Cost of Beverages	711,653.85	31.07%	6,009,458.48	25.77%
Total Cost of Sales	2,321,719.52	34.20%	23,316,534.62	35.89%
Food and Beverage Gross Profit	5,480,498.95	70.24%	50,863,125.00	68.57%
Food and Beverage Department Exp:				
Coffee Shop	216,207.95	2.77%	2,168,134.51	2.92%
Room Service	174,164.35	2.23%	1,922,835.48	2.59%
Steak House	181,186.59	2.32%	1,147,539.61	1.55%
Fine Dining	130,043.65	1.67%	1,154,175.98	1.56%
Show Lounge	44,240.33	0.57%	483,589.50	0.65%
Lobby Bar	58,234.95	0.75%	612,995.35	0.83%
Roof Top Restaurant and Bar	145,647.37	1.87%	1,287,107.09	1.74%
Meeting Space	128,731.79	1.65%	881,287.92	1.19%
Kitchen	115,984.41	1.49%	1,276,825.85	1.72%
Total Non Food and Beverage Expense	1,194,441.39	15.31%	10,934,491.29	14.74%
Food & Beverage Operating Profit or Loss	4,286,057.56	54.93%	39,928,633.71	53.83%

Fig 10:5 Part 2

Departmentalized Income Statements provides us with other options and that is what I call the summarized Food and Beverage income and expenses. That is found Fig 10:5

 Now what if you want to know how each food and beverage department performed financially as a stand-alone entity? What would you recommend if you were an outside consultant? Fig 10 6 covers the following pages.

Income Statement for Deacon Management Corporation
For the Month Ending December 31st, 2003

Revenues	Current Month	Percent	Year to Date	Percent
Revenue Coffee Shop Food	577,468.95	92.13%	6,125,090.72	94.30%
Revenue Coffee Shop Liquor	49,345.08	7.87%	370,198.60	5.70%
Total Revenue	626,814.03	100.00%	6,495,289.32	100.00%
Cost of Sales:				
Coffee Shop Cost of Food	236,762.77	41.00%	2,286,654.88	37.33%
Coffee Shop Cost of Liquor	17,764.23	36.00%	117,710.67	31.80%
Total Cost of Sales	254,527.00	77.00%	2,404,365.55	37.33%
Gross Profit Margin	372,287.03	59.39%	4,090,923.77	62.98%
Expenses				
Coffee Shop Gross Payroll	144,840.00	23.11%	1,608,100.36	24.76%
Employer Payroll Taxes	15,235.00	2.43%	168,445.03	2.59%
Coffee Shop Vacation and Sick	13,035.60	2.08%	132,050.52	2.03%
Coffee Shop Employer Medical	4,200.00	0.67%	45,600.00	0.70%
Employer Life and Disability	384.00	0.06%	4,140.00	0.06%
Coffee Shop Employer 401k	3,041.64	0.49%	30,319.76	0.47%
Employee Benefits Other	1,250.00	0.20%	1,650.00	0.03%
Cutlery Crockery and Linens	24,321.08	3.88%	24,321.08	0.37%
Coffee Stationery and Office	284.35	0.05%	3,422.83	0.05%
Coffee Shop Copy Paper	1,592.36	0.25%	14,215.87	0.22%
Coffee Copy Machine Supplies	0.00	0.00%	0.00	0.00%
Coffee Shop Managers Meals	329.28	0.05%	1,682.27	0.03%
Coffee Telephone Calls Local	0.00	0.00%	0.00	0.00%
Telephone Calls Long Distance	0.00	0.00%	0.00	0.00%
Telephone Calls Cellular	0.00	0.00%	0.00	0.00%
Coffee Non Inventory Supplies	157.05	0.03%	3,202.79	0.05%
Coffee Shop Travel	103.76	0.02%	1,466.49	0.02%
Coffee Shop Uniforms	0.00	0.00%	11,723.64	0.18%
Coffee Shop Miscellaneous	153.91	0.02%	1,615.95	0.02%
Printing and Design	0.00	0.00%	44,973.74	0.69%
Coffee Shop Signage	257.60	0.04%	5,550.10	0.09%
Decorating Expenses	2,311.27	0.37%	7,818.30	0.12%
Coffee Shop Laundy	4,396.78	0.70%	53,701.11	0.83%
Coffee Shop Dry cleaning	314.27	0.05%	4,134.67	0.06%
Coffee Shop Postage	0.00	0.00%	0.00	0.00%
Total Non Cost of Sales Expenses	216,207.95	34.49%	2,168,134.51	33.38%
Coffee Shop Profit or Loss	156,079.08	24.90%	1,922,789.26	29.60%
Revenue Room Service Food	28,025.79	60.78%	304,400.88	72.54%
Revenue Room Service Liquor	13,055.31	28.31%	69,321.91	16.52%
Total Revenue	41,081.10	89.09%	373,722.79	89.06%
Room Service Delivery Charge	5,029.31	10.91%	45,886.65	10.94%

Fig 10:6 Part 1

Income Statement for Deacon Management Corporation
For the Month Ending December 31st, 2003

Revenues	Current Month	Percent	Year to Date	Percent
Total Room Service Revenue	46,110.41	100.00%	419,609.44	100.00%
Room Service Cost of Food	10,089.28	36.00%	118,530.88	38.94%
Room Service Cost of Beverage	4,308.25	15.37%	29,370.99	9.65%
Total Cost of Sales	14,397.53	51.37%	147,901.87	38.94%
Gross Profit Margin	31,712.88	68.78%	271,707.57	64.75%
Room Service Gross Payroll	128,520.00	278.72%	1,420,233.53	338.47%
Employer Payroll Taxes	13,518.38	29.32%	153,582.63	36.60%
Vacation and Sick	11,566.80	25.09%	148,945.03	35.50%
Employer Medical	2,800.00	6.07%	40,900.00	9.75%
Employer Life and Disability	256.00	0.56%	3,720.00	0.89%
Room Service Employer 401k	2,698.92	5.85%	34,753.88	8.28%
Employee Benefits Other	550.00	1.19%	550.00	0.13%
Cutlery Crockery and Linens	8,214.87	17.82%	8,214.87	1.96%
Stationery and Office	298.57	0.65%	3,173.98	0.76%
Room Service Copy Paper	1,671.98	3.63%	17,774.25	4.24%
Copy Machine Supplies	0.00	0.00%	0.00	0.00%
Room Service Managers Meals	103.42	0.22%	1,185.82	0.28%
Telephone Calls Local	0.00	0.00%	0.00	0.00%
Telephone Calls Long Distance	0.00	0.00%	0.00	0.00%
Telephone Calls Cellular	0.00	0.00%	0.00	0.00%
Non Inventory Supplies	49.27	0.11%	1,969.15	0.47%
Room Service Travel	146.69	0.32%	1,227.92	0.29%
Room Service Uniforms	0.00	0.00%	14,289.04	3.41%
Room Service Miscellaneous	67.44	0.15%	707.99	0.17%
Room ServicPrinting and Design	0.00	0.00%	24,654.23	5.88%
Room Service Signage	622.24	1.35%	12,369.12	2.95%
Room ServiceDecorating Expense	524.26	1.14%	6,925.77	1.65%
Room Service Laundry	2,198.39	4.77%	24,629.18	5.87%
Room Service Dry cleaning	357.12	0.77%	3,029.09	0.72%
Room Service Postage	0.00	0.00%	0.00	0.00%
Total Non Cost of Sales Expenses	174,164.35	377.71%	1,922,835.48	458.24%
Room Service Profit or Loss	(142,451.47)	-2832.43%	(1,651,127.91)	-3598.28%
Steak House Food	777,360.34	94.71%	11,170,992.89	92.73%
Steak House Liquor	43,398.31	5.29%	875,721.15	7.27%
Total Revenue	820,758.65	100.00%	12,046,714.04	100.00%
Cost of Sales:				
Steak House Cost of Food	279,849.72	36.00%	4,031,086.44	36.09%
Steak House Cost of Liquor	12,585.51	29.00%	253,498.43	28.95%
Total Cost of Sales	292,435.23	65.00%	4,284,584.87	36.09%
Gross Profit Margin	528,323.42	64.37%	7,762,129.17	64.43%

Fig 10:6 Part 2

Income Statement for Deacon Management Corporation
For the Month Ending December 31st, 2003

Revenues	Current Month	Percent	Year to Date	Percent
Expenses				
Steak House Gross Payroll	65,348.00	7.96%	724,355.32	6.01%
Steak House Employer Taxes	6,873.63	0.84%	76,984.65	0.64%
Steak House Vacation and Sick	5,881.32	0.72%	60,421.91	0.50%
Steak House Employer Medical	3,500.00	0.43%	38,000.00	0.32%
Employer Life and Disbality	320.00	0.04%	3,450.00	0.03%
Steak House Employer 401k	1,372.31	0.17%	14,097.94	0.12%
Employee Benefits Other	600.00	0.07%	600.00	0.00%
Cutlery Crockery and Linens	84,210.00	10.26%	84,210.00	0.70%
Stationery and Office	312.79	0.04%	3,321.27	0.03%
Steak House Copy Paper	1,751.60	0.21%	17,134.21	0.14%
Copy Machine Supplies	0.00	0.00%	0.00	0.00%
Steak House Managers Meals	385.21	0.05%	2,295.63	0.02%
Telephone Calls Local	0.00	0.00%	0.00	0.00%
Telephone Calls Long Distance	0.00	0.00%	0.00	0.00%
Telephone Calls Cellular	0.00	0.00%	0.00	0.00%
Non Inventory Supplies	57.05	0.01%	3,605.70	0.03%
Steak House Travel	657.05	0.08%	1,742.10	0.01%
Steak House Uniforms	0.00	0.00%	29,342.25	0.24%
Steak House Miscellaneous	118.80	0.01%	1,343.89	0.01%
Steak HousePrinting and Design	0.00	0.00%	11,099.30	0.09%
Steak House Signage	131.99	0.02%	1,387.68	0.01%
Decorating Expense	2,225.37	0.27%	5,547.34	0.05%
Steak House Laundy	2,931.19	0.36%	39,134.11	0.32%
Steak House Dry cleaning	399.98	0.05%	5,352.46	0.04%
Steak House Postage	0.00	0.00%	0.00	0.00%
Entertainment Expense	4,110.30	0.50%	24,113.85	0.20%
Total Non Cost of Sales Expenses	181,186.59	22.08%	1,147,539.61	9.53%
Steak House Profit or Loss	347,136.83	42.29%	6,614,589.56	54.91%
Fine Dining Food	1,147,424.49	78.24%	13,869,059.10	92.47%
Fine Dining Liquor	319,171.52	21.76%	1,128,859.35	7.53%
Total Revenue	1,466,596.01	100.00%	14,997,918.45	100.00%
Cost of Sales:				
Fine Dining Cost of Food	458,969.80	40.00%	5,505,001.62	39.69%
Fine Dining Cost of Liquor	73,409.45	23.00%	349,941.16	31.00%
Total Cost of Sales	532,379.25	63.00%	5,854,942.78	39.69%
Gross Profit Margin	934,216.76	63.70%	9,142,975.67	60.96%
Expenses				
Fine Dining Gross Payroll	71,721.30	4.89%	773,772.04	5.16%
Employer Payroll Taxes	7,544.01	0.51%	84,242.32	0.56%
Fine Dining Vacation and Sick	6,454.92	0.44%	70,841.03	0.47%

Fig 10:6 Part 3

Income Statement for Deacon Management Corporation
For the Month Ending December 31st, 2003

Revenues	Current Month	Percent	Year to Date	Percent
Fine Dining Employer Medical	4,200.00	0.29%	49,800.00	0.33%
Employer Life and Disability	364.00	0.03%	4,524.00	0.03%
Fine Dining Employer 401k	1,506.14	0.10%	16,529.58	0.11%
Employee Benefits Other	900.00	0.06%	1,500.00	0.01%
Cutlery Crockery and Linens	16,111.09	1.10%	16,111.09	0.11%
Stationey and Office	398.09	0.03%	3,727.14	0.02%
Fine Dining Copy Paper	1,433.12	0.10%	13,406.38	0.09%
Copy Machine Supplies	0.00	0.00%	0.00	0.00%
Fine Dining Managers Meals	174.85	0.01%	958.23	0.01%
Telephone Calls Local	0.00	0.00%	0.00	0.00%
Telephone Calls Long Distance	0.00	0.00%	0.00	0.00%
Telephone Calls Cellular	0.00	0.00%	0.00	0.00%
Non Inventory Supplies	383.89	0.03%	8,980.91	0.06%
Fine Dining Travel	611.89	0.04%	2,612.34	0.02%
Fine Dining Uniforms	0.00	0.00%	9,600.60	0.06%
Fine Dining Miscellaneous	2,021.46	0.14%	3,393.42	0.02%
Printing and Design	0.00	0.00%	16,404.68	0.11%
Fine Dining Signage	47.07	0.00%	4,716.34	0.03%
Decorating Expense	3,848.21	0.26%	13,587.34	0.09%
Fine Dining Laundry	3,297.59	0.22%	39,163.84	0.26%
Fine Dining Dry cleaning	411.41	0.03%	4,439.13	0.03%
Fine Dining Postage	0.00	0.00%	0.00	0.00%
Entertainment Expense	8,594.61	0.59%	15,865.57	0.11%
Total Non Cost of Sales Expenses	130,043.65	8.87%	1,154,175.98	7.70%
Fine Dining Profit or Loss	804,173.11	54.83%	7,988,799.69	53.27%
Show Lounge Food	64,419.28	8.53%	733,614.49	11.16%
Show Lounge Liquor	24,046.24	3.18%	132,408.91	2.01%
Total Show Lounge Food & Bev	88,465.52	11.71%	866,023.40	0.13
Show Lounge Entertainment Fee	666,710.00	88.29%	5,706,210.00	86.82%
Total Revenue	755,175.52	100.00%	6,572,233.40	100.00%
Show Lounge Cost of Food	21,258.36	33.00%	259,069.84	35.31%
Show Lounge Cost of Liquor	5,530.64	23.00%	40,154.52	30.33%
Total Cost of Sales	26,789.00	56.00%	299,224.36	35.31%
Gross Profit	728,386.52	96.45%	6,273,009.04	95.45%
Show Lounge Gross Payroll	15,725.00	2.08%	174,375.24	2.65%
Employer Payroll Taxes	1,654.04	0.22%	17,942.60	0.27%
Show Lounge Vacation and Sick	516.15	0.07%	15,351.32	0.23%
Show Lounge Employer Medical	2,800.00	0.37%	33,200.00	0.51%
Empployer Life and Disability	256.00	0.03%	3,016.00	0.05%
Show Lounge Employer 401k	330.23	0.04%	3,614.03	0.05%
Employee Benefits Other	2,250.00	0.30%	2,250.00	0.03%

Fig 10:6 Part 4

Income Statement for Deacon Management Corporation
For the Month Ending December 31st, 2003

Revenues	Current Month	Percent	Year to Date	Percent
Lobby Bar Decorating Expenses	5,279.26	0.67%	14,736.66	0.20%
Lobby Bar Laundry	0.00	0.00%	0.00	0.00%
Lobby Bar Dry cleaning	0.00	0.00%	0.00	0.00%
Lobby Bar Postage	0.00	0.00%	0.00	0.00%
Total Non Cost of Sales Expenses	58,234.95	7.40%	612,995.35	8.42%
Lobby Bar Profit or Loss	437,662.08	55.60%	4,123,485.20	56.65%
Revenue Roof Top Rest and Lounge Food	1,415,656.46	56.79%	11,073,551.90	54.64%
Revenue Roof Top Rest and Lounge Bev	948,648.94	38.06%	8,128,458.82	40.11%
Total Food and Beverage	2,364,305.40	94.85%	19,202,010.72	94.75%
Entertainment Fees	128,290.05	5.15%	1,062,967.74	5.25%
Total Roof Top and Bar Revenue	2,492,595.45	100.00%	20,264,978.46	100.00%
Roof Top Rest Cost of Food	481,323.03	34.00%	4,116,380.71	37.17%
Roof Top Rest Cost of Liquor	284,594.18	30.00%	2,519,598.12	31.00%
Total Cost of Sales	765,917.21	64.00%	6,635,978.83	37.17%
Gross Profit Margin	1,726,678.24	69.27%	13,628,999.63	67.25%
Roof Top Restaurant Gross Pay	66,300.00	2.66%	790,587.77	3.90%
Roof Top Rest Employer taxes	10,790.41	0.43%	81,922.82	0.40%
Roof Top Rest Vacation & Sick	9,232.65	0.37%	70,095.95	0.35%
Roof Top Rest Employer Medical	11,200.00	0.45%	87,200.00	0.43%
Employer Life and Disability	1,024.00	0.04%	7,924.00	0.04%
Roof Top Rest Employer 401k	1,392.30	0.06%	15,077.00	0.07%
Employee Benefits Other	3,300.00	0.13%	4,515.97	0.02%
Cutlery Crockery and Linens	21,439.87	0.86%	21,439.87	0.11%
Stationery and Office	739.31	0.03%	7,859.36	0.04%
Roof Top Rest Copy Paper	1,910.83	0.08%	20,313.43	0.10%
Roof Top Copy Machine Supplies	0.00	0.00%	0.00	0.00%
Roof Top Rest Managers Meals	367.88	0.01%	1,393.84	0.01%
Telephone Calls Local	0.00	0.00%	0.00	0.00%
Telephone Calls Long Distance	0.00	0.00%	0.00	0.00%
Telephone Calls Cellular	0.00	0.00%	0.00	0.00%
Non Inventory Expenses	666.15	0.03%	4,059.56	0.02%
Roof Top Rest Travel	723.81	0.03%	2,744.02	0.01%
Roof Top Rest Uniforms	0.00	0.00%	22,579.26	0.11%
Roof Top Rest Miscellaneous	142.15	0.01%	1,554.77	0.01%
Printing and Design	0.00	0.00%	15,572.82	0.08%
Roof Top Rest Signage	55.96	0.00%	2,229.27	0.01%
Decorating Expenses	4,403.01	0.18%	19,858.25	0.10%
Roof Top Rest Laundry	4,396.78	0.18%	53,701.11	0.26%
Roof Top Rest Dry cleaning	399.98	0.02%	4,885.24	0.02%
Roof Top Rest Postage	0.00	0.00%	0.00	0.00%
Entertainment Expense	7,162.28	0.29%	51,591.95	0.25%

Fig 10:6 Part 6

Income Statement for Deacon Management Corporation
For the Month Ending December 31st, 2003

Revenues	Current Month	Percent	Year to Date	Percent
Total Non Cost of Sales Expenses	145,647.37	5.56%	1,287,107.09	6.10%
Roof Top Restaurant and Bar Profit or Loss	1,581,030.87	63.43%	12,341,892.54	60.90%
Revenue Meeting Space Food	487,250.83	60.38%	3,131,617.87	51.30%
Revenue Meeting Space Liquor	105,811.75	13.11%	575,036.88	9.42%
Revenue Meeting Space Fully Catered	0.00	0.00%	0.00	0.00%
Revenue Meeting Space Room Rental	202,675.00	25.11%	2,189,088.10	35.86%
Revenue Meeting Space Cash Bar	0.00	0.00%	0.00	0.00%
Revenue Meeting Space Audio Visual	11,292.67	1.40%	208,414.64	3.41%
Total Meeting Space Revenue	807,030.25	100.00%	6,104,157.49	100.00%
Meeting Space Cost of Food	121,812.71	25.00%	990,351.77	31.62%
Meeting Space Cost of Liquor	22,220.47	21.00%	156,906.12	27.29%
Total Cost of Sales	144,033.18	46.00%	1,147,257.89	31.62%
Gross Profit Margin	662,997.07	82.15%	4,956,899.60	81.21%
Meeting Space Gross Payroll	94,260.00	11.68%	524,523.26	8.59%
Employer Payroll Taxes	6,098.10	0.76%	50,962.20	0.83%
Meeting Space Vacation & Sick	5,217.75	0.65%	43,608.51	0.71%
Employer Medical	2,450.00	0.30%	48,050.00	0.79%
Employer Life and Sick	224.00	0.03%	4,364.00	0.07%
Meetling Space Emploer 401k	1,217.47	0.15%	10,175.34	0.17%
Employee Benefits Other	6,300.00	0.78%	7,600.00	0.12%
Stationery and Office	526.05	0.07%	5,592.24	0.09%
Meeting Space Copy Paper	2,945.87	0.37%	32,784.93	0.54%
Copy Machine Supplies	155.63	0.02%	1,900.86	0.03%
Meeting Space Managers Meals	303.42	0.04%	1,385.82	0.02%
Telephone Calls Local	1,426.65	0.18%	17,424.74	0.29%
Telephone Calls Long Distance	1,858.97	0.23%	22,704.96	0.37%
Telephone Calls Cellular	268.47	0.03%	3,279.01	0.05%
Meeting Non Inventory Supplies	267.05	0.03%	5,986.14	0.10%
Meeting Space Travel	427.06	0.05%	1,975.65	0.03%
Meeting Space Uniforms	0.00	0.00%	17,157.21	0.28%
Meeting Space Miscellanous	334.11	0.04%	1,659.05	0.03%
Printing and Design	0.00	0.00%	8,356.07	0.14%
Meeting Space Signage	52.25	0.01%	5,089.88	0.08%
Meeting Decrating Expense	0.00	0.00%	13,247.15	0.22%
Meeting Space Laundry	4,030.39	0.50%	49,226.04	0.81%
Meeting Space Dry cleaning	368.55	0.05%	4,234.86	0.07%
Meeting Space Postage	0.00	0.00%	0.00	0.00%
Total Non Cost of Sales Expenses	128,731.79	15.95%	881,287.92	14.44%
Meeting Space Profit or Loss	534,265.28	66.20%	4,075,611.68	66.77%

Fig 10:6 Part 7

214

Revenues	Current Month	Percent	Year to Date	Percent
Kitchen Gross Payroll	84,150.00	72.55%	932,581.88	73.04%
Kitchen Employer Payroll Taxes	8,851.32	7.63%	99,134.77	7.76%
Kitchen Vacation and Sick	7,573.50	6.53%	84,823.24	6.64%
Kitchen Employer Payroll Taxes	3,150.00	2.72%	37,350.00	2.93%
Employer Life and Disability	288.00	0.25%	3,393.00	0.27%
Kitchen Employer 401k	1,767.15	1.52%	19,791.77	1.55%
Employee Benefits Other	3,100.00	2.67%	3,100.00	0.24%
Stationery and Office	810.40	0.70%	8,615.00	0.67%
Kitchen Copy Paper	4,538.23	3.91%	50,244.37	3.94%
Kitchen Copy Machine Supplies	0.00	0.00%	0.00	0.00%
Kitchen Managers Meals	0.00	0.00%	0.00	0.00%
Telephone Calls Local	0.00	0.00%	0.00	0.00%
Telephone Calls Long Distance	0.00	0.00%	0.00	0.00%
Telephone Calls Cellular	0.00	0.00%	0.00	0.00%
Kitchen Non Inventory Supplies	853.40	0.74%	12,486.20	0.98%
Kitchen Travel	620.75	0.54%	1,772.65	0.14%
Kitchen Uniforms	0.00	0.00%	19,653.28	1.54%
Kicthen Miscellaneous	53.10	0.05%	843.12	0.07%
Kitchen Printing and Design	0.00	0.00%	245.00	0.02%
Kitchen Signage	0.00	0.00%	0.00	0.00%
Kitchen Decorating Expense	0.00	0.00%	0.00	0.00%
Kitchen Laundry	0.00	0.00%	0.00	0.00%
Kitchen Dry cleaning	228.56	0.20%	2,791.57	0.22%
Kitchen Postage	0.00	0.00%	0.00	0.00%
Kitchen Cooking Utensils	0.00	0.00%	0.00	0.00%
Total Kitchen Expenses	115,984.41	100.00%	1,276,825.85	100.00%

Fig 10:6 Part 8

The following ten (Fig 10:7) pages show the remaining parts of the Departmentalized Income Statement. Note how many Sub Categories there are within the groups. After that, I will list, and add a few comments to the Chart of Accounts, and the essentials in getting this right at the time of setting up the General Ledger. Fig 10:7 this is the last of in the Income Statement series.

Income Statement for Deacon Management Corporation
For the Month Ending December 31st, 2003

Revenues	Current Month	Percent	Year to Date	Percent
Rooms Corporate Individual	2,798,096.84	29.81%	59,975,413.52	56.30%
Rooms Corporate Group	30,512.00	0.33%	2,119,667.81	1.99%
Rooms Leisure Individual	3,159,100.00	33.65%	24,600,896.37	23.09%
Rooms Leisure Groups	170,277.00	1.81%	1,409,614.50	1.32%
Rooms Group Meeting	2,765,145.36	29.46%	12,911,011.33	12.12%
Rooms Airline and Travel	52,766.00	0.56%	248,176.09	0.23%
Rooms No Show	23,534.00	0.25%	1,080,433.13	1.01%
Rooms Permanent and Office	387,500.00	4.13%	4,188,750.00	3.93%
Total Room Revenue	9,386,931.20	100.00%	106,533,962.75	100.00%
Expenses				
Rooms Gross Payroll	658,067.14	55.83%	6,925,167.37	59.05%
Employer Payroll Taxes	69,218.49	5.87%	735,841.89	6.27%
Rooms Vacation and Sick	59,226.04	5.02%	629,612.31	5.37%
Rooms Employer Medical	26,625.00	2.26%	314,175.00	2.68%
Employer Life and Disability	1,775.00	0.15%	21,300.00	0.18%
Rooms Employer 401k	13,819.41	1.17%	146,909.42	1.25%
Employee Benefits Other	9,500.00	0.81%	10,300.00	0.09%
Rooms Linen	49,250.00	4.18%	49,250.00	0.42%
Rooms Cleaning Supplies	8,710.88	0.74%	34,612.92	0.30%
Regular Room Supp	67,724.13	5.75%	472,374.15	4.03%
Special Amenities and Other	38,530.50	3.27%	177,456.10	1.51%
Rooms Stationery and Office	3,270.13	0.28%	8,842.39	0.08%
Rooms Copy Paper	6,512.12	0.55%	50,606.77	0.43%
Rooms Copy Machine Supplies	0.00	0.00%	0.00	0.00%
Rooms Managers Meals	653.64	0.06%	3,308.20	0.03%
Rooms Telephone Local	0.00	0.00%	0.00	0.00%
Rooms Telephone Long Distance	0.00	0.00%	0.00	0.00%
Rooms Tellephone Cellular	0.00	0.00%	0.00	0.00%
Rooms Non Inventory Supplies	3,162.84	0.27%	44,763.60	0.38%
Rooms Tavel	696.54	0.06%	11,585.12	0.10%
Rooms Uniforms	0.00	0.00%	13,442.32	0.11%
Rooms Miscellaneous	310.40	0.03%	4,505.57	0.04%
Rooms Printing and Design	0.00	0.00%	58,051.26	0.49%
Rooms Signage	389.09	0.03%	3,206.36	0.03%
Rooms Decorating Expense	6,975.60	0.59%	48,936.83	0.42%
Rooms Laundry	11,724.76	0.99%	237,972.50	2.03%
Rooms Dry cleaning	564.27	0.05%	6,966.38	0.06%
Rooms Postage	77.82	0.01%	950.46	0.01%
Travel Agent Commission Expens	93,869.41	7.96%	1,162,790.03	9.91%
Rooms Reservation Expense	48,136.94	4.08%	555,453.40	4.74%
Total Expenses	1,178,790.15	12.56%	11,728,380.35	11.01%
Rooms Net Profit or Loss	8,208,141.05	87.44%	94,805,582.40	88.99%

Fig 10:7 Part 1

Revenues	Current Month	Percent	Year to Date	Percent
Revenue Spa General Useage	40,894.73	12.72%	211,355.39	6.80%
Revenue Spa Professional Massage	51,010.75	15.87%	301,365.84	9.70%
Revenue Spa Products	6,552.83	2.04%	112,012.44	3.61%
Revenue Spa - Sauna	42,523.31	13.23%	233,697.72	7.52%
Revenue Spa Memberships Current Month	126,167.17	39.26%	1,446,506.01	46.57%
Revenue Spa Memberships Six Months	0.00	0.00%	0.00	0.00%
Revenue Spa Memeberships One Year	0.00	0.00%	0.00	0.00%
Revenue Spa Swim Memberships Only	48,417.15	15.06%	724,435.56	23.32%
Revenue Spa Relaxing CD's	1,922.11	0.60%	13,002.74	0.42%
Revenue Spa Video Sales	3,900.77	1.21%	63,741.83	2.05%
Total Reveue Spa and Fitness	321,388.82	87.28%	3,106,117.53	93.20%
Spa and Fitness Gross Payroll	65,280.00	68.39%	723,457.46	70.19%
Employer Payroll Taxes	6,866.48	7.19%	76,915.56	7.46%
Vacation and Sick	5,875.20	6.16%	65,802.24	6.38%
Employer Medical	2,450.00	2.57%	29,050.00	2.82%
Employer Life and Disabiltiy	224.00	0.23%	2,639.00	0.26%
Spa and Fitness Employer 401k	1,370.88	1.44%	15,333.86	1.49%
Employee Benefits Other	2,100.00	2.20%	2,100.00	0.20%
Stationery and Office	952.57	1.00%	9,170.39	0.89%
Spa and Fitness Copy Paper	5,334.41	5.59%	53,364.09	5.18%
Copy Machine Supplies	51.88	0.05%	581.17	0.06%
Spa and Fitness Managers Meals	290.49	0.30%	1,337.69	0.13%
Telephone Calls Local	0.00	0.00%	0.00	0.00%
Telephone Calls Long Distance	0.00	0.00%	0.00	0.00%
Telephone Calls Cellular	0.00	0.00%	0.00	0.00%
Spa and Fitness Non Inventory	725.83	0.76%	2,719.61	0.26%
Spa and Fitness Travel	429.21	0.45%	858.77	0.08%
Spa and Fitness Uniforms	0.00	0.00%	8,338.20	0.81%
Spa and Fitness Miscellaneous	645.65	0.68%	2,830.11	0.27%
Printing and Design	0.00	0.00%	2,155.68	0.21%
Spa and Fitness Signage	65.68	0.07%	478.42	0.05%
Spa and Fitness Decorating Exp	0.00	0.00%	0.00	0.00%
Spa and Fitness Laundry	2,564.79	2.69%	31,325.68	3.04%
Spa and Fitness Dry cleaning	157.13	0.16%	1,474.95	0.14%
Spa and Fitness Postage	69.17	0.07%	844.82	0.08%
Total Expenses Spa and Fitness	95,453.37	29.70%	1,030,775.70	33.19%
Spa and Fitness Net Profit or Loss	225,935.45	57.58%	2,075,341.83	60.01%
Revenue Local Telephone Calls	61,369.65	29.30%	651,148.56	28.63%
Revenue Long Distance Calls	138,680.82	66.22%	1,470,361.61	64.66%
Revenue Internet Connections Fee	5,522.09	2.64%	111,537.39	4.90%
Revenue Eight Hundred Call Toll	3,865.46	1.85%	41,006.18	1.80%
Total Rooms Phone Revenue	209,438.02	100.00%	2,274,053.74	100.00%

Fig 10:7 Part 2

Income Statement for Deacon Management Corporation
For the Month Ending December 31st, 2003

Revenues	Current Month	Percent	Year to Date	Percent
Telephone Gross Payroll	6,072.00	10.00%	585,094.51	48.28%
Employer Payroll Taxes	638.68	1.05%	71,131.56	5.87%
Telephone Vacation and Sick	3,378.24	5.56%	63,694.43	5.26%
Telephone Employer Medical	0.00	0.00%	29,750.00	2.45%
Employer Life and Disability	0.00	0.00%	2,703.00	0.22%
Telephone Employer 401k	127.52	0.21%	14,221.29	1.17%
Employee Benefits Other	1,000.00	1.65%	1,000.00	0.08%
Stationery and Office	426.53	0.70%	4,534.77	0.37%
Telephone Copy Paper	56.87	0.09%	904.58	0.07%
Copy Machine Supplies	25.94	0.04%	316.82	0.03%
Telephone Managers Meals	112.93	0.19%	248.23	0.02%
Telephone Calls Local	19,387.95	31.92%	161,667.12	13.34%
Telephone Calls Long Distance	25,263.08	41.60%	206,990.44	17.08%
Telephone Calls Cellular	3,648.46	6.01%	36,485.34	3.01%
Non Inventory Supplies	211.81	0.35%	641.19	0.05%
Telephone Travel	70.26	0.12%	328.88	0.03%
Telephone Uniform	0.00	0.00%	16,167.26	1.33%
Telephone Miscellaneous	28.43	0.05%	239.93	0.02%
Printing and Design	0.00	0.00%	9,309.62	0.77%
Telephone Signage	86.37	0.14%	1,912.36	0.16%
Telephone Decorating Expense	0.00	0.00%	0.00	0.00%
Telephone Laundry	0.00	0.00%	0.00	0.00%
Telephone Dry cleaning	199.99	0.33%	4,515.76	0.37%
Telephone Postage	0.00	0.00%	0.00	0.00%
Total Telephone Department Expenses	60,735.06	29.00%	1,211,857.09	53.29%
Telephone Department Net Profit or Loss	148,702.96	71.00%	1,062,196.65	46.71%
Revenue Business Center Color Copies	826.31	1.43%	12,919.01	2.99%
Revenue Business Center Regular Copies	621.24	1.08%	16,526.13	3.83%
Revenue Business Center Work Stations	51,769.59	89.61%	347,354.27	80.44%
Revenue Business Center Phone Calls	414.16	0.72%	9,641.77	2.23%
Revenue Business Center Internet Conn	4,141.57	7.17%	45,373.87	10.51%
Toal Business Center Income	57,772.87	100.00%	431,815.05	100.00%
Business Center Gross Payroll	41,976.00	69.89%	545,510.06	69.86%
Employer Payroll Taxes	4,415.24	7.35%	58,064.65	7.44%
Vacation and Sick	3,777.84	6.29%	49,682.16	6.36%
Employer Medical	1,400.00	2.33%	16,600.00	2.13%
Employer Life and Disability	128.00	0.21%	1,508.00	0.19%
Business Center Employer 401k	881.50	1.47%	13,120.82	1.68%
Employee Benefits Other	750.00	1.25%	1,350.00	0.17%
Stationery and Office	523.30	0.87%	6,034.37	0.77%
Business Center Copy Paper	1,194.27	1.99%	18,050.58	2.31%
Copy Machine Supplies	285.33	0.48%	3,537.39	0.45%

Fig 10:7 Part 3

Income Statement for Deacon Management Corporation
For the Month Ending December 31st, 2003

Revenues	Current Month	Percent	Year to Date	Percent
Fine Dining Employer Medical	4,200.00	0.29%	49,800.00	0.33%
Employer Life and Disability	384.00	0.03%	4,524.00	0.03%
Fine Dining Employer 401k	1,506.14	0.10%	16,529.58	0.11%
Employee Benefits Other	900.00	0.06%	1,500.00	0.01%
Cutlery Crockery and Linens	16,111.09	1.10%	16,111.09	0.11%
Stationey and Office	398.09	0.03%	3,727.14	0.02%
Fine Dining Copy Paper	1,433.12	0.10%	13,406.38	0.09%
Copy Machine Supplies	0.00	0.00%	0.00	0.00%
Fine Dining Managers Meals	174.85	0.01%	958.23	0.01%
Telephone Calls Local	0.00	0.00%	0.00	0.00%
Telephone Calls Long Distance	0.00	0.00%	0.00	0.00%
Telephone Calls Cellular	0.00	0.00%	0.00	0.00%
Non Inventory Supplies	383.89	0.03%	8,980.91	0.06%
Fine Dining Travel	611.89	0.04%	2,612.34	0.02%
Fine Dining Uniforms	0.00	0.00%	9,600.60	0.06%
Fine Dining Miscellaneous	2,021.46	0.14%	3,393.42	0.02%
Printing and Design	0.00	0.00%	16,404.68	0.11%
Fine Dining Signage	47.07	0.00%	4,716.34	0.03%
Decorating Expense	3,848.21	0.26%	13,587.34	0.09%
Fine Dining Laundry	3,297.59	0.22%	39,163.84	0.26%
Fine Dining Dry cleaning	411.41	0.03%	4,439.13	0.03%
Fine Dining Postage	0.00	0.00%	0.00	0.00%
Entertainment Expense	8,594.61	0.59%	15,865.57	0.11%
Total Non Cost of Sales Expenses	130,043.65	8.87%	1,154,175.98	7.70%
Fine Dining Profit or Loss	804,173.11	54.83%	7,988,799.09	53.27%
Show Lounge Food	64,419.28	8.53%	733,614.49	11.16%
Show Lounge Liquor	24,046.24	3.10%	132,408.91	2.01%
Total Show Lounge Food & Bev	88,465.52	11.71%	866,023.40	0.13
Show Lounge Entertainment Fee	666,710.00	88.29%	5,706,210.00	86.82%
Total Revenue	755,175.52	100.00%	6,572,233.40	100.00%
Show Lounge Cost of Food	21,258.36	33.00%	259,069.84	35.31%
Show Lounge Cost of Liquor	5,530.64	23.00%	40,154.52	30.33%
Total Cost of Sales	26,789.00	56.00%	299,224.36	35.31%
Gross Profit	728,386.52	96.45%	6,273,009.04	95.45%
Show Lounge Gross Payroll	15,725.00	2.08%	174,375.24	2.65%
Employer Payroll Taxes	1,654.04	0.22%	17,942.60	0.27%
Show Lounge Vacation and Sick	516.15	0.07%	15,351.32	0.23%
Show Lounge Employer Medical	2,800.00	0.37%	33,200.00	0.51%
Empployer Life and Disability	256.00	0.03%	3,016.00	0.05%
Show Lounge Employer 401k	330.23	0.04%	3,614.03	0.05%
Employee Benefits Other	2,250.00	0.30%	2,250.00	0.03%

Fig 10:7 Part 4

Income Statement for Deacon Management Corporation
For the Month Ending December 31st, 2003

Revenues	Current Month	Percent	Year to Date	Percent
Front of House Copy Paper	7,421.75	5.48%	22,114.15	1.60%
Copy Machine Supplies	103.76	0.08%	1,267.26	0.09%
Front of House Managers Meals	293.91	0.22%	2,322.52	0.17%
Telephone Calls Local	0.00	0.00%	0.00	0.00%
Telephone Calls Long Distance	0.00	0.00%	0.00	0.00%
Telephone Calls Cellular	0.00	0.00%	0.00	0.00%
Non Inventory Supplies	784.73	0.58%	6,980.93	0.50%
Front of House Travel	523.28	0.39%	2,370.12	0.17%
Front of House Uniforms	0.00	0.00%	24,165.46	1.75%
Front of House Miscellaneous	17.28	0.01%	898.26	0.06%
Printing and Design	0.00	0.00%	6,555.23	0.47%
Front of House Signage	95.52	0.07%	9,926.66	0.72%
Decorating Expenses	334.50	0.25%	11,890.71	0.86%
Front of House Laundry	0.00	0.00%	0.00	0.00%
Front of House Dry cleaning	285.70	0.21%	3,489.46	0.25%
Front of House Postage	0.00	0.00%	0.00	0.00%
Total Expenses Front of the House	135,443.08	100.00%	1,382,459.23	100.00%
Doormen & Other Gross Payroll	54,468.00	76.64%	603,044.80	75.45%
Employer Payroll Taxes	5,729.22	8.06%	64,158.23	8.03%
Doormen Vacation and Sick	4,902.12	6.90%	54,903.74	6.87%
Employer Medical	2,450.00	3.45%	30,800.00	3.85%
Employer Life and Disability	224.00	0.32%	2,799.00	0.35%
Doormen & Other Employer 401k	1,113.83	1.57%	12,780.88	1.60%
Employee Benefits Other	600.00	0.84%	600.00	0.08%
Non Inventory Supplies	612.97	0.86%	1,257.93	0.16%
Doormen & Other Travel	87.18	0.12%	483.17	0.06%
Doormen & Other Uniforms	0.00	0.00%	17,032.80	2.13%
Doormen & Other Miscellaneous	298.30	0.42%	2,636.22	0.33%
Printing and Design	0.00	0.00%	252.80	0.03%
Doormen & Other Signage	110.66	0.16%	684.81	0.09%
Decorating Expenses	134.50	0.19%	3,647.48	0.46%
Doormen & Other Laundy	0.00	0.00%	0.00	0.00%
Doormen & Other Dry cleaning	342.84	0.48%	4,187.36	0.52%
Doormen & Other Postage	0.00	0.00%	0.00	0.00%
Total Expenses Doormen and Other	71,073.62	100.00%	799,269.22	100.00%
Repairs Maintenance Gross Pay	89,760.00	20.52%	994,754.04	27.28%
Employer Payroll Taxrd	9,441.41	2.16%	105,743.71	2.90%
Vacation and Sick	8,078.40	1.85%	90,477.90	2.48%
Employer Medical	4,200.00	0.96%	49,800.00	1.37%
Employer Life and Disability	384.00	0.09%	4,524.00	0.12%
Repairs MaintenanEmployer 401k	1,011.49	0.23%	18,524.92	0.51%
Employee Benefits Other	1,960.00	0.45%	2,860.00	0.08%
Utilities - Heating	62,227.51	14.22%	627,031.99	17.20%
Utilities - Electricity	42,602.04	9.74%	752,934.40	20.65%

Fig 10:7 Part 5

Income Statement for Deacon Management Corporation
For the Month Ending December 31st, 2003

Revenues	Current Month	Percent	Year to Date	Percent
Utilities - Water	56,482.78	12.91%	336,313.79	9.22%
Repairs Maintenance Building	76,847.74	17.56%	269,102.69	7.38%
Repairs Maintenance Equipment	40,108.64	9.17%	167,965.46	4.61%
Repairs Maintenance Electical	38,739.10	8.85%	135,136.62	3.71%
Stationery and Office	299.05	0.07%	3,063.47	0.08%
Repairs Maintenance Copy Paper	0.00	0.00%	5,939.56	0.16%
Copy Machine Supplies	129.70	0.03%	1,584.07	0.04%
Managers Meals	255.13	0.06%	2,179.41	0.06%
Telephone Calls Local	1,426.65	0.33%	17,424.74	0.48%
Telephone Calls Long Distance	1,858.97	0.42%	22,704.96	0.62%
Telephone Calls Cellular	268.47	0.06%	3,279.01	0.09%
Telephone Calls Local	0.00	0.00%	1,076.24	0.03%
Repairs Maintenance Travel	337.18	0.08%	1,902.91	0.05%
Repairs Maintenance Uniforms	0.00	0.00%	25,696.57	0.70%
Repairs Maintenance Miscellane	753.10	0.17%	2,105.37	0.06%
Printing and Design	0.00	0.00%	45.00	0.00%
Repairs Maintenance Signage	0.00	0.00%	0.00	0.00%
Repairs Maintenance Decorating	0.00	0.00%	0.00	0.00%
Repairs Maintenance Laundry	0.00	0.00%	0.00	0.00%
Dry cleaning	342.84	0.08%	4,187.36	0.11%
Repairs Maintenance Postage	0.00	0.00%	0.00	0.00%
Repairs Maintenance Building	0.00	0.00%	0.00	0.00%
Repairs Maintenance Equipment	0.00	0.00%	0.00	0.00%
Repairs Maintenance Electrical	0.00	0.00%	0.00	0.00%
Total Repairs and Maintennce	437,514.20	100.00%	3,646,358.19	100.00%
Security Gross Payroll	54,400.00	74.60%	602,919.02	73.94%
Employer Payroll Taxes	5,722.06	7.85%	64,087.11	7.86%
Security Vacation and Sick	4,896.00	6.71%	54,655.20	6.70%
Security Employer Medical	1,750.00	2.40%	20,750.00	2.54%
Employer Life and Disability	160.00	0.22%	1,885.00	0.23%
Security Employer 401k	1,142.40	1.57%	12,979.70	1.59%
Employee Benefits Other	1,440.00	1.97%	1,440.00	0.18%
Security Stationery and Office	142.18	0.19%	2,036.58	0.25%
Security Copy Paper	42.65	0.06%	1,412.07	0.17%
Copy Machine Supplies	77.82	0.11%	950.46	0.12%
Security Managers Meals	377.57	0.52%	1,189.36	0.15%
Telephone Calls Local	855.99	1.17%	10,454.84	1.28%
Telephone Calls Long Distance	1,115.38	1.53%	11,328.41	1.39%
Telephone Calls Cellular	161.08	0.22%	1,967.40	0.24%
Security Non Inventory Expense	140.15	0.19%	1,947.79	0.24%
Security Travel	37.78	0.05%	742.16	0.09%
Security Uniforms	0.00	0.00%	17,887.53	2.19%
Security Miscellaneous	265.75	0.36%	2,000.39	0.25%
Security Printing and Design	0.00	0.00%	56.71	0.01%
Security Signage	0.00	0.00%	0.00	0.00%
Security Decorating Expense	0.00	0.00%	0.00	0.00%

Fig 10:7 Part 6

Income Statement for Deacon Management Corporation
For the Month Ending December 31st, 2003

Revenues	Current Month	Percent	Year to Date	Percent
Security Laundry	0.00	0.00%	0.00	0.00%
Security Dry cleaning	171.42	0.24%	4,388.23	0.54%
Security Postage	25.94	0.04%	316.82	0.04%
Outside Security Contracts	0.00	0.00%	0.00	0.00%
Total Security	72,924.17	100.00%	815,394.78	100.00%
Human Resources Gross Payroll	24,150.00	60.18%	261,711.39	44.74%
Employer Payroll Taxes	2,540.21	6.33%	27,816.21	4.76%
Vacation and Sick	2,173.50	5.42%	23,800.50	4.07%
Human ResoucesEmployer Medical	1,750.00	4.36%	20,750.00	3.55%
Employer Life and Disability	160.00	0.40%	1,885.00	0.32%
Human Resources Employer 401k	507.15	1.26%	5,553.45	0.95%
Employee Benefits Other	2,100.00	5.23%	4,583.24	0.78%
Stationery and Office	675.31	1.68%	1,662.68	0.28%
Human Resources Copy Paper	579.62	1.44%	2,593.59	0.44%
Copy Machine Supplies	181.57	0.45%	2,034.21	0.35%
Human Resouces Managers Meals	390.49	0.97%	2,505.35	0.43%
Telephone Calls Local	1,141.32	2.84%	12,809.15	2.19%
Telephone Calls Long Distance	1,487.18	3.71%	18,163.96	3.11%
Telephone Calls Cellular	214.78	0.54%	2,623.24	0.45%
Human Resouces Non Inventory	663.06	1.65%	2,837.33	0.49%
Human Resources Laundry	0.00	0.00%	0.00	0.00%
Human Resources Dry cleaning	205.70	0.51%	2,749.66	0.47%
Human Resouces Postage	95.11	0.24%	1,162.03	0.20%
Human Resources Staff Training	0.00	0.00%	55,220.00	9.44%
Staff Advertising	1,117.10	2.78%	134,443.20	22.99%
Human Resources Staffing Other	0.00	0.00%	0.00	0.00%
Total Human Resouces	40,132.10	100.00%	584,904.19	100.00%
Sales and Marketing Gross Pay	54,403.85	14.12%	578,080.59	17.40%
Employer Payroll Taxes	5,722.47	1.49%	61,454.34	1.85%
Vacation and Sick	4,896.35	1.27%	52,582.48	1.58%
Employer Medical	2,800.00	0.73%	33,200.00	1.00%
Employer Life and Disability	256.00	0.07%	3,016.00	0.09%
Employer 401k	1,142.47	0.30%	12,269.67	0.37%
Employee Beneifts Other	1,800.00	0.47%	1,800.00	0.05%
Stationery and Office	2,639.76	0.69%	8,635.52	0.26%
Sales and Marketing Copy Paper	1,919.44	0.50%	19,853.99	0.60%
Copy Machine Supplies	651.07	0.17%	7,477.34	0.23%
Managers Meals	229.28	0.06%	1,708.51	0.05%
Telephone Calls Local	2,853.30	0.74%	35,507.59	1.07%
Telephone Calls Long Distance	3,717.94	0.96%	47,891.35	1.44%
Telephone Calls Cellular	536.94	0.14%	6,558.84	0.20%
Non Inventory Supplies	0.00	0.00%	3,494.38	0.11%
Sales and Marketing Travel	0.00	0.00%	207,985.72	6.26%
Sales and Marketing Uniforms	0.00	0.00%	944.31	0.03%

Fig 10:7 Part 7

Income Statement for Deacon Management Corporation
For the Month Ending December 31st, 2003

Revenues	Current Month	Percent	Year to Date	Percent
Sales and Marketing Miscellane	1,138.91	0.30%	3,353.16	0.10%
Printing and Design	0.00	0.00%	1,704.26	0.05%
Sales and Marketing Signage	0.00	0.00%	0.00	0.00%
Sales and Marketing Decorating	0.00	0.00%	0.00	0.00%
Sales and Marketing Laundry	0.00	0.00%	0.00	0.00%
Sales and Marketing Dry cleani	131.42	0.03%	1,908.48	0.06%
Sales and Marketing Postage	216.16	0.06%	2,640.12	0.08%
Sales and Promtion Materials	25,000.00	6.49%	185,000.00	5.57%
Gifts and Giveaways	26,591.13	6.90%	174,802.62	5.26%
Trade Show Promotions	13,809.40	3.58%	333,059.31	10.03%
Advertising Contract Print	71,240.28	18.49%	294,155.74	8.86%
Advertising Contract Media	65,563.47	17.01%	351,907.98	10.59%
Entertaining Client	98,087.26	25.45%	890,875.26	26.82%
Total Sales and Marketing	385,346.90	100.00%	3,321,867.56	100.00%
Accounting Gross Pay	40,603.85	3.61%	431,345.41	3.85%
Employer Payroll Taxes	4,270.92	0.38%	45,566.03	0.41%
Accounting Vacation and Sick	3,654.35	0.32%	39,721.13	0.35%
Accounting Employer Medical	2,450.00	0.22%	28,573.35	0.26%
Employer Life and Disability	224.00	0.02%	2,639.00	0.02%
Accounting Employer 401k	852.67	0.08%	9,649.10	0.09%
Employee Benefits Other	1,250.00	0.11%	3,150.00	0.03%
Stationery and Office	4,682.44	0.42%	11,255.29	0.10%
Accounting Copy Paper	3,587.55	0.32%	27,568.50	0.25%
Copy Machine Supplies	622.54	0.06%	13,292.73	0.12%
Accounting Managers Meals	432.70	0.04%	2,704.67	0.02%
Telephone Calls Local	1,997.33	0.18%	24,394.66	0.22%
Telephone Calls Long Distance	2,722.55	0.24%	26,974.28	0.24%
Telephone Calls Cellular	375.86	0.03%	4,590.63	0.04%
Accounting Non Inventory Exp	420.75	0.04%	5,932.08	0.05%
Accounting Travel	0.00	0.00%	65,485.49	0.59%
Accounting Uniform	0.00	0.00%	160.72	0.00%
Accounting Miscellaneous	1,109.81	0.10%	3,045.53	0.03%
Accounting Printing and Design	0.00	0.00%	2,633.24	0.02%
Accounting Signage	0.00	0.00%	0.00	0.00%
Accounting Decorating Exp	0.00	0.00%	0.00	0.00%
Accounting Laundry	0.00	0.00%	0.00	0.00%
Accounting Dry cleaning	0.00	0.00%	6,426.97	0.06%
Accounting Postage	190.22	0.02%	2,323.31	0.02%
Entertaining Client and House	1,957.82	0.17%	70,966.57	0.63%
Licenses and Permits	11,469.88	1.02%	18,207.88	0.16%
Penalties and Fines	0.00	0.00%	3,643.44	0.03%
Software Expense	14,490.25	1.29%	37,128.61	0.33%
Software Licenses	7,000.00	0.62%	85,426.00	0.76%
Server Maintenance Contracts	4,000.00	0.36%	30,800.00	0.28%
Postage Machine Monthly Rental	587.94	0.05%	6,968.01	0.06%
Copy Machine Maintenance Contr	0.00	0.00%	0.00	0.00%

Fig 10:7 Page 8

223

Income Statement for Deacon Management Corporation
For the Month Ending December 31st, 2003

Revenues	Current Month	Percent	Year to Date	Percent
Outside Contract Cleaners	18,000.00	1.60%	167,000.00	1.49%
Bad Debt Expense	182,694.78	16.24%	3,433,201.47	30.67%
Outside Collection Agency Fees	29,495.60	2.62%	191,533.63	1.71%
Credit Card Commission Expense	617,161.36	54.86%	4,510,584.67	40.30%
Payroll Processing Fee	3,157.82	0.28%	14,606.84	0.13%
Bank Fees	425.00	0.04%	2,006.57	0.02%
Cashier over and Short	1,978.66	0.18%	15,986.01	0.14%
Professional Fees Legal	139,422.66	12.39%	1,378,271.59	12.31%
Proffesional Fees- Auditors	18,238.78	1.62%	225,444.26	2.01%
Professional Fees Consulting	4,154.65	0.37%	202,642.91	1.81%
Insurance Workers Compensation	1,296.96	0.12%	40,830.16	0.36%
Total General and Administrative	1,124,979.70	100.00%	11,192,683.74	100.00%
Executive Office Gross Payroll	404,723.18	83.08%	1,324,350.63	60.04%
Employer Payroll Taxes	13,749.22	2.82%	111,619.85	5.06%
Vacation and Sick	8,598.46	1.77%	92,339.97	4.19%
Employer Medical	1,750.00	0.36%	19,000.00	0.86%
Employer Life and Disability	160.00	0.03%	1,725.00	0.08%
Executive Office Employer 401k	9,710.32	1.99%	29,249.95	1.33%
Employee Benefits Other	0.00	0.00%	0.00	0.00%
Stationery and Office	1,255.92	0.26%	6,042.60	0.27%
Executive Office Copy Paper	1,433.12	0.29%	16,235.06	0.74%
Copy Machine Supplies	308.67	0.06%	12,120.16	0.55%
Executive Managers Meals	319.70	0.07%	1,468.57	0.07%
Telephone Calls Local	3,994.62	0.82%	48,789.25	2.21%
Telephone Calls Long Distance	5,205.11	1.07%	60,995.69	2.77%
Telephone Calls Cellular	751.73	0.15%	9,181.26	0.42%
Non Inventory Supplies	0.00	0.00%	2,702.01	0.12%
Executive Offices Travel	0.00	0.00%	180,420.73	8.18%
Executive Offices Uniforms	0.00	0.00%	720.87	0.03%
Executive Offices Miscellaneou	0.00	0.00%	1,088.77	0.05%
Printing and Design	0.00	0.00%	32.97	0.00%
Executive Offices Signage	0.00	0.00%	0.00	0.00%
Executive Offices Decorating	0.00	0.00%	0.00	0.00%
Executive Offices Laundry	0.00	0.00%	0.00	0.00%
Executive Offices Dry cleaning	131.42	0.03%	835.11	0.04%
Executive Offices Postage	129.70	0.03%	1,584.06	0.07%
Entertaining-Client and House	34,936.72	7.17%	285,380.04	12.94%
Total Ececutive Office Expenses	487,157.89	100.00%	2,205,882.55	100.00%
Net Operating Income Exc. Food & Beverage	6,389,503.07		79,705,138.84	
Insurance - Fire	90,000.00	0.89%	1,170,000.00	1.01%
Insurance - General	120,000.00	1.18%	1,163,333.00	1.00%
Insurance - Business	23,200.00	0.23%	229,466.00	0.20%
Insurance - Terror	150,000.00	1.48%	2,420,140.71	2.09%

Fig 10:7 Page 9

224

Management Fee Minimum	112,500.00	1.11%	1,277,500.00	1.10%
Management Fee Additional	1,142,818.01	11.24%	12,194,723.50	10.52%
Trademark and Other	1,019,973.90	10.03%	11,456,021.36	9.89%
Depreciation Expense	3,662,065.30	36.02%	40,379,253.92	34.84%
Interest Expense Short Term	3,150,404.14	30.99%	38,562,614.28	33.27%
Interest Expense Long Term	0.00	0.00%	0.00	0.00%
Interest Pref Stock 5%	0.00	0.00%	0.00	0.00%
Interest Pref Stock 7%	0.00	0.00%	0.00	0.00%
Interest Pref Stock 9%	0.00	0.00%	0.00	0.00%
Taxes - Property	325,000.00	3.20%	4,587,982.20	3.96%
Taxes - Income Tax Federal	273,995.18	2.70%	1,798,725.57	1.55%
Taxes Income State and Local	96,755.92	0.95%	650,960.08	0.56%
Taxes - Excise and Use taxes	0.00	0.00%	0.00	0.00%
Gain or Loss Dispos of Assets	0.00	0.00%	0.00	0.00%
Gain or Loss Other	0.00	0.00%	0.00	0.00%
Total Non Operating Expenses	10,166,712.45	100.00%	115,890,720.62	100.00%

Fig 10:7 Part 10

 This quantity of detail isn't for everybody. Some entities can't support it. I have said it in practice, and I will say it again. Entities setting up the General Ledger and Subsidiary Ledgers initially are well advised to spend eighty percent of the time design phase. Too many entities of all sizes designed the General Ledger for today only!

If there are more then one departments utilizing, for example, Stationery and Office and one department is allocated Account Number 30105, for the other department try keeping the last two or three numbers the same, such as 40105.

Try characterizing or grouping expenses together within categories. It's frustrating locating Long Distance Phone, Cell Phone, Internet connections and calls all over the place. The next fifteen pages list the Chart of Accounts for the hotel project for this book.

Deacon Management Corporation
Chart of Accounts

Account ID	Account Description	Active ?	Account Type
10010	Cash on Hand	Yes	Cash
10101	Cash Operating Account	Yes	Cash
10102	Cash - Payroll Account	Yes	Cash
10103	Cash Certificate of Deposits	Yes	Cash
10200	Rooms In House Ledger	Yes	Accounts Receivable
10201	A/R House Expenses	Yes	Accounts Receivable
10202	A/R Corporate Accounts	Yes	Accounts Receivable
10203	Accounts Receivable	Yes	Accounts Receivable
10204	A/R Diners Club	Yes	Accounts Receivable
10205	A/R Discover	Yes	Accounts Receivable
10206	A/R Mastercard and Visa	Yes	Accounts Receivable
10207	A/R Space Rental & Garage Inc	Yes	Accounts Receivable
10208	A/R Other	Yes	Accounts Receivable
10209	Reserve for Bad Debts	Yes	Accounts Receivable
10301	Prepayments & Security Deposit	Yes	Other Current Assets
10302	Prepay-Sales & Promotion Mat	Yes	Other Current Assets
10303	Prepay-Insurance Fire	Yes	Other Current Assets
10304	Prepay-Insurance General	Yes	Other Current Assets
10305	Prepay-Insurance Other	Yes	Other Current Assets
10306	Prepay-Insurance Terror	Yes	Other Current Assets
10307	Prepay-Software Licenses	Yes	Other Current Assets
10308	Prepay-Server Maint Contracts	Yes	Other Current Assets
10309	Prepay-Postage Machine Rental	Yes	Other Current Assets
10310	Prepay-Contract Cleaners	Yes	Other Current Assets
10311	Security Dep Sales Tax	Yes	Other Current Assets
10312	Security Dep - Water and Power	Yes	Other Current Assets
10313	Security Dep - Telephone	Yes	Other Current Assets
10314	Security Dep - Food Liquor Ven	Yes	Other Current Assets
10401	Furniture Fittings & Equipment	Yes	Fixed Assets
10402	Accumulated Depreciation	Yes	Accumulated Depreciation
10500	Org Cost & Pre Opening Exp	Yes	Other Assets
10501	Land and Buildings	Yes	Other Assets
10502	Accumulated Depreciation	Yes	Accumulated Depreciation
10602	Cleaning Supplies	Yes	Inventory
10603	Regular Room Supp	Yes	Inventory
10604	Other Room Supplies	Yes	Inventory
10605	Food Inventory	Yes	Inventory
10606	Liquor and Soft Drinks	Yes	Inventory
10607	Statonery Office and Other	Yes	Inventory
10608	Inventory - Other	Yes	Inventory
15100	Accounts Payable Trade	Yes	Accounts Payable
15101	Payables - Affiliates	Yes	Accounts Payable
15102	Taxes Payable Sales and Use	Yes	Other Current Liabilities
15103	Taxes - Income Federal & State	Yes	Other Current Liabilities
15104	Interest Payable	Yes	Other Current Liabilities
15105	Commissions Payable	Yes	Other Current Liabilities
15106	Accrued Expense Payable	Yes	Other Current Liabilities
15107	Spa Memberships	Yes	Other Current Liabilities
15108	Deposits - Customers Rooms	Yes	Other Current Liabilities

Deacon Management Corporation
Chart of Accounts

Account ID	Account Description	Active ?	Account Type
15109	Deposits - Customers Other	Yes	Other Current Liabilities
15110	Security Deposits-Show Case	Yes	Other Current Liabilities
15111	Security Deposits-Lobby Shop	Yes	Other Current Liabilities
15112	Security Deposits-Starbucks	Yes	Other Current Liabilities
15113	Security Deposits-Amex Office	Yes	Other Current Liabilities
15114	Security Deposits-Garage	Yes	Other Current Liabilities
15201	Payroll Signed Gratuities	Yes	Other Current Liabilities
15202	Medical Insurance Payable	Yes	Other Current Liabilities
15203	Life and Disability Insurance	Yes	Other Current Liabilities
15204	401k Contributions Payable	Yes	Other Current Liabilities
15205	Payroll Tax & Emp Ded - State	Yes	Other Current Liabilities
15206	Payroll Tax & Emp Ded - Fedl	Yes	Other Current Liabilities
15207	Payroll Net Payroll Payable	Yes	Other Current Liabilities
15301	Accrued Vacation Personal Sick	Yes	Other Current Liabilities
26101	Mortgage Payable	Yes	Long Term Liabilities
26102	Construction Loan	Yes	Long Term Liabilities
26103	Bond Issue 30 year Coupon 7%	Yes	Long Term Liabilities
26201	Preferred Stock 7% Interest	Yes	Equity-doesn't close
26202	Preferred Stock 5% Interest	Yes	Equity-doesn't close
26203	Preferred Stock 9% Interest	Yes	Equity-doesn't close
26502	Common Stock $1.00 Par Value	Yes	Equity-doesn't close
26503	Additional Paid in Capital	Yes	Equity-doesn't close
26504	Retained Earnings	Yes	Equity-Retained Earnings
26505	Treasury Stock	Yes	Equity-doesn't close
26506	Dividends Paid	Yes	Equity-doesn't close
30102	Rooms Gross Payroll	Yes	Expenses
30103	Employer Payroll Taxes	Yes	Expenses
30104	Rooms Vacation and Sick	Yes	Expenses
30105	Rooms Employer Medical	Yes	Expenses
30106	Employer Life and Disability	Yes	Expenses
30107	Rooms Employer 401k	Yes	Expenses
30108	Employee Benefits Other	Yes	Expenses
30109	Towels, Sheets and Linens	Yes	Expenses
30110	Rooms Cleaning Supplies	Yes	Expenses
30111	Regular Room Supp	Yes	Expenses
30112	Special Amenities and Other	Yes	Expenses
30115	Rooms Stationery and Office	Yes	Expenses
30116	Rooms Copy Paper	Yes	Expenses
30117	Rooms Copy Machine Supplies	Yes	Expenses
30118	Rooms Managers Meals	Yes	Expenses
30119	Rooms Telephone Local	Yes	Expenses
30120	Rooms Telephone Long Distance	Yes	Expenses
30121	Rooms Tellephone Cellular	Yes	Expenses
30122	Rooms Non Inventory Supplies	Yes	Expenses
30123	Rooms Tavel	Yes	Expenses
30124	Rooms Uniforms	Yes	Expenses
30125	Rooms Miscellaneous	Yes	Expenses
30126	Rooms Printing and Design	Yes	Expenses
30127	Rooms Signage	Yes	Expenses
30128	Rooms Decorating Expense	Yes	Expenses

Deacon Management Corporation
Chart of Accounts

Account ID	Account Description	Active ?	Account Type
30129	Rooms Laundry	Yes	Expenses
30130	Rooms Dry cleaning	Yes	Expenses
30131	Rooms Postage	Yes	Expenses
30132	Travel Agent Commission Expens	Yes	Expenses
30133	Rooms Reservation Expense	Yes	Expenses
30200	Coffee Shop Cost of Food	Yes	Cost of Sales
30201	Coffee Shop Cost of Liquor	Yes	Cost of Sales
30202	Coffee Shop Gross Payroll	Yes	Expenses
30203	Employer Payroll Taxes	Yes	Expenses
30204	Coffee Shop Vacation and Sick	Yes	Expenses
30205	Coffee Shop Employer Medical	Yes	Expenses
30206	Employer Life and Disability	Yes	Expenses
30207	Coffee Shop Employer 401k	Yes	Expenses
30208	Employee Benefits Other	Yes	Expenses
30209	Cutlery Crockery and Linens	Yes	Expenses
30215	Coffee Stationery and Office	Yes	Expenses
30216	Coffee Shop Copy Paper	Yes	Expenses
30217	Coffee Copy Machine Supplies	Yes	Expenses
30218	Coffee Shop Managers Meals	Yes	Expenses
30219	Coffee Telephone Calls Local	Yes	Expenses
30220	Telephone Calls Long Distance	Yes	Expenses
30221	Telephone Calls Cellular	Yes	Expenses
30222	Coffee Non Inventory Supplies	Yes	Expenses
30223	Coffee Shop Travel	Yes	Expenses
30224	Coffee Shop Uniforms	Yes	Expenses
30225	Coffee Shop Miscellaneous	Yes	Expenses
30226	Printing and Design	Yes	Expenses
30227	Coffee Shop Signage	Yes	Expenses
30228	Decorating Expenses	Yes	Expenses
30229	Coffee Shop Laundy	Yes	Expenses
30230	Coffee Shop Dry cleaning	Yes	Expenses
30231	Coffee Shop Postage	Yes	Expenses
30300	Room Service Cost of Food	Yes	Cost of Sales
30301	Room Service Cos tof Liquor	Yes	Cost of Sales
30302	Room Service Gross Payroll	Yes	Expenses
30303	Employer Payroll Taxes	Yes	Expenses
30304	Vacation and Sick	Yes	Expenses
30305	Employer Medical	Yes	Expenses
30306	Employer Life and Disablility	Yes	Expenses
30307	Room Service Employer 401k	Yes	Expenses
30308	Employee Benefits Other	Yes	Expenses
30309	Cutlery Crockery and Linens	Yes	Expenses
30315	Stationery and Office	Yes	Expenses
30316	Room Service Copy Paper	Yes	Expenses
30317	Copy Machine Supplies	Yes	Expenses
30318	Room Service Managers Meals	Yes	Expenses
30319	Telephone Calls Local	Yes	Expenses
30320	Telephone Calls Long Distance	Yes	Expenses
30321	Telephone Calls Cellular	Yes	Expenses
30322	Non Inventory Supplies	Yes	Expenses

Deacon Management Corporation
Chart of Accounts

Account ID	Account Description	Active ?	Account Type
30323	Room Service Travel	Yes	Expenses
30324	Room Service Uniforms	Yes	Expenses
30325	Room Service Miscellaneous	Yes	Expenses
30326	Room ServicPrinting and Design	Yes	Expenses
30327	Room Service Signage	Yes	Expenses
30328	Room ServiceDecorating Expense	Yes	Expenses
30329	Room Service Laundry	Yes	Expenses
30330	Room Service Dry cleaning	Yes	Expenses
30331	Room Service Postage	Yes	Expenses
30400	Steak House Cost of Food	Yes	Cost of Sales
30401	Steak House Cost of Liquor	Yes	Cost of Sales
30402	Steak House Gross Payroll	Yes	Expenses
30403	Steak House Employer Taxes	Yes	Expenses
30404	Steak House Vacation and Sick	Yes	Expenses
30405	Steak House Employer Medical	Yes	Expenses
30406	Employer Life and Disbality	Yes	Expenses
30407	Steak House Employer 401k	Yes	Expenses
30408	Employee Benefits Other	Yes	Expenses
30409	Cutlery Crockery and Linens	Yes	Expenses
30415	Stationery and Office	Yes	Expenses
30416	Steak House Copy Paper	Yes	Expenses
30417	Copy Machine Supplies	Yes	Expenses
30418	Steak House Managers Meals	Yes	Expenses
30419	Telephone Calls Local	Yes	Expenses
30420	Telephone Calls Long Distance	Yes	Expenses
30421	Telephone Calls Cellular	Yes	Expenses
30422	Non Inventory Supplies	Yes	Expenses
30423	Steak House Travel	Yes	Expenses
30424	Steak House Uniforms	Yes	Expenses
30425	Steak House Miscellaneous	Yes	Expenses
30426	Steak HousePrinting and Design	Yes	Expenses
30427	Steak House Signage	Yes	Expenses
30428	Decorating Expense	Yes	Expenses
30429	Steak House Laundy	Yes	Expenses
30430	Steak House Dry cleaning	Yes	Expenses
30431	Steak House Postage	Yes	Expenses
30434	Entertainment Expense	Yes	Expenses
30500	Fine Dining Cost of Food	Yes	Cost of Sales
30501	Fine Dining Cost of Liquor	Yes	Cost of Sales
30502	Fine Dining Gross Payroll	Yes	Expenses
30503	Employer Payroll Taxes	Yes	Expenses
30504	Fine Dining Vacation and Sick	Yes	Expenses
30505	Fine Dining Employer Medical	Yes	Expenses
30506	Employer Life and Disability	Yes	Expenses
30507	Fine Dining Employer 401k	Yes	Expenses
30508	Employee Benefits Other	Yes	Expenses
30509	Cutlery Crockery and Linens	Yes	Expenses
30515	Stationey and Office	Yes	Expenses
30516	Fine Dining Copy Paper	Yes	Expenses
30517	Copy Machine Supplies	Yes	Expenses

Deacon Management Corporation
Chart of Accounts

Account ID	Account Description	Active ?	Account Type
30518	Fine Dining Managers Meals	Yes	Expenses
30519	Telephone Calls Local	Yes	Expenses
30520	Telephone Calls Long Distance	Yes	Expenses
30521	Telephone Calls Cellular	Yes	Expenses
30522	Non Inventory Supplies	Yes	Expenses
30523	Fine Dining Travel	Yes	Expenses
30524	Fine Dining Uniforms	Yes	Expenses
30525	Fine Dining Miscellaneous	Yes	Expenses
30526	Printing and Design	Yes	Expenses
30527	Fine Dining Signage	Yes	Expenses
30528	Decorating Expense	Yes	Expenses
30529	Fine Dining Laundry	Yes	Expenses
30530	Fine Dining Dry cleaning	Yes	Expenses
30531	Fine Dining Postage	Yes	Expenses
30534	Entertainment Expense	Yes	Expenses
30600	Show Lounge Cost of Food	Yes	Cost of Sales
30601	Show Lounge Cost of Liquor	Yes	Cost of Sales
30602	Show Lounge Gross Payroll	Yes	Expenses
30603	Employer Payroll Taxes	Yes	Expenses
30604	Show Lounge Vacation and Sick	Yes	Expenses
30605	Show Lounge Employer Medical	Yes	Expenses
30606	Empployer Life and Disability	Yes	Expenses
30607	Show Lounge Employer 401k	Yes	Expenses
30608	Employee Benefits Other	Yes	Expenses
30615	Stationery and Office	Yes	Expenses
30616	Show Lounge Copy Paper	Yes	Expenses
30617	Copy Machine Supplies	Yes	Expenses
30618	Show Lounge Managers Meals	Yes	Expenses
30619	Telephone Calls Local	Yes	Expenses
30620	Telephone Calls Long Distance	Yes	Expenses
30621	Telephone Calls Cellular	Yes	Expenses
30622	Non Inventory Supplies	Yes	Expenses
30623	Show Lounge Travel	Yes	Expenses
30624	Show Lounge Uniforms	Yes	Expenses
30625	Show Lounge Miscellaneous	Yes	Expenses
30626	Show Lounge Printing & Design	Yes	Expenses
30627	Show Liounge Signage	Yes	Expenses
30628	Decorating Expenses	Yes	Expenses
30629	Show Lounge Laundry	Yes	Expenses
30630	Show Lounge Dry cleaning	Yes	Expenses
30631	Show Lounge Postage	Yes	Expenses
30634	Entertainment Expense	Yes	Expenses
30700	Lobby Bar Cost of Food	Yes	Cost of Sales
30701	Lobby Bar Cost of Liquor	Yes	Cost of Sales
30702	Lobby Bar Gross Payroll	Yes	Expenses
30703	Employer Payroll Taxes	Yes	Expenses
30704	Lobby Bar Vacation and Sick	Yes	Expenses
30705	Loby Bar Employer Medical	Yes	Expenses
30706	Employer Life and Disability	Yes	Expenses
30707	Lobby Bar Employer 401k	Yes	Expenses

Deacon Management Corporation
Chart of Accounts

Account ID	Account Description	Active ?	Account Type
30708	Employee Benefits Other	Yes	Expenses
30715	Stationery and Office	Yes	Expenses
30716	Lobby Bar Copy Paper	Yes	Expenses
30717	Copy Machine Supplies	Yes	Expenses
30718	Lobby Bar Managers Meals	Yes	Expenses
30719	Telephone Calls Local	Yes	Expenses
30720	Telephone Calls Long Disrance	Yes	Expenses
30721	Telephone Calls Cellular	Yes	Expenses
30722	Non Inventory Supplies	Yes	Expenses
30723	Lobby Bar Travel	Yes	Expenses
30724	Lobby Bar Uniforms	Yes	Expenses
30725	Lobby Bar Miscellaneous	Yes	Expenses
30726	Lobby Bar Printing and Design	Yes	Expenses
30727	lobby Bar Signage	Yes	Expenses
30728	Lobby Bar Decorating Expenses	Yes	Expenses
30729	Lobby Bar Laundry	Yes	Expenses
30730	Lobby Bar Dry cleaning	Yes	Expenses
30731	Lobby Bar Postage	Yes	Expenses
30800	Roof Top Rest Cost of Food	Yes	Cost of Sales
30801	Roof Top Rest Cost of Liquor	Yes	Cost of Sales
30802	Roof Top Restaurant Gross Pay	Yes	Expenses
30803	Roof Top Rest Employer taxes	Yes	Expenses
30804	Roof Top Rest Vacation & Sick	Yes	Expenses
30805	Roof Top Rest Employer Medical	Yes	Expenses
30806	Employer Life and Disability	Yes	Expenses
30807	Roof Top Rest Employer 401k	Yes	Expenses
30808	Employee Benefits Other	Yes	Expenses
30809	Cutlery Crockery and Linens	Yes	Expenses
30815	Stationery and Office	Yes	Expenses
30816	Roof Top Rest Copy Paper	Yes	Expenses
30817	Roof Top Copy Machine Supplies	Yes	Expenses
30818	Roof Top Rest Managers Meals	Yes	Expenses
30819	Telephone Calls Local	Yes	Expenses
30820	Telephone Calls Long Distance	Yes	Expenses
30821	Telephone Calls Cellular	Yes	Expenses
30822	Non Inventory Expenses	Yes	Expenses
30823	Roof Top Rest Travel	Yes	Expenses
30824	Roof Top Rest Uniforms	Yes	Expenses
30825	Roof Top Rest Miscellaneous	Yes	Expenses
30826	Printing and Design	Yes	Expenses
30827	Roof Top Rest Signage	Yes	Expenses
30828	Decorating Expenses	Yes	Expenses
30829	Roof Top Rest Laundry	Yes	Expenses
30830	Roof Top Rest Dry cleaning	Yes	Expenses
30831	Roof Top Rest Postage	Yes	Expenses
30834	Entertainment Expense	Yes	Expenses
30900	Meeting Space Cost of Food	Yes	Cost of Sales
30901	Meeting Space Cost of Liquor	Yes	Cost of Sales
30902	Meeting Space Gross Payroll	Yes	Expenses
30903	Employer Payroll Taxes	Yes	Expenses

231

Deacon Management Corporation
Chart of Accounts

Account ID	Account Description	Active ?	Account Type
30904	Meeting Space Vacation & Sick	Yes	Expenses
30905	Employer Medical	Yes	Expenses
30906	Employer Life and Sick	Yes	Expenses
30907	Meetiing Space Emploer 401k	Yes	Expenses
30908	Employee Benefits Other	Yes	Expenses
30915	Stationery and Office	Yes	Expenses
30916	Meeting Space Copy Paper	Yes	Expenses
30917	Copy Machine Supplies	Yes	Expenses
30918	Meeting Space Managers Meals	Yes	Expenses
30919	Telephone Calls Local	Yes	Expenses
30920	Telephone Calls Long Distance	Yes	Expenses
30921	Telephone Calls Cellular	Yes	Expenses
30922	Meeting Non Inventory Supplies	Yes	Expenses
30923	Meeting Space Travel	Yes	Expenses
30924	Meeting Space Uniforms	Yes	Expenses
30925	Meeting Space Miscellanous	Yes	Expenses
30926	Printing and Design	Yes	Expenses
30927	Meeting Space Signage	Yes	Expenses
30928	Meeting Decrating Expense	Yes	Expenses
30929	Meeting Space Laundry	Yes	Expenses
30930	Meeting Space Dry cleaning	Yes	Expenses
30931	Meeting Space Postage	Yes	Expenses
31002	Telephone Gross Payroll	Yes	Expenses
31003	Employer Payroll Taxes	Yes	Expenses
31004	Telephone Vacation and Sick	Yes	Expenses
31005	Telephone Employer Medical	Yes	Expenses
31006	Employer Life and Disability	Yes	Expenses
31007	Telephone Employer 401k	Yes	Expenses
31008	Employee Benefits Other	Yes	Expenses
31015	Stationery and Office	Yes	Expenses
31016	Telephone Copy Paper	Yes	Expenses
31017	Copy Machine Supplies	Yes	Expenses
31018	Telephone Managers Meals	Yes	Expenses
31019	Telephone Calls Local	Yes	Expenses
31020	Telephone Calls Long Distance	Yes	Expenses
31021	Telephone Calls Cellular	Yes	Expenses
31022	Non Inventory Supplies	Yes	Expenses
31023	Telephone Travel	Yes	Expenses
31024	Telephone Uniform	Yes	Expenses
31025	Telephone Miscellaneous	Yes	Expenses
31026	Printing and Design	Yes	Expenses
31027	Telephone Signage	Yes	Expenses
31028	Telephone Decorating Expense	Yes	Expenses
31029	Telephone Laundry	Yes	Expenses
31030	Telephone Dry cleaning	Yes	Expenses
31031	Telephone Postage	Yes	Expenses
31102	Front of House Gross Payroll	Yes	Expenses
31103	Employer Payroll Taxes	Yes	Expenses
31104	Vacation and Sick	Yes	Expenses
31105	Employer Medical	Yes	Expenses

Deacon Management Corporation
Chart of Accounts

Account ID	Account Description	Active ?	Account Type
31106	Employer Life and Disabiltiy	Yes	Expenses
31107	Front of House Employer 401k	Yes	Expenses
31108	Employee Benefits Other	Yes	Expenses
31115	Stationery and Office	Yes	Expenses
31116	Front of House Copy Paper	Yes	Expenses
31117	Copy Machine Supplies	Yes	Expenses
31118	Front of House Managers Meals	Yes	Expenses
31119	Telephone Calls Local	Yes	Expenses
31120	Telephone Calls Long Distance	Yes	Expenses
31121	Telephone Calls Cellular	Yes	Expenses
31122	Non Inventory Supplies	Yes	Expenses
31123	Front of House Travel	Yes	Expenses
31124	Front of House Uniforms	Yes	Expenses
31125	Front of House Miscellaneous	Yes	Expenses
31126	Printing and Design	Yes	Expenses
31127	Front of House Signage	Yes	Expenses
31128	Decorating Expenses	Yes	Expenses
31129	Front of House Laundry	Yes	Expenses
31130	Front of House Dry cleaning	Yes	Expenses
31131	Front of House Postage	Yes	Expenses
31202	Doormen & Other Gross Payroll	Yes	Expenses
31203	Employer Payroll Taxes	Yes	Expenses
31204	Doormen Vacation and Sick	Yes	Expenses
31205	Employer Medical	Yes	Expenses
31206	Employer Life and Disability	Yes	Expenses
31207	Doormen & Other Employer 401k	Yes	Expenses
31208	Employee Benefits Other	Yes	Expenses
31222	Non Inventory Supplies	Yes	Expenses
31223	Doormen & Other Travel	Yes	Expenses
31224	Doormen & Other Uniforms	Yes	Expenses
31225	Doormen & Other Miscellaneous	Yes	Expenses
31226	Printing and Design	Yes	Expenses
31227	Doormen & Other Signage	Yes	Expenses
31228	Decorating Expenses	Yes	Expenses
31229	Doormen & Other Laundy	Yes	Expenses
31230	Doormen & Other Dry cleaning	Yes	Expenses
31231	Doormen & Other Postage	Yes	Expenses
31302	Repairs Maintenance Gross Pay	Yes	Expenses
31303	Employer Payroll Taxrd	Yes	Expenses
31304	Vacation and Sick	Yes	Expenses
31305	Employer Medical	Yes	Expenses
31306	Employer Life and Disability	Yes	Expenses
31307	Repairs MaintenanEmployer 401k	Yes	Expenses
31308	Employee Benefits Other	Yes	Expenses
31309	Utilities - Heating	Yes	Expenses
31310	Utilities - Electricity	Yes	Expenses
31311	Utilities - Water	Yes	Expenses
31312	Repairs Maintenance Building	Yes	Expenses
31313	Repairs Maintenance Equipment	Yes	Expenses
31314	Repairs Maintenance Electical	Yes	Expenses

Deacon Management Corporation
Chart of Accounts

Account ID	Account Description	Active ?	Account Type
31315	Stationery and Office	Yes	Expenses
31316	Repairs Maintenance Copy Paper	Yes	Expenses
31317	Copy Machine Supplies	Yes	Expenses
31318	Managers Meals	Yes	Expenses
31319	Telephone Calls Local	Yes	Expenses
31320	Telephone Calls Long Distance	Yes	Expenses
31321	Telephone Calls Cellular	Yes	Expenses
31322	Telephone Calls Local	Yes	Expenses
31323	Repairs Maintenance Travel	Yes	Expenses
31324	Repairs Maintenance Uniforms	Yes	Expenses
31325	Repairs Maintenance Miscellane	Yes	Expenses
31326	Printing and Design	Yes	Expenses
31327	Repairs Maintenance Signage	Yes	Expenses
31328	Repairs Maintenance Decorating	Yes	Expenses
31329	Repairs Maintenance Laundry	Yes	Expenses
31330	Dry cleaning	Yes	Expenses
31331	Repairs Maintenance Postage	Yes	Expenses
31332	Repairs Maintenance Building	Yes	Expenses
31333	Repairs Maintenance Equipment	Yes	Expenses
31334	Repairs Maintenance Electrical	Yes	Expenses
31402	Kitchen Gross Payroll	Yes	Expenses
31403	Kitchen Employer Payroll Taxes	Yes	Expenses
31404	Kitchen Vacation and Sick	Yes	Expenses
31405	Kitchen Employer Payroll Taxes	Yes	Expenses
31406	Employer Life and Disability	Yes	Expenses
31407	Kitchen Employer 401k	Yes	Expenses
31408	Employee Benefits Other	Yes	Expenses
31415	Stationery and Office	Yes	Expenses
31416	Kitchen Copy Paper	Yes	Expenses
31417	Kitchen Copy Machine Supplies	Yes	Expenses
31418	Kitchen Managers Meals	Yes	Expenses
31419	Telephone Calls Local	Yes	Expenses
31420	Telephone Calls Long Distance	Yes	Expenses
31421	Telephone Calls Cellular	Yes	Expenses
31422	Kitchen Non Inventory Supplies	Yes	Expenses
31423	Kitchen Travel	Yes	Expenses
31424	Kitchen Uniforms	Yes	Expenses
31425	Kicthen Miscellaneous	Yes	Expenses
31426	Kitchen Printing and Design	Yes	Expenses
31427	Kitchen Signage	Yes	Expenses
31428	Kitchen Decorating Expense	Yes	Expenses
31429	Kitchen Laundry	Yes	Expenses
31430	Kitchen Dry cleaning	Yes	Expenses
31431	Kitchen Postage	Yes	Expenses
31435	Kitchen Cooking Utensils	Yes	Expenses
31502	Security Gross Payroll	Yes	Expenses
31503	Employer Payroll Taxes	Yes	Expenses
31504	Security Vacation and Sick	Yes	Expenses
31505	Security Employer Medical	Yes	Expenses
31506	Employer Life and Disability	Yes	Expenses

Deacon Management Corporation
Chart of Accounts

Account ID	Account Description	Active ?	Account Type
31507	Security Employer 401k	Yes	Expenses
31508	Employee Benefits Other	Yes	Expenses
31515	Security Stationery and Office	Yes	Expenses
31516	Security Copy Paper	Yes	Expenses
31517	Copy Machine Supplies	Yes	Expenses
31518	Security Managers Meals	Yes	Expenses
31519	Telephone Calls Local	Yes	Expenses
31520	Telephone Calls Long Distance	Yes	Expenses
31521	Telephone Calls Cellular	Yes	Expenses
31522	Security Non Inventory Expense	Yes	Expenses
31523	Security Travel	Yes	Expenses
31524	Security Uniforms	Yes	Expenses
31525	Security Miscellaneous	Yes	Expenses
31526	Security Printing and Design	Yes	Expenses
31527	Security Signage	Yes	Expenses
31528	Security Decorating Expense	Yes	Expenses
31529	Security Laundry	Yes	Expenses
31530	Security Dry cleaning	Yes	Expenses
31531	Security Postage	Yes	Expenses
31536	Outside Security Contracts	Yes	Expenses
31602	Business Center Gross Payroll	Yes	Expenses
31603	Employer Payroll Taxes	Yes	Expenses
31604	Vacation and Sick	Yes	Expenses
31605	Employer Medical	Yes	Expenses
31606	Employer Life and Disability	Yes	Expenses
31607	Business Center Employer 401k	Yes	Expenses
31608	Employee Benefits Other	Yes	Expenses
31615	Stationery and Office	Yes	Expenses
31616	Business Center Copy Paper	Yes	Expenses
31617	Copy Machine Supplies	Yes	Expenses
31618	Business Center Managers Meals	Yes	Expenses
31619	Telephone Calls Local	Yes	Expenses
31620	Telephone Calls Long Distance	Yes	Expenses
31621	Telephone Calls Cellular	Yes	Expenses
31622	Non Inventory Expenses	Yes	Expenses
31623	Business Center Travel	Yes	Expenses
31624	Business Center Uniforms	Yes	Expenses
31625	Business Center Miscellaneous	Yes	Expenses
31626	Printing and Design	Yes	Expenses
31627	Business Center Signage	Yes	Expenses
31628	Business Center Decorating	Yes	Expenses
31629	Business Center Laundry	Yes	Expenses
31630	Business Center Dry cleaning	Yes	Expenses
31631	Business Center Postage	Yes	Expenses
31702	Spa and Fitness Gross Payroll	Yes	Expenses
31703	Employer Payroll Taxes	Yes	Expenses
31704	Vacation and Sick	Yes	Expenses
31705	Employer Medical	Yes	Expenses
31706	Employer Life and Disabiltiy	Yes	Expenses
31707	Spa and Fitness Employer 401k	Yes	Expenses

Deacon Management Corporation
Chart of Accounts

Account ID	Account Description	Active ?	Account Type
31708	Employee Benefits Other	Yes	Expenses
31715	Stationery and Office	Yes	Expenses
31716	Spa and Fitness Copy Paper	Yes	Expenses
31717	Copy Machine Supplies	Yes	Expenses
31718	Spa and Fitness Managers Meals	Yes	Expenses
31719	Telephone Calls Local	Yes	Expenses
31720	Telephone Calls Long Distance	Yes	Expenses
31721	Telephone Calls Cellular	Yes	Expenses
31722	Spa and Fitness Non Inventory	Yes	Expenses
31723	Spa and Fitness Travel	Yes	Expenses
31724	Spa and Fitness Uniforms	Yes	Expenses
31725	Spa and Fitness Miscellaneous	Yes	Expenses
31726	Printing and Design	Yes	Expenses
31727	Spa and Fitness Signage	Yes	Expenses
31728	Spa and Fitness Decorating Exp	Yes	Expenses
31729	Spa and Fitness Laundry	Yes	Expenses
31730	Spa and Fitness Dry cleaning	Yes	Expenses
31731	Spa and Fitness Postage	Yes	Expenses
31802	Human Resources Gross Payroll	Yes	Expenses
31803	Employer Payroll Taxes	Yes	Expenses
31804	Vacation and Sick	Yes	Expenses
31805	Human ResoucesEmployer Medical	Yes	Expenses
31806	Employer Life and Disability	Yes	Expenses
31807	Human Resources Employer 401k	Yes	Expenses
31808	Employee Benefits Other	Yes	Expenses
31815	Stationery and Office	Yes	Expenses
31816	Human Resources Copy Paper	Yes	Expenses
31817	Copy Machine Supplies	Yes	Expenses
31818	Human Resouces Managers Meals	Yes	Expenses
31819	Telephone Calls Local	Yes	Expenses
31820	Telephone Calls Long Distance	Yes	Expenses
31821	Telephone Calls Cellular	Yes	Expenses
31822	Human Resouces Non Inventory	Yes	Expenses
31829	Human Resources Laundry	Yes	Expenses
31830	Human Resources Dry cleaning	Yes	Expenses
31831	Human Resouces Postage	Yes	Expenses
31837	Human Resources Staff Training	Yes	Expenses
31838	Staff Advertising	Yes	Expenses
31839	Human Resources Staffing Other	Yes	Expenses
31902	Sales and Marketing Gross Pay	Yes	Expenses
31903	Employer Payroll Taxes	Yes	Expenses
31904	Vacation and Sick	Yes	Expenses
31905	Employer Medical	Yes	Expenses
31906	Employer Life and Disability	Yes	Expenses
31907	Employer 401k	Yes	Expenses
31908	Employee Beneifts Other	Yes	Expenses
31915	Stationery and Office	Yes	Expenses
31916	Sales and Marketing Copy Paper	Yes	Expenses
31917	Copy Machine Supplies	Yes	Expenses
31918	Managers Meals	Yes	Expenses

Deacon Management Corporation
Chart of Accounts

Account ID	Account Description	Active ?	Account Type
31919	Telephone Calls Local	Yes	Expenses
31920	Telephone Calls Long Distance	Yes	Expenses
31921	Telephone Calls Cellular	Yes	Expenses
31922	Non Inventory Supplies	Yes	Expenses
31923	Sales and Marketing Travel	Yes	Expenses
31924	Sales and Marketing Uniforms	Yes	Expenses
31925	Sales and Marketing Miscellane	Yes	Expenses
31926	Printing and Design	Yes	Expenses
31927	Sales and Marketing Signage	Yes	Expenses
31928	Sales and Marketing Decorating	Yes	Expenses
31929	Sales and Marketing Laundry	Yes	Expenses
31930	Sales and Marketing Dry cleani	Yes	Expenses
31931	Sales and Marketing Postage	Yes	Expenses
31940	Sales and Promtion Materials	Yes	Expenses
31941	Gifts and Giveaways	Yes	Expenses
31942	Trade Show Promotions	Yes	Expenses
31943	Advertising Contract Print	Yes	Expenses
31944	Advertising Contract Media	Yes	Expenses
31945	Entertaining Client	Yes	Expenses
32002	Accounting Gross Pay	Yes	Expenses
32003	Employer Payroll Taxes	Yes	Expenses
32004	Accounting Vacation and Sick	Yes	Expenses
32005	Accounting Employer Medical	Yes	Expenses
32006	Employer Life and Disability	Yes	Expenses
32007	Accounting Employer 401k	Yes	Expenses
32008	Employee Benefits Other	Yes	Expenses
32015	Stationery and Office	Yes	Expenses
32016	Accounting Copy Paper	Yes	Expenses
32017	Copy Machine Supplies	Yes	Expenses
32018	Accounting Managers Meals	Yes	Expenses
32019	Telephone Calls Local	Yes	Expenses
32020	Telephone Calls Long Distance	Yes	Expenses
32021	Telephone Calls Cellular	Yes	Expenses
32022	Accounting Non Inventory Exp	Yes	Expenses
32023	Accounting Travel	Yes	Expenses
32024	Accounting Uniform	Yes	Expenses
32025	Accounting Miscellaneous	Yes	Expenses
32026	Accounting Printing and Design	Yes	Expenses
32027	Accounting Signage	Yes	Expenses
32028	Accounting Decorating Exp	Yes	Expenses
32029	Accounting Laundry	Yes	Expenses
32030	Accounting Dry cleaning	Yes	Expenses
32031	Accounting Postage	Yes	Expenses
32045	Entertaining Client and House	Yes	Expenses
32046	Licenses and Permits	Yes	Expenses
32047	Penalties and Fines	Yes	Expenses
32048	Software Expense	Yes	Expenses
32049	Software Licenses	Yes	Expenses
32050	Server Maintenance Contracts	Yes	Expenses
32051	Postage Machine Monthly Rental	Yes	Expenses

Deacon Management Corporation
Chart of Accounts

Account ID	Account Description	Active ?	Account Type
32052	Copy Machine Maintenance Contr	Yes	Expenses
32053	Outside Contract Cleaners	Yes	Expenses
32054	Bad Debt Expense	Yes	Expenses
32055	Outside Collection Agency Fees	Yes	Expenses
32056	Credit Card Commission Expense	Yes	Expenses
32057	Payroll Processing Fee	Yes	Expenses
32058	Bank Fees	Yes	Expenses
32059	Cashier over and Short	Yes	Expenses
32060	Professional Fees Legal	Yes	Expenses
32061	Proffesional Fees- Auditors	Yes	Expenses
32062	Professional Fees Consulting	Yes	Expenses
32063	Insurance Workers Compensation	Yes	Expenses
32102	Executive Office Gross Payroll	Yes	Expenses
32103	Employer Payroll Taxes	Yes	Expenses
32104	Vacation and Sick	Yes	Expenses
32105	Employer Medical	Yes	Expenses
32106	Employer Life and Disability	Yes	Expenses
32107	Executive Office Employer 401k	Yes	Expenses
32108	Employee Benefits Other	Yes	Expenses
32115	Stationery and Office	Yes	Expenses
32116	Executive Office Copy Paper	Yes	Expenses
32117	Copy Machine Supplies	Yes	Expenses
32118	Executive Managers Meals	Yes	Expenses
32119	Telephone Calls Local	Yes	Expenses
32120	Telephone Calls Long Distance	Yes	Expenses
32121	Telephone Calls Cellular	Yes	Expenses
32122	Non Inventory Supplies	Yes	Expenses
32123	Executive Offices Travel	Yes	Expenses
32124	Executive Offices Uniforms	Yes	Expenses
32125	Executive Offices Miscellaneou	Yes	Expenses
32126	Printing and Design	Yes	Expenses
32127	Executive Offices Signage	Yes	Expenses
32128	Executive Offices Decorating	Yes	Expenses
32129	Executive Offices Laundry	Yes	Expenses
32130	Executive Offices Dry cleaning	Yes	Expenses
32131	Executive Offices Postage	Yes	Expenses
32145	Entertaining-Client and House	Yes	Expenses
32280	Insurance - Fire	Yes	Expenses
32281	Insurance - General	Yes	Expenses
32282	Insurance - Business	Yes	Expenses
32283	Insurance - Terror	Yes	Expenses
32284	Management Fee Minimum	Yes	Expenses
32285	Management Fee Additional	Yes	Expenses
32286	Trademark and Other	Yes	Expenses
32287	Depreciation Expense	Yes	Expenses
32288	Interest Expense Short Term	Yes	Expenses
32289	Interest Expense Long Term	Yes	Expenses
32290	Interest Pref Stock 5%	Yes	Expenses
32291	Interest Pref Stock 7%	Yes	Expenses
32292	Interest Pref Stock 9%	Yes	Expenses

Deacon Management Corporation
Chart of Accounts

Account ID	Account Description	Active ?	Account Type
32293	Taxes - Property	Yes	Expenses
32294	Taxes- Income Tax Federal	Yes	Expenses
32295	Taxes Income State and Local	Yes	Expenses
32296	Taxes - Excise and Use taxes	Yes	Expenses
32397	Gain or Loss Dispos of Assets	Yes	Expenses
32398	Gain or Loss Other	Yes	Expenses
40100	Rooms Corporate Individual	Yes	Income
40101	Rooms Corporate Group	Yes	Income
40102	Rooms Leisure Individual	Yes	Income
40103	Rooms Leisure Groups	Yes	Income
40104	Rooms Group Meeting	Yes	Income
40105	Rooms Airline and Travel	Yes	Income
40106	Rooms No Show	Yes	Income
40107	Rooms Permanent and Office	Yes	Income
40200	Coffee Shop Food	Yes	Income
40201	Coffee Shop Liquor	Yes	Income
40300	Room Service Food	Yes	Income
40301	Room Service Liquor	Yes	Income
40302	Room Service Delivery Charge	Yes	Income
40400	Steak House Food	Yes	Income
40401	Steak House Liquor	Yes	Income
40500	Fine Dining Food	Yes	Income
40501	Fine Dining Liquor	Yes	Income
40600	Show Lounge Food	Yes	Income
40601	Show Lounge Liquor	Yes	Income
40602	Show Lounge Entertainment Fee	Yes	Income
40603	Lobby Bar Beverage Revenue	Yes	Income
40700	Roof Top Restaurant Bar Food	Yes	Income
40701	Roof Top Restaurant Bar Liquor	Yes	Income
40702	Roof Top Restaurant Bar Entert	Yes	Income
40800	Meeting Space Food	Yes	Income
40801	Meeting Space Liquor	Yes	Income
40802	Meeting Space Fully Catered	Yes	Income
40803	Meeting Space Room Rental	Yes	Income
40804	Meeting Space Cash Bar	Yes	Income
40805	Meeting Space Audio Visual	Yes	Income
40900	Spa General Useage	Yes	Income
40901	Spa Professional Massage	Yes	Income
40902	Spa Products	Yes	Income
40903	Spa - Sauna	Yes	Income
40904	Spa Memberships Current Month	Yes	Income
40905	Spa Memberships Six Months	Yes	Income
40906	Spa Memeberships One Year	Yes	Income
40907	Spa Swim Memberships Only	Yes	Income
40908	Spa Relaxing CD's	Yes	Income
40909	Spa Video Sales	Yes	Income
41000	Parking - Overnight	Yes	Income
41001	Parking - Minimum Rent	Yes	Income
41002	Parking - Participation	Yes	Income
41200	Laundry	Yes	Income

Deacon Management Corporation
Chart of Accounts

Account ID	Account Description	Active ?	Account Type
41201	Valet and Dry Cleaning	Yes	Income
41300	In Room Movies	Yes	Income
41400	Local Telephone Calls	Yes	Income
41401	Long Distance Calls	Yes	Income
41402	Internet Connections Fee	Yes	Income
41403	Eight Hundred Call Toll	Yes	Income
41500	Business Center Color Copies	Yes	Income
41501	Business Center Regular Copies	Yes	Income
41502	Business Center Work Stations	Yes	Income
41503	Business Center Phone Calls	Yes	Income
41504	Business Center Internet Conn	Yes	Income
41600	Show Case Display Rental	Yes	Income
41601	Bank ATM Machine	Yes	Income
41602	Lobby Shop	Yes	Income
41603	Mini Starbucks Stand	Yes	Income
41603	American Express Full Service	Yes	Income

 It's time, for now to say Good Bye. Thank you for choosing, reading and studying this book on Financial Accounting.

I hope it has ignited the first of many steps, in extending your knowledge and the understanding of this important subject and I hope you will find it an excellent reference guide whenever you need to go back and review these basic steps.

Remember: The Accountant is only as good as his or her client!

Regards

Errol Deacon

How do I obtain additional copies of this book?

 I want to use this book for our corporate introductory accounting class. Are volume discounts available?

 How do I know if a new or a second addition has been launched? Has Deacon considered an online newsletter?

 Is Deacon planning strategic alliances with others in the business world to offer seminars, workshops and newsletters on accounting and other business subjects and issues of the day?

 I Have heard that Financial Accounting is the first in a "GET IT STRAIGHT" series of business related subjects presented in this format. How do I keep up to date?

 How do I know if and when Financial Accounting GET IT STRAIGHT will be available on CD/DVD presented in a live seminar?

 Is Deacon available to speak on this subject to our corporate group?

 Is there an on-line newsletter?

Contact: Deacon Media Company

WWW.DEACONMEDIA.COM

Deacon Media Company

Www.deaconmeadia.com

Printed in the United States
51303LVS00002B/1